REGENERATE

W. D. BEAMAN

First Edition

Fulton Books, Inc.
Meadville, PA

Published by Fulton Books 2021

ISBN 978-1-63710-367-8 (paperback)
ISBN 978-1-63710-368-5 (digital)

Printed in the United States of America

CONTENTS

"Who are your people?" It's a question often asked by Southerners when they meet a stranger. Most of us know very little of our ancestors. John Bishop XIII was born into a line of wealthy, savvy, thrifty Scottish descendants who made him a very wealthy man, but his parents had never wanted children. He was conceived by accident, and his father tried to have the fetus aborted. John's mother did love him, but he was relegated to a place behind her illustrious musical career. His father simply ignored him. Their self-centered lack of empathy would lead to their murders and to several attempts on John's life. John found solace in his own music as he struggled to regenerate himself.

CHAPTER 1

Homecoming

"Dad, can I go worship my Ramsay ancestors? Why do we only worship Mom's Williams ancestors?"

"Where in the world did you get this idea, John?"

"Eddie told me that Uncle Charlie and Aunt Rosilyn are taking him to Charleston this weekend to organize his cousin in the cathedral. Uncle Charlie told him that they worship their ancestors and eat rice when they're in Charleston, so I want to go worship my Ramsay ancestors. Where do they live?"

"Ah. I get it. Come over here and sit with me for a few minutes."

"I want to practice my music before Mom gets back. She says I play too loud. How do people get organized in the cathedral? Can I get organized at St. Philip's?"

"I know she does, but let's see if I can answer your questions first."

Six-year-old John Bishop Ramsay walked across the granite-paved terrace and sat on the teak bench beside his father, Hew. Hew and Alexis had decided before their marriage that they wanted a large family. Hew was an only child, and Alexis had an older brother. She became pregnant three months after the wedding, so they bought five contiguous large houses on Riverside Drive on the Southeast side of the Chattahoochie River near Atlanta, Georgia. He demolished the old houses and had his favorite architect design a new house that was at once a study in Greek proportions but very modernist, minimalistic, and environmentally sensitive. She had grown up in a superb architecturally designed contemporary house along a golf fairway, so she was partial to the style. From a pair of stainless-steel gates designed to look like tall waving grasses, a long graveled driveway stretched along the south property line until it finally curved 180 degrees around the east property line and ended at a large motor court in front of the house. There was a gated service entrance off Riverside Drive that led to the lower-level garages. The south, east, and west property lines were heavily planted with native evergreens to screen out prying eyes. They even added stands of historic southern long leaf pine trees to the borders. The area inside the semi-oval drive was a simple green rolling meadow of restored native southeastern prairie grasses that had been curated by specialists at Clemson University. To the untrained eye, the site had the look of an abandoned nineteenth-century cotton farm, but any local horticulturist would drool at the sight. Alexis hated having the children run into the house covered in beggar lice, but Hew just laughed it off. She made him pick the freeloaders off the children's clothes.

The new house was perched high over the river with views to the northwest toward the Appalachian Mountains. There was a nature preserve on the other side of the river affording them complete privacy. From the driveway, the house appeared to be a simple gray and brown linear dry stacked stone wall but the continuous pitched black solar roof panels promised something more complex. A thin row of glass under the low eave separated the roof from the stone wall. The roof covering changed to include a large skylight and projected forward over the translucent glass entry doors to form a porch. Inside the wide foyer, a glass spiral stair descended two levels to Hew's library. The southern sun penetrated to the lower levels, giving the entire space a solarium effect. At Christmas, they placed a large tall fir tree in the center of the stairwell. The foyer opened onto a great room with sixteen-foot-high continuous glass windows overlooking the terrace and the view. The pale-colored oak floor was accented with large worn Oriental carpets that created islands for their International Style furnishings. The matte black plain slab cabinets in the kitchen at the west end of the room receded into the background. A large island covered with absolute black granite separated the cooking zone from the entertaining area. A large native dry stacked stone fireplace commanded the east wall of the room.

A corridor on the east side of the foyer led to the family's bedrooms, and a corridor off the West side led to the wine cellar, bar, butler's pantry, and service areas. The butler's pantry was a large three-story balconied space with a large elevator. It allowed deliveries at the garage level, service to the guest rooms on the second level under the family bedrooms, and then opened to the main level service corridor.

The library / music room was a two-story space with a balcony of books along three sides and a wall of glass on the view side. His Flentrop pipe organ stood near the west wall, and a stone fireplace supporting the fireplace above occupied the east wall. A passage ran behind the fireplace to a small spiral stair near the glass wall. Hew moved everything from his penthouse in Atlanta to the new house.

Hew, like his late mother, was a fine musician. Hew had been baptized John Bishop XIII, but after an attempt on his life when he was fifteen, he changed his name to Charteris Hew Ramsay and moved to Atlanta to live with his grandfather's law partner, Edward Hardy and family. He took the name of a Scottish ancestor.

John, a tall boy for his age, looked like Hew. His unruly mop of golden curls would never be tamed by a brush or comb. His sky-blue eyes twinkled when his mischievous personality bubbled to the surface. He had the face of an angel—most of the time—but his temper could exceed the normal artistic temperament of most musicians. The boy had long legs that were perfect for the pedalboard, and he inherited his ancestor's long slim fingers. He was already more musically advanced than Hew had been at the same age, but Hew had been suppressed by his father's total lack of interest in him. John's three-year-old identical twin sisters, Elizabeth and Courtney, looked like Alexis.

"Okay, John. First, take my iPhone and Google *ordination*." He spelled it for him.

"I see. It's a church service where someone becomes a priest. Is that where they worship him?"

Hew laughed. "No, Eddie has it confused. Charlie's Charleston cousin studied for the priesthood at the University of the South in Sewanee, Tennessee—that's north of here in the mountains. It also has an Episcopal seminary, and our dean at St. Philip's studied there too, but many years earlier. Charlie's cousin is his relative. Relatives are living family members. Ancestors are dead family members. Taken together, they are the people from whom you are descended. Uncle Charlie's comment about worshiping ancestors is not nice, and don't ever repeat it. Many people just fondly remember their ancestors and tell stories about them to later generations to keep their memories alive. They don't really worship them."

"So where do my Ramsay, um, relatives live?"

"All of your relatives on my side of your family are dead." Hew told the truth, but not the whole truth.

"Where did they live? Can I go to their graves?"

Avoiding the complete truth again, Hew said, "The Ramsay's are Scottish, but many of your ancestors are buried in the cemetery at Swan Bay Farm in Virginia. We're flying up there in a few weeks for Thanksgiving, so I'll tell you more about your ancestors when we get there. That's where they all lived."

"Well, I love Swan Bay. Why don't we live there?"

"That's a very long story, and it will make more sense when we're there, and I can take you to a few places where they lived."

"Can Eddie go with us, please?"

"Ah! Now that's a great idea. We'll invite the whole Hardy family. It'll be like old times."

"Old times for you maybe."

Hew tousled his son's unruly mop of blond curls. "Off you go to your music, wise guy."

About thirty minutes later, Alexis walked out onto the terrace with three-year-old Elizabeth in tow. She had two glasses of red Franciscan Magnificat wine on a silver tray.

"I brought you a glass of your favorite wine. John's playing too loudly again."

Hew ignored the criticism. "Thanks for the wine. How was lunch with the Hardy women?"

"Fine. They're taking the jet to Charleston tomorrow."

"Oh, I've already heard from John. Eddie's gotten him asking questions about my ancestors."

"What did you tell him? We knew that would come up at some point."

"I told him that they were dead and that I'd tell him more when we get to Virginia. I just don't know how much to tell a six-year-old boy. Some parts are still too horrible even for me to remember. Oh, and I want to invite the Hardys for Thanksgiving."

"That'll be fun. Why don't we start John researching my family. Let's go to Greenville this weekend and let my grandfather tell his tales of growing up in the South Carolina foothills. It would be nice to get it written down while there's still time. They can sit on the deck, and John can take notes."

"Actually, it would be better if he made a video for posterity. He can transcribe it later. I can get some software to do that, so okay, but for now let's just sit here and watch the sunset over the mountains while I think about what I'm going to say."

She reached over and took his hand, and they watched as the blue autumn sky made its decrescendo into brilliant shades of pink, purple, orange, and yellow. A chilled breeze blew up from the rushing river below, and Hew shivered, partly from the wind and partly from his memories. Suddenly, he had a bad memory of arriving at Swan Bay from his school in Bogota, Colombia, South America. Though eighteen years had passed, and he was now twenty-eight, the horrible memories of that day were still raw.

Eighteen Years Earlier

They had barely managed to snatch him from the abductors who had murdered his parents, and now the rescue team was about to deliver young John Bishop XIII safely to his grandfather at the Bishop family ancestral tobacco farm. A faint glow in the east at the mouth of the James River was slowly separating the water from the sky. It promised another beautiful day for the folks of Tidewater, Virginia. The stark-white twin-engine jet roared down the private airstrip at Swan Bay Farm on the western side of the James River near Claremont, Virginia, and stopped at the end of the runway in front of the hangar. Technically, the runway was more than adequate for this plane, but the seasoned pilots still took advantage of approaching the strip from over the James River, dropping altitude as quickly as possible. They lined up with the grass lawn that sloped gently from the manor house down to the river, and by the time the nose was over the end of the runway, they were barely airborne. Swan Bay was now known worldwide as a modern premier equine breeding center, but that was really just a cover.

Spring was usually the beginning of a busy time for the breeders, but there were no horse owners aboard on this May morning. As the plane approached, the entire staff, who had been waiting inside the warm hangar, gathered near the stairs to pay their respects to their fallen members. It would be the saddest day and the worst loss in a single day in the entire 368 years of the farm's existence. When the cabin door opened, the bright lights in the plane's interior temporarily blinded those gathered nearby, but as their vision cleared, a lone backlit figure started down the stairs. He was carrying the heavily sedated fourteen-year-old boy John Bishop XIII on his back and shoulders, fireman rescue style. Without acknowledging any of those present, Jeffrey Beverly walked directly over to the SUV where his weeping wife, Mary, was standing and carefully laid the boy on the back seat. He then turned, and with his back to the waiting mourners, he gently gathered her into his arms and buried his head into her spasming neck to comfort her. He was grateful that her long auburn hair hid his face because he was struggling mightily to maintain his composure, and he was barely winning the fight. He held her and gently stroked her back, but he knew he didn't dare speak; he didn't trust his voice. She knew her husband well and finally gathered her wits and willed her brain to move into operations mode.

"Is he dead?"

Jefferey was finally able to speak in a whisper. "Oh no, Mary. No! No! He's just still knocked out."

"How much did you give him?"

"The entire syringe. He fought us like a tiger, and I need to warn you, he got me in my eye with a right hook too."

That broke the tension, and she laughed. Her big retired special forces guy got sucker punched in the face by a fourteen-year-old! Really!

Jeffrey pulled back a few inches. "I've asked Pink to ride with you back to the house and take John upstairs to our guest room. When he wakes in a few hours, I don't want him to hurt himself or anyone else."

"Why is he wrapped in a bedsheet like a corpse? I thought he had died en route!"

"He fought so hard we had to wrap him up and stick him with the entire contents of the syringe to get him to stop. The dorm room was a mess, clothes piled everywhere, so we didn't have a chance to sort out his clothes. Maybe one of the guys has something he can wear. He's only wearing boxers."

Pinkney "Pink" Summey had come down the stairs and walked over to the SUV. "I'll drive, Mary. You've been up all night, and this day is only gonna get worse."

After confirmation had come in the day before by sat phone, she had thought of nothing else except the sadness of this situation. Yesterday's mascara had streaked her normally beautiful cheeks, and her face was drawn. She suddenly yawned, gratefully opened the passenger door, and slumped into the seat. She was secretly glad that she was spared from having to watch the next event. Twelve members of the Ops Center staff walked up to the far side of the plane to start the gruesome task. As was the family tradition, all family members were buried in the family cemetery in coffins built from the ancient long leaf pine trees that had grown on the land. These prized, precious old boards had been salvaged from trees that had fallen over the years. Those gathered at the ramp stood ramrod stiff as they heard the unmistakable sounds of the electric drills forcing the waxed brass screws into the ancient pine. The sounds of the screaming screws only made the grief worse.

Jeffrey walked over and stood beside his old friend, John Bishop the eleventh. John was the owner of the farm and the grandfather of the boy. He was the father and father-in-law of the two people in the coffins. Jeffrey didn't dare touch or speak to him because he could see that his old friend was barely holding it together. The staff gathered into two columns and quietly followed as the pallbearers walked slowly toward the rising sun.

Many were openly sobbing. Husbands were holding onto their wives. Had anyone noticed, they would have seen that John Bishop, known to all simply by his nickname, XI, from the Roman numerals for eleven—his full name was John Bishop XI—was clenching his fists as tightly as possible in an effort to trick his brain into feeling the pain in his palms rather than producing tears. Bishop men had been trained from birth to stifle their emotions.

XI stood quietly between the heavy custom crimson French silk damask window drapes as he stared out from one of the Georgian-style double-hung windows in the front withdrawing room of the Swan Bay manor house. Standing six feet, six inches tall, he was absent-mindedly twisting one of the elaborately hand-worked metallic gold braided tie-back passementerie as he tried to gather his thoughts. As was the family tradition, both bodies were lying in repose in this room. Following another ancient family custom, their caskets were draped with their respective Scottish tartans. After a long pause, he spoke to the group of staff gathered there. Among them were his law partner, Edward Hardy; his Ops Center and farm manager, Jeffrey Beverly; and the managing partner of the Bogota, Colombia, branch of their law firm, Luis Torres. Luis had merged his firm with Bishop Hardy a few years earlier to continue the environmental work in South America.

"There can be no death certificates, no coroner's report, no media, or police." He paused again and took a deep breath. "But we must bury them immediately. I'll send out a press release later announcing that they were lost in a storm in the Andes...probably fell over a cliff or something, and their bodies have not been recovered."

The men all looked at each other and quietly nodded their heads. Two others, trusted workers on the farm, finally spoke. "We'll go and prepare the graves, sir."

"Thank you," he said. "Put my son—John Bishop XII was known simply as JB—in the family plot next to his mother, and bury Liz beside him. For now, make it look as undisturbed as possible."

Jeffrey asked, "Has anyone thought to call the rector?"

"No. It's too early to bother Jack, and I want to do this as quickly as possible. We'll follow the rites of the church. *The Book of Common Prayer* allows a lay reader to read the Burial Office. Jeffrey, I'd like you to read it...and, Luis...if you will, the twenty-third psalm and the lessons."

Both responded that it would be their honor.

An hour later, the group dispersed from the old Bishop family cemetery. Mac MacLennan, one of the Ops Center team members and a former Scottish regimental pipe major, walked up to XI. "Sir, I brought my pipes, if you think a tune would be in order."

"Oh, yes, Mac. Thank you. Your Great Highland Bagpipes will be perfect, but make it lively. JB hated dirges."

Mac began to play an old jig they all loved known as "Highland Laddie."

*****

As the group approached the manor, the skirl of the pipes woke young John. He warily looked around the room, which bore no resemblance to any of the rooms at his school. He pulled the comforter up around him and stared at the man sitting in a chair at the foot of the bed. Pink was second in command to Jeffrey. "Pink? He captured you too? How? Where are we?"

Pink gazed at him before speaking. "We're in Virginia at the farm."

"Quit lying to me and tell them to just get it over with. Torture me, kill me, do whatever the hell it is they're going to do, but just *do* it!"

"None of that's going to happen, John. As I said, you're no longer in South America. I know you probably don't remember being rescued and brought here, but you're now in the United States, and you're safe."

"Where's my mother? I need to call her."

Pink gestured toward the bathroom door. "Why don't you take a shower? I'm sure it will make you feel better. There's a borrowed set of clothes that should fit you hanging in the closet."

Head pounding, John finally swung his feet to the side of the bed. He took a few unsteady steps toward the bathroom and then closed and locked the door behind him. A sudden wave of nausea overtook him, and he knelt over the toilet. There was nothing but dry heaves. He couldn't remember when he'd last eaten.

When he finally stood, he moved to the window. *There must be a way to escape*, he thought.

When he pulled the curtain back, though, the view was comforting. There were no bars, no jungle, no men with assault rifles—only a massive red barn and pastures that seemed to go on forever. Men and women in work clothes led some of the most beautiful horses he'd ever seen around pens near the barn. He knew this place. He had spent the last summer here while his parents summered in their RV high in the Andes. He hated the Andes. One summer there had been more than enough. He refused to go back, so his parents packed him off to Virginia. That suited JB because he had never wanted a child. Liz agreed because she knew that to do otherwise would just make everyone miserable.

His weakness returned, and he sat down in a chair in front of an antique vanity. When the nausea passed, he stripped off his boxers and stepped into the shower. As he stood letting the warmth of the water revive him, thoughts raced through his head. *Did the cartel drug me? Am I just dreaming from a cocaine-induced haze? Are my parents here?*

Dressed in the ill-fitting clothes from the closet, John opened the door of the bathroom. Pink was still there, so he decided that it must be real. "Feel better?" Pink asked.

John said nothing.

Pink gestured toward the door. "Then let's go downstairs." The two descended a massive staircase and entered a room even larger than the bedroom.

He chose a Queen Anne chair near a window through which even more endless pastures could be seen. A woman wearing a bright red-and-blue plaid tartan apron carrying a tray with tomato juice and some small buttered biscuits entered from a side door. "Ms. Mamie! Now I know it's real! I couldn't hallucinate your buttered biscuits, and Espinis wouldn't know that I hate orange juice."

Not completely understanding the comment, she said as she hugged him, "We're all just glad you're safe, honey! It's near lunch-time, but your grandfather thought you might like something to eat before."

The door opened, and Mamie left as XI entered the room and sat down on a love seat across from him. He leaned forward and poured another glass of juice for the boy.

John wasted no more time. "Why am I here during school term? Where are my parents?"

A look of sadness swept over XI's face. Despite his best efforts, tears began to well up in his eyes, and he was forced to turn away.

CHAPTER 2

Confession

"John, I'm not really hungry at the moment, so unless you want more, please come with me outside. We need to talk, and I need some fresh air." XI led John out to an old, well-preserved log cabin, and they sat in wooden rocking chairs on the often-restored porch.

"I will tell you everything. I won't leave out anything unless you decide it's too much. I'm afraid I have very bad news." XI began to tremble. He couldn't hold it any longer. "I'm sorry." He managed to blurt out between sobs, "Your parents are dead."

Astonished and shocked, John began to cry. DEAD? "My mother's DEAD? NO! No!"

John jumped up screaming and started running. His sudden movements startled Jeffrey's chocolate Lab, Buster. Buster jumped up and ran after him.

Pink was walking by, saw John run, and started after him, but XI sighed and quietly said, "No, let him run. We've still got the GPS chip tracking him. He needs to be alone. I need to be alone too. It's just too much for one day. Buster will keep him safe.

At sundown, Pink took the ATV out and found the boy in a pine grove propped up asleep under a massive old tree. The effects of the drug hadn't fully worn off.

The noise woke him. "Come on back, boy. It's suppertime, and everyone wants to see you."

John's stomach was growling.

Supper was a sumptuous feast served in the formal dining room. Ms. Mamie had outdone herself to welcome John home. The table seated twenty-six in fine Chippendale chairs around an eighteenth-century English Chippendale table, and many of the farm staff were waiting there. The eighteenth-century Chippendale sideboard groaned with all the heaping dishes of food. There were fires in both fireplaces to warm the room from the spring evening chill. XI introduced the rescue team, and John was careful to thank them even though he still didn't understand what had actually happened.

During supper, XI casually mentioned, "I need to leave for a few days, but I would like it if you would stay here for a while. I need to sort out some details about all of this, and I need to be in New York and Washington to do it. This is your ancestral home, and one day, you'll inherit all of this—sooner than planned, as it turns out—so it would be good if you would start getting to know more about it. There's a whole history that you don't know. I know you've been here before, but you spent most of your summers sitting in the ballroom practicing your music. Do you know that the cabin with the porch where we were sitting this morning was built by your first American ancestor after he arrived in 1638 from Scotland? Perhaps you would like to live there while I make other arrangements."

John was still in shock about his parents' murders, but to clear his mind, he asked, "May I go to New York with you? I need to buy some clothes."

"I think you need to stay here for a while." XI didn't want to tell him that there might still be a threat against his life, and he wasn't comfortable turning him loose in New York. The rescue helicopter had been airborne less than five minutes when the trucks arrived at the school gate. The pilot had seen the bright lights off in the distance as the chopper headed for the airport, and he turned for a moment to watch them enter the gates. "Pink can take you to Williamsburg tomorrow to shop. Buy a week's worth of everything, but I don't think you've stopped growing, so don't buy the high-end stuff yet."

"Can we at least sail over in the boat? I don't want to keep growing. I'm fine the way I am!" John was a six-foot, two-inch blond, blue-eyed slim but not skinny boy, with a movie star boyish-type clear face.

"Maybe if the weather is good."

Pink chimed in, "I'll be glad to take you. I need a few things myself."

"I like the quietness here, but can we at least move Mother's little portative organ from the Cali apartment up here?"

XI laughed. "Yes. I'll have the apartment closed and the contents moved here right away."

"Thank you. It's really the only thing I want from there, but I wish I had my journals from my dorm room in that hellhole of a school."

Ignoring the reference to what he considered as the finest boys' boarding school in South America, XI told him, "I also think we should get you a complete physical exam just in case you're carrying some 'jungle bug' which could come back to haunt you sometime in the future. You'll probably need inoculations too. All of this will take a few days, and I need to get some paperwork made for you."

After supper, XI asked him to sit with him for a while in the little study behind the withdrawing room. He tried again, this time with more success. He reached for his little nosing glass, took a small sip of his favorite eighteen-year-old Macallan single-malt scotch, swirled it around in his mouth, and began. "I'm an attorney, and this is the only way I know to handle this situation. I'm sorry I dropped such a bomb on you this morning. Obviously, you were still under the effects of the drugs, and it wasn't fair of me to have done it that way, but unfortunately, both your parents were murdered, near the mountain village. Apparently they stumbled into a cocaine field. We found their bodies using their GPS chips just as we did you. They are buried here now. I know you have questions, but please, just let me start at the beginning, and I think things will make more sense to you."

John unconsciously reached for his own chip hidden behind his right ear. His nerves were raw. He had never really understood why it had been necessary to have a chip, but now, suddenly, it occurred to him that he may have been responsible for the murders. Was it one of the Colombian drug lord Espinis's fields? Maybe that's why he was rescued so quickly. He needed to change the subject as fear began to run rampant in his mind. "Sir, what is that you're sipping?"

He told him that it was one of the finest drinks Scotland produced. "We're descended from Scots, you know."

"Yes, that's one of the few civil conversations my father ever had with me. May I try a little? I think that's the same stuff my father drank, but he wouldn't ever let me taste it."

"For good reason! You're too young for alcohol, but perhaps a little, a wee dram, as the Scots call it, might help you settle down a bit. We'll call it a medicinal dram just for tonight." XI walked over to the small bar, took down another nosing glass, and poured a small amount. "This is a nosing glass. Notice that the neck is shaped like a little clear glass chimney to concentrate the aroma. Sniff it deeply first and then sip. Let it roll around in your mouth before you swallow."

"It burns my throat a little, but the taste is nice."

"Well, it's an acquired taste, but don't get used to it. You must be twenty-one before you can drink alcohol. I want to begin with Scotland and the family history. I have here on the table a book we call a journal. It's the daily log of our ancestor, the first John Bishop. He was a sea captain and a planter, and these are his recordings of his voyages and of his years in Virginia. This is a copy. I have given all the originals to the University of Virginia's rare book library. Each succeeding generation kept a journal. Well, actually they're a collection of ship's logs, ledgers, diaries, day books, and such. So far, there are ten in all. They cover everything from the operations of the farms, the weather, politics, and family events. You're welcome to read them at any time."

"So I guess yours isn't finished yet, number eleven, I mean."

He laughed. "I haven't started yet. I'll get to it when I retire. I only have notes at the moment." Continuing, he added, "We're going to have the condo in Cali emptied and then sold, unless you want to keep it."

"No way! No! I'm never going back to Colombia for ANY reason. You can sell that stupid camping trailer too. Get rid of it all!"

"Okay, okay. Settle down. It's yours now, so I just wanted to ask before making decisions for you."

"I really do want that little organ. You can sell the Yamaha concert grand piano in the Cali penthouse if you want. I prefer the Bosendorfer Concert Grand here."

"I'm sure that can be arranged, but now, back to Captain John. While I'm away, I want you to read about him. This transcription with commentary will be much easier to read than the original."

CHAPTER 3

Spring 1638

James River, Virginia

Since he had slept for most of the last twenty-four hours, John settled into a black leather recliner in the cabin and began to read chapter one of the manuscript.

*****

"We're so close, so close, Mr. Bishop. Ye bloody fog rolled in just as we passed through ye breakwater, and ye wind and tide died straight away. I'm so sorry, sir, but I had to drop anchor. I can't see me hand in front of me face, sir."

"Bloody hell, laddie, but ye did good, Mr. Bonner. Now go on down and warm yerself. We'll all need our strength for this adventure. I'll take the helm. The sun's a-coming. I can almost feel warmth on me back."

Ramrod straight, six feet, six inches tall, narrow at the waist, and broad in the shoulders, John Bishop had been pacing the fo'c's'le deck of his ship, Swan, *for hours waiting for the sun to burn the fog off. Unruly, curly blond hair and watery blue eyes marked him as a Viking, but he was all Scot. His pale white skin would soon become a deep brown. His four-month-old beard accentuated his appearance.*

In Tidewater, Virginia, the results of the spring temperature change produced thick fog on the rivers. Visibility was zero. At least there was a dull glow in the eastern sky. The spring days were getting warmer, but their nights were still cold. There was nothing to do but wait and hope the sun would quickly burn it off.

*****

John Bishop; his wife, Elizabeth; their young son, John Jr.; three indentured men; and a seasoned sea captain hired to teach John the ways of the sea had left his older brother James's new dock on the River Clyde at Greenock Port near Glasgow on Christmas Day. Since the dour Lords of the Congregation no longer allowed Christmas celebrations, they hadn't missed anything. Bitter battles with his father, Sir Knight William Bishop the Elder, and his mother, Charteris Hew Lady Elizabeth Ramsay of Clatto, Midlothian, Scotland, had waged on for months. His oldest brother, Sir Knight William Bishop the Younger, would inherit the title and the land, and he had finally convinced their parents that since John and James couldn't inherit, they should seek their fortunes out in the world. Often, younger sons went into the clergy, but John and his brother James were adventurous and wanted no part of that! As children, they had been convinced that the local Scots preacher must live in hell during the week since he knew so much about it and never stopped railing about it during his intolerably long Sunday sermons, and they were sure his soot-black clothes must have been singed by the fires he always ranted about. The preacher never smiled, but he loved to drop by and consume an entire bottle of Sir William's whiskey after Sunday service.

Finally, Sir William decided that John could sail to Virginia and grow tobacco. The Bishops and the Ramsays had long distinguished histories in the service of the Scottish monarchs, not the least of whom was King John. John was married to Elizabeth Booker, and her brother was one of London's successful tobacco brokers. The Bookers were a family of prominence in London. John sailed to London and left Elizabeth and John Jr. at Elizabeth's brother's town house. John Jr. and his cousin would enter boarding school in the fall. Using the family's connections, Sir William had agreed to finance his sons' plans. England forbade Scotland to trade with the colonies in the seventeenth century, so these family ties were crucial. John could sell his tobacco to his brother-in-law at the docks in London. Sir William's mother claimed ties to King James, and so did Lady Elizabeth. Lady Elizabeth's uncle had saved the life of King James's in an incident known as the Gowrie Conspiracy. One of her family members, Sir Thomas Bishop, married the king's third cousin. The king never forgot the Bishop family. John Bishop's tobacco preferments were therefore linked to the king. John and James had grand plans of becoming wealthy. In England, tobacco was already being referred to as brown gold. King James I hated tobacco—he even wrote a treatise condemning the noxious weed, but being a savvy Scot, he convinced Parliament to pass heavy taxes on it.

A fair wind on the Atlantic reduced the voyage to only four months, including the stay in London. Leaving Scotland during the winter took courage, but old sailors told legendary tales of terrible storms that swept up the Atlantic seaboard of America during the late summer and fall. John was eager to get settled and start planting. *Swan* was not the largest ship on the high seas, but it belonged to him. It rode at anchor in the mouth of the James River, waiting on a little warmth, a breeze, and a flooding tide. With him, he'd brought three passengers: John Tompkins, John Bonner, and John Wright. They were indentured to him and would work off their financial obligations by helping him clear the land. Indentures only lasted a few years, so John was in a hurry. He had also hired a fine captain for this voyage. The captain taught James the basics needed to sail the Atlantic, and then the captain caught the next ship sailing from James Citty back to England.

*****

The sun burned off the fog, the winds rose out of the southeast, and the tide began its late morning flood. By midday, Swan *landed safely at the new English settlement of James Citty, where the river was six fathoms deep at the dock so the ships merely tied off to the trees on the river bank. John Bishop was twenty-six years old when he first stepped onto the ground. When he disembarked, John went in search of his distant cousin, Thomas Gray. John was afraid Thomas might be out on one of his farms, but luckily, he found him in town. Having read the sealed letters of introduction, Thomas agreed to grant John a land patent in Virginia.*

The two men sat to talk. Thomas, one of the men known as an Ancient Planter, arrived at James Fort when he was fifteen and somehow managed to survive. Thomas explained the regulations as established by the London Company. John knew them all but sat patiently and listened. When Thomas stopped speaking, John nodded and asked, "May I ask you about tobacco, please? I want to know as much as possible afore I start planting."

Thomas filled the bowl of his long-stemmed pipe. "Spanish Conquistadors found the plant growing in the Andes while searching for gold. Native Caribs had domesticated it and had been smoking it since the beginning of time. The first Europeans discovered the natives here using the very same plant for religious and ceremonial purposes. The Conquistadors imported it to Spain, where it became immensely popular, and Spain jealously guarded it. John Rolfe managed to acquire new, untested seeds and brought them with him when he landed here from Bermuda about the same time as I did. The seeds are very tiny and must be started in pots until the danger of frost has passed. They must be strong before they can be planted in the fields."

Thomas paused. "The work is backbreaking. From the clearing of the trees, to the planting of seeds, to the weeding of the rows, to the cutting the leaves, to the drying and packing, and finally to the moving of the heavy barrels, this work is not for weak men. The ancient plants are known as Nicotiana rustica, but Rolfe's improved seeds were called Nicotiana tobacum. Rolfe took his leaves to London, where they were an immediate hit. His tobacco leaves are light tan and much less bitter than the Spanish and Indian rustica. The land here is perfect for growing it, but over time, the land seems to stop growing it. We must keep clearing more land to continue to supply the Europeans. Fortunately, we have more land than we need."

John smiled. "Is Mr. Rolfe living? I'd like to meet him."

Thomas shook his head. "No. He died in 1622, but I can tell you, and everyone here will agree, he saved this colony by introducing the new tobacco."

"Tell me about Africans."

"One of the sea captains landed near here about 1619. He had captured a Portuguese ship bound for Bermuda. Actually, I believe he pirated it, but the cargo hold was loaded with Africans headed for the sugar cane fields. The planters saw the value of having these workers and started purchasing them at the dock. At first, they were treated as indentured servants, like your three fellows, but we soon realized they were too valuable to let them go."

John was doing quick calculations in his head. His startup was going to be expensive. "Why was the smoke so popular?"

"Who knows? It's one of life's little pleasures. As you remember, since ancient times, many houses had holes in the roof to let most of the smoke out from fires built on the earthen floors of the central rooms. The danger of fire, especially to the thatched roofs, was always a fear. As brick and stone fireplaces replaced the holes in the roof, the houses became less smokey. Maybe the tobacco smoke replaced the older, familiar smells of home. Tobacco can be smoked by rolling a few ground leaves into a stick, or it can be dipped, or it can be snuffed up the nose."

"Yes, I saw all of that in Glasgow."

"Now, please tell me more about the colony."

Thomas was growing tired, but he filled another bowl with his tobacco. He offered one to John, but he declined. "James Citty, sometimes spelled C-i-t-t-i-e, was founded in May 1607 as a business enterprise first called James Fort. The town barely survived the early hardships, but now tobacco is allowing the town to thrive."

"Thank you for your time. I'll be back to meet with you when my patent is ready for signatures."

Walking through town, John noticed timber-framed two-story houses, shops, and a wooden church. Several men were sawing logs into timber. John was not very familiar with wooden houses like these. He had seen the ancient half-timbered houses, but he was more familiar with stone buildings in Scotland. The secretary to the colony was constructing a new brick house, and there was talk of building a brick custom house. Clay for making bricks was very plentiful, and the local shellfish were being made into lime for mortar. The religious denomination of James Citty was Church of England. The Bishop family had originally been Roman Catholic and loyal to Mary, Queen of Scots, but John's father joined the new Protestant Church of Scotland. The Lords of the Congregation made it nearly impossible for anyone who wanted to remain within the social and business relationships to resist conversion. His heart wasn't in it, but business was business. In Scotland, the Church of England began to compete with the Lords of the Congregation. When Scottish James VI ascended the throne of England, he took the name James I and automatically became the head of the Church of England. The Lords of the Congregation hated the English Church, however, and began murdering Scottish clergymen who dared to profess the faith of the English Church. The truth was, religion was simply not an issue for James Bishop. He was there to make money.

*On November 9, 1638, Thomas Grey granted John Bishop his first land patent for 150 acres of land in James Citty County. The patent is described as being "**at the head of Tappahonnock Creek, Northerly upon a path, Wly towards a reedy swamp, E. towards a sunken marsh & sly into the woods. Due for trans of 3 pers: John Tompkins, John Bonner, John Wright.**"*

John and his workers spent their first months in Virginia working with the planters, learning about growing and curing tobacco, but he was not really ready for the extent of work required to clear the land. The huge trees required several men to fell, and then there were the stumps. They needed to wait until the ground thawed to dig around the stumps and cut the upper roots with their ax. They finally pilled the dead branches around the stumps and burned them out pulling out whatever remained using horses. It was time-consuming hard work, but they simply planted between the largest stumps when they had no other choice. He finally came to the conclusion that he would need more experienced men to help him get started. It would take the four of them entirely too long to clear the land by themselves. He was able to find the help he needed, but the price was high. Finally, after purchasing food supplies to replenish their stores, they set sail for the wilderness of the North American frontier. The patent was about seventy miles from James Citty by land, but James sailed down the James River into Chesapeake Bay, and then north into the Tappahannock.

To save time, and for safety, rather than build houses, they lived aboard the ship. They worked hard at the backbreaking job of clearing the land and getting the plants started. He used the first timber to build a barn for his horses, mules, cow, and chickens. Bugs! Swarms of biting insects plagued them. He laid awake at night, swatting the biting insects, trying to determine a plan for his enterprise. His main worry was the cost of labor. The simple answer was to buy slaves, but he thought the price was very high, and they needed training. John barely knew the growing process himself, so he didn't think that trying to work and teach slaves was an efficient way forward. He thought that on his next trip to England, he could just stop in Africa and buy slaves there much cheaper than at the dock in James Citty, but he had seen, heard, and smelled enough slave ships to know that he didn't really want that. Then just before he drifted off one night, he had an idea. There were plenty of others in Scotland who would come as indentured servants. If he brought a few every trip, he could stagger his workforce so training would be easier. They spoke the same language, traveled free except for the cost of provisions on the voyage, and were willing workers.

After all, once their indenture was over, the colony would give them fifty acres of land, and the colony would give him land for bringing the new servants. He only needed to get the crop up and running.

Once they were sure the natives wouldn't attack, John started planning to build houses and a barn for curing the tobacco. On his next provisioning trip to James Citty, he went to the sawmill and asked if he might buy the owner a pint. In the tavern, John asked about building with wood.

"I'm not familiar with wood construction," confessed John. "What might it cost me to have your men construct four houses and a tobacco barn on my land?"

Ever the frugal Scot, John didn't like the terms. So he asked if the man would take his timber in trade. The sawyer, a Swede, was a shrewd businessman. He quoted John a price. John liked his price for the timber, but he still thought the Swede's construction and material costs were high.

"Well," said the sawyer, "here's another idea you might like. I notice you've brought pine and some very fine poplar. We Swedes had been building our houses from poplar since the beginning of time. It's one of the preferred timbers in our country. It's much warmer in winter because it's thicker than the thin stuff the English prefer."

John liked the idea of that. "How do I build with the logs?"

"Strip the bark from the logs and cut the lengths that you need. Hew them flat on all four sides. They will shed water better than the round surfaces. Cut notches into the ends and stack them. Then pack the spaces between the logs with moss from the riverbanks or mud and small stones. Here, let me draw it for you."

While the sawyer drew, John bought another round. When the pints arrived, the Swede took a draught and pointed to his drawings. "Your logs are large enough that you can split them down the middle and get two logs for every length. These you brought are wide enough you won't need to stack them but four high. It won't take you and your men long to stack enough to get them to eave height. Set the bottom course on stone piers to keep the wet earth away. You can build your fireplace and chimney with logs, but line the interior with thick mud to keep them from burning."

Having already calculated his savings, he decided to buy a few bricks and some lime for mortar for his chimneys. He traded his logs for doors and windows from the Swede's supply. He also hired one sawyer and an apprentice to teach them to build the first cabin.

During the next year, John's land produced fine tobacco, but he wanted to be closer to the town. By 1643, he had established another 891-acre farm nearer to James Citty. He built a larger log cabin for himself on the new land and a larger log barn and curing barns, and he built log cabins for his growing number of indentured servants. He could already see the value of his idea. His profits were steadily rising because his labor costs were less than the planters who bought Africans or didn't own their own ship.

On his return voyage from England that year, his wife, Elizabeth, came with him. By then, other members of her family were living in Virginia and trading with her brother in London too. He stopped in Bermuda and bought one slave woman to help his wife with the house-

hold chores and cooking. As a well-bred English woman, Elizabeth had never had to cook, much less clean a house or wash clothes.

Before long, John was established in the community. He was elected as burgess of Charles City in 1644 and became a captain of the Charles City Militia as a Royalist in support of King Charles I. He also had been elected to the vestry of Westover Church in Charles City. Known by the villagers as Capt'n John, his fortune continued to quickly rise, and he and Elizabeth returned to England, this time bringing their children to America. John had always left his profits in England because he didn't really trust the Virginia currency. His Loyalist tendencies, though, were causing problems with the English government, and he knew it was too dangerous to leave the children there. His eldest son, John, was sixteen. He moved his now considerable profits to Scotland. In 1651, he established another farm of three hundred acres on Upper Chippokes Creek on the south side of the James River across from Jamestown and Charles City.

John and his son sat on their horses, surveying the land. "Father, is that it?" Asked John Jr.

"Aye, laddie. Read this paper and see if you agree."

*Young John took the papers and read, "**Mr. John Bishop, 300 acs, lying upon the S side of Upper Chipoaks Cr., commonly called by the name of Swan Bay. Due sd. Bishop for trans, of 6 persons: John Bishopp, Eliza Bishopp, Mary Bishop, one Negro wench, Ann Ingleton, Jno Bishop, Junr. 9 Apr. 1651, p.323.**" The boy looked at his father and down at the paper again. "Jno Bishop Junr. That be me?"*

"Aye, laddie. That be you."

John decided to keep the name Swan Bay. The best located of his three tracts, the land sloped gently down to the creek which was deep enough for him to build a dock. Now, he could fill larger barrels and simply roll them onto the ship.

At breakfast the next morning, Elizabeth was oddly silent. It was clear to John that Elizabeth had something on her mind. "What are you thinking about, Mrs. Bishop?" he asked.

"Mr. Bishop," she responded, "I want a new English house, not a log cabin. I want a place for my Flemish virginal. The children must keep up with their music lessons."

He thought about it for a minute and countered, "But the logs are free, and the English boards are not. The log house will be warmer in winter."

"But hot in summer!"

"Aye. I will build you a fine covered porch and locate the cabin in the trees at the top of that gently sloped meadow. There will be space for the virginal, but the lad must work the land."

"He's a fine musician. He will practice at night."

John was as good as his word. He built a large log cabin for his family, two tobacco barns, a barn for the livestock, and several cabins for his workers. He also built a large brick kitchen away from the cabin, which boasted a large brick fireplace and oven. His slave woman who lived above the kitchen made good use of it. She was a fine cook.

One afternoon, John and his son sat on their front porch discussing the farm. "Laddie," said John, "this is fine land. You must never lose it. Here you and your sister will regenerate the Bishop clan in America."

John Jr. turned to his father. "What does 'regenerate' mean?"

"Get the Book of Common Prayer and turn to the service of Baptism." Archbishop Thomas Cranmer created this word. The boy obeyed, and when he returned, John said, "Read the opening Baptismal Prayer."

*"**Dearly Beloved,**" began John Jr., "**forasmuch as all men be conceived and born into sin, and that our Savior Christ saith, None can enter into the kingdom of God except he be regenerate...**"*

"I see," said the boy looking up at his father. "Because we will start our new family line in America, it will be like we have been regenerated."

John smiled at his son. "Aye, laddie. Aye."

*****

John was getting sleepy. The two extra medicinal drams of scotch had worked their magic. "Okay. That's enough for tonight." My god, what a story! Who knew.

*****

The next morning, John walked barefooted into the kitchen. His borrowed clothes were too tight. The hem of the jeans was above his ankles, and he couldn't button the top two buttons of the plaid shirt.

"You hungry, honey?"

"Yes, ma'am. May I still have breakfast, please?"

"Yes, sir. You just sit down right here and tell Ms. Mamie what you want."

Ms. Mamie was about five feet, five inches tall and very thin and fit.

John thought that she talked funny.

"I would like some of your blueberry pancakes, please."

"Not today. Too late in the season. Here's a plate of some of Ms. Mamie's finest breakfast, sugar. Grits, red-eye gravy, country ham, buttered biscuits, and homemade cherry jam. You want milk and sugar in yo' coffee?

"Ms. Mamie, don't you remember that I don't like grits, gravy, and that ham? It's too salty."

"I thought you learned to eat real food in that school. The good Lord made salt to season food."

"The good Lord made the eggs too, and if he had wanted them to be salty, he would have added it, but he didn't."

"Now don't you go giving me no sass, city boy. We don't eat bagels and yogurt here. We eat what I make. Everybody loves my cooking. You can start fixing your own breakfast."

"Now, Ms. Mamie, you know I love your cooking, just not the salty stuff. I don't drink coffee either. It comes from Colombia, but I'll take a cup of tea if it's no trouble—no sugar or milk, just a slice of lemon, please. I would love several of your delicious little biscuits too."

"Uh-huh, but, honey, you gonna be in trouble around here. This place runs on coffee. Even our rector over at the Westover Episcopal Church says coffee is the third sacrament on Sundays. Where are your shoes, sugar? You can't be walking around all barefoot around here. Catch some nastiness and then it'll be me who has to look after you."

"They belong to someone else, and they were too tight this morning."

"Uh-huh. You're a growing boy, honey. I'll talk with Mary. She'll get you fixed up. Ms. Mamie will whip up some special pancakes for you tomorrow." She beamed.

Honey, sugar, uh-huh. John was still having trouble with the Virginia language.

Jeffrey came in while John was eating the buttered biscuits and joined him at the old kitchen table. Afterward, as they walked back out to the old porch and when they were out of Mamie's hearing, Jeffrey said, "So you don't like our grits and red-eye gravy?"

"No, sir, or that salty ham. And I think that red-eye gravy must have coffee in it."

"Don't worry about it. That pot of grits has been cooking all night. She feeds breakfast and lunch to the entire staff five days a week. I'm afraid one night the pot is going to burn this kitchen down, but it has been that way ever since the kitchen was built, I suppose. Someone else will eat it. You should know Ms. Mamie is a direct descendant of Capt'n John's first Negro woman. She's been cooking for the farm all of her life. Her family has lived and worked on this land for twelve, now with you, thirteen generations. Her ancestors are buried in the Bishop family cemetery alongside all of your family. She and her husband live in Scotland, Virginia, just down the road. He works on the James River ferry boat, *Pocahontas*, between Scotland and Jamestown. This whole area loves and depends on him. They have raised three children, and XI sent each of them to college. Her eldest son is in medical school at George Washington University in DC on a full scholarship.

"Did you notice the large fireplace over beyond the kitchen table? That's Capt'n John's original kitchen fireplace. The table is original too. The white plaster on the fireplace wall is the original lime plaster made from oyster shells. It's never been painted, and it's still in great condition. XI had the kitchen remodeled and brought up to modern restaurant standards when he restored the house. The iron hardware is original. During the winter, she still bakes in the little brick oven. I promise you can taste the difference in her winter biscuits. In the fall, she still roasts large game in the fireplace, but she sure does love the new dishwashers, the two big gas Viking ranges, and the air-conditioning! What do you want to do today? Have you finished the book?"

"It's not really a book yet. It's just chapter one, but it's one hell of a tale. Life was much different then, but I'm just now beginning to discover that I've got a lot to learn about this place. I've noticed that there are more men around than seems necessary to run this place. What do they all do? And how were stable hands able to kidnap—I mean, rescue me and recover my parents' bodies?"

Jeffrey knew that this issue would come up sooner or later, but he wasn't in a position to discuss it at the moment. "You need to talk to XI about that."

"Okay. Then I want to have a tour of the farm. I'll view it with different eyes this time, I think. After the tour, Pink's taking me to buy new clothes."

CHAPTER 4

The Best Man

XI's jet left Swan Bay at 6:00 a.m. for the quick flight to Teterboro Airport in New Jersey. His driver picked him up, and just as he was settling in for the drive across the Hudson, his phone rang. His secretary called to say she had a man named David Dale on the line asking to meet with him today if possible.

"Do I know him? Oh yes, JB's best man. Of course. What does he want? Okay, make some time for him. Okay, five thirty, and make a reservation downstairs for dinner for two if he's available. We've got a lot to discuss. I want to pick his brain, and it'll take a while.

XI's offices were in the Seagram Building in midtown Manhattan. The bronze and glass building had been designed by the famous midcentury German architect Ludwig Mies van der Rohe. XI's private suite occupied the entire southern end of the top floor. His secretary sat in a spacious reception room between the conference room and his private office. His large conference room occupied the southeast corner, and his private office occupied the southwest corner. There was a small vestibule between the reception room and his office that allowed total privacy. A door to his private toilet and shower opened off the vestibule. The walls in the entire suite were covered with either book and butt matched French walnut panels or pale gray Scottish wool fabric. There was a large Picasso in his reception room and a large Canaletto in the conference room. He didn't have the usual trophy wall of diplomas and pictures with famous people in his office, but there were two more Picassos on the wall behind his desk. The furnishings were all midcentury modern, and the guest chairs were Miesian Barcelona chairs of black leather and chrome carefully placed on a large antique silk rug.

David walked in precisely at 5:30 p.m. XI offered him a drink.

"Yes, please. Macallan 18. JB drank it and taught me to love it. Mr. Bishop, I know you're very busy, but Kayla and I just wanted to give you our condolences for JB and Liz. We are just heartbroken. They were our oldest friends. We've known them since we first met at Exeter."

"Thank you, David. That means a lot to me. And please call me XI. Everyone does. Unfortunately, I know very little about JB's time at Philips Exeter and Harvard. If you have some time, I'd like it very much if you could tell me everything you can remember. Since they are gone, you won't be betraying their confidences or memory. I'm left to raise their son, and he is very inquisitive. When he starts to ask questions about his parents, I don't want to appear to be the disinterested parent that I obviously now see that I was. I need to not make the same mistakes this time with young John. Perhaps we can start with my telling you about my relationship with my son."

"Yes, sir. That would be helpful, and take all the time you need. I'm in no hurry."

"JB was a happy child, but he was restless." He sighed. "Perhaps if he had had a sibling, but that just never happened. The last several generations of Bishops only produced single sons. He hated the house in DC, but he loved Swan Bay. Truth be told, he ran my staff ragged when he was there, but on cold winter days, he loved to stretch out on the rug in front of the fire with a pillow and read about faraway places. After his mother died, we both went into a shell. I lost myself in my work, and he went back to boarding school, and well, I guess that was that. It seemed easier at the time to not discuss it."

David took a sip. "May I ask about your wife's death, sir, er, XI?"

XI took a sip. "Certainly. In thinking back over this during the last few days, I think it's key in understanding the whole series of events. We were a happy family. Lorraine and I were childhood sweethearts. Our families were parishioners at Westover Episcopal Church. We had been for generations. We were members of the same hunt club, that sort of thing, but she lived on the east side of the James River, and we lived on the west side." He laughed. "Getting married simplified our lives. The boys in my family have always gone to boarding schools. John Jr., that's John number two, was left in England at school when his father came to Jamestown. In the early years of America, there really weren't any suitable schools for very young boys here, but once Philips Exeter opened, the boys were sent there. We are Scots at heart, you know, and it was easier, faster, and less expensive to sail to New England than make additional Atlantic crossings even though they were constantly back and forth with the tobacco trade. We were in the first class at Exeter and have been students there ever since. We sent JB to board at a fine primary school near our home in DC, and he seemed happy there among the other boys. After that graduation, he, as you know, moved to Exeter and then Harvard."

"But there were fine colleges in early America. The College of William and Mary was near your farm."

"Well, yes, and William and Mary is historically Anglican, whereas Harvard is historically Congregational, but apparently the family believed that an education away from home would give the boys a broader life experience."

"I knew that you were an Exonian, but I didn't know about everyone else. That's where you got your nickname I believe, but JB didn't seem to know that story."

"Yes, well, it's simple. I had a chip on my shoulder, you might say. I didn't want to be there. I wanted to fly. My father, John X, was known as DoX because he studied medicine at Harvard and was the local doctor. He was also the local crop duster. He started a very profitable company that serviced many of the fields in the South. He had no idea about the actual damage he was unleashing on the environment, but we can't judge the morals, mores, and knowledge of our ancestors using today's standards, can we? He and I fought over my wanting to take over the flying business rather than going off to school, but my mother got him to bribe me. She had him buy a larger plane, and we all flew back and forth to Exeter. They let me sit in the copilot seat until I learned to fly long distances. Of course, she had an ulterior motive. On the trips back from dropping me off, she got to shop in Manhattan. She even got him to buy the apartment in the Carlisle Hotel where Liz and JB lived before they moved to Cali. I still use it when I'm in New York. The Latin word for eleven is *Undecim*, Undie, as they tried to call me, and I fought to keep from being tagged with that!"

David laughed.

"I bloodied so many noses that the boys gave in and just called me by two letters *X* and *I* for the roman numerals. But I digress. On a very fine late November day, Lorraine picked JB up from school, and they were driving to Swan Bay for Thanksgiving. I was here in New York, and I was to fly down to Swan Bay next day. She drove an old mint-condition red Ford Thunderbird convertible. It had a hardtop that stowed in the trunk, and on that afternoon, they had the top down, the windows up, and the heater blasting. They were fighting over the radio station. As they approached a stop sign, JB reached over to change the station—there were no seat belts in those days. Lorraine slowed to stop, but the woman behind them didn't stop. The impact shoved their car through the intersection. The other woman went through her windshield and was t-boned by a semi. I still cringe to think that if it had happened a few seconds later..." His voice trailed off.

"That woman died at the scene. Lorraine and JB were transported to the hospital. JB broke his arm, but his position at that moment saved him from going through the windshield. Lorraine hit the steering wheel and broke both arms, but her main injury was with her spine when her head bounced back. It's called whiplash. The investigating officer said that the top in the trunk took much of the impact. The other woman was high on cocaine. Lorraine had several surgeries but became addicted to the painkillers. I didn't realize that she had started using cocaine to supplement the painkillers until she overdosed a few years later. By the time we found her, she was gone, and our lives were never the same."

"Oh my god. How awful! He never talked about that, but that may explain why he always rubbed his arm when he was stressed."

"Interesting. I never noticed."

"Do you still fly? Oh, and tell me more about Swan Bay."

"I can still fly, but now the firm has a policy that makes me travel with two engines and a professional pilot and copilot, and I must admit, it's very comfortable to ride in the back. Swan Bay has a long history. Until recently we always grew tobacco. We have eight thousand acres. Today we grow longleaf pine trees, peanuts, and pasture grasses for our breeding center. My vets keep the horses on a strict diet, which helps make us one of the best breeding centers in America."

"But won't those grasses also attract birds? That would be a problem with flying I would think."

"Yes, but we grow the feed in a large pasture away from the airstrip. The airstrip is fenced, and we also keep dogs. They are free to roam within the fenced airstrip and are trained to keep the birds away."

"Tell me about the manor house, as JB called it. As I recall, it has quite a history."

"Yes, and Cap'n John's cabin of square hewn poplar logs and his timber-framed tobacco barns are still in great but much restored condition. The workers' cabins and barns were later moved further away from the main house, but Cap'n John's cabin is in its original location near the main house. It has been converted to a modern guest house with all the best amenities. John Bishop IV built the main house in 1745 in the Tidewater, Virginia, style. On his 1742 trip to England, he persuaded his young distant Scottish cousin James Stuart, later to become famously known as James 'Anthenian' Stuart, to sketch out a modest house for Swan Bay. James was broke but looking for money to fund a grand tour of Europe, so he took the commission, calling it a 'small provincial country house.' Once back in Virginia, John IV had to greatly reduce and simplify the grand plans to fit his Scot's budget.

"We still have the original drawings. He kept the basic plan, but tobacco prices were dropping in London. He assumed it would be temporary, but he was wrong. Even George Washington and Thomas Jefferson suffered from the drop in value. Because he was trading with his family in London, he avoided losing the land, but he rotated the crops in some of his fields, planting corn and squash to survive. He didn't know that the years of growing tobacco had broken down the soil into a mixture which would grow food crops more easily. His gamble paid off, but the cost of building and furnishing even the greatly reduced house in that economy was very costly."

David nodded his head. "There must have been other hardships too. Having one family hold that much land for over three hundred years is amazing."

XI laughed. "During the Revolutionary War, John V served as a major. He was stationed with the quartermaster of Washington's Army and procured goods and food for them. He saw an advantage and rotated most of his fields to food crops. He grew enough tobacco to help supply Washington's inner circle of men, since trade with England was stopped. When the war ended, he returned to planting tobacco."

"How could anyone have been so lucky?"

XI smiled. "There's a funny story recorded in one of the family's daily journals."

"Journals? They kept journals?"

"Yes. We're very fortunate. Cap'n John started a ship's log before he left Glasgow and kept a daily journal throughout his entire life. All the others have done the same. I recently had them rebound."

"My god. That's most of the history of America!"

"Well, our little piece of it anyway. They contain the ledgers and daily comments about the staff and current events, depending on who wrote them, of course. While John V was away at war, his wife concocted a story saying the barns were full of sick soldiers. The land was posted with numerous signs warning the English that the barns were being used as hospitals and were full of soldiers with typhoid and dysentery. If the Brits got too close, her workers would come out of the barns with brick-filled coffins and, with great ceremony, walk to the cemetery. Her younger brother would come out of the main house dressed in a clerical dog collar and black gown and, in a loud voice so no one could miss it, read the Anglican burial office. The Brits recognized the English ceremony, and it usually did the trick. To be careful, all the silver was buried in the cemetery in carefully marked plots. They built a separate storage vault there with a crypt and hid most of the better furniture and paintings in it. They put a few coffins near the door to discourage exploration. His journal records that the slop pots were occasionally emptied just outside the door to further discourage visitors."

"Those folks were ingenious, weren't they?

"It gets better. While John VIII was serving as an officer under General Lee in the Civil War, his wife used the same hospital ruse with the same effect. No one knows the number of empty unmarked coffins buried in the old family cemetery. Occasionally, grave diggers uncover one, and everyone on the farm stops and merrily toasts 'the dearly departed.'"

"You're right, that's even better," quipped David. "So is the house unchanged since 1745? That would be remarkable in itself."

"No. The eastern riverfront is original, but in 1790, John V remodeled the western front to include a large portico in the classical style. He redecorated the interiors of the principal rooms. He moved the working buildings away from the house and added a large oval of grass surrounded by a drive to allow carriages to arrive under the portico.

"Travel was moving away from the river as the population spread west, so he added massive wrought iron gates with a ten-foot-tall overwork of heavy wrought iron. There are carved swans on the stone gate posts, and there is a wrought iron shield that resembles a bishop's miter in the center of the overwork. I'm told it's called a Clairvoyee. Beyond, he planted a grand allée with magnolia grandiflora trees on both sides of the drive. The lower branches of these old trees have rooted where they touched the ground, and rings of new trees surrounded the mother trees. Some are now nearly eighty feet in diameter."

"How did all of this survive reconstruction? Without slaves, I can't imagine they could continue to grow tobacco."

XI shrugged. “Scot’s ingenuity and guts. They reduced the planting area to the original three hundred acres. They also didn’t know about addiction. Turns out that people will always buy alcohol, tobacco, and now drugs, despite the economy. The journals show that the so-called reconstruction period was another hell on earth for the local landowners. John VIII’s journals record that after the war ended, when the Yankee government sent tax men to punish the Southern landowners and make them pay for the war, he quietly organized the other owners. They expected a herd of Hell’s Minions, as they called them, to swarm over the South, and they were worried that Virginia, being so close to the Devil’s Lair in Washington, would get the top-ranked opportunists.

“The owners met at Swan Bay. John VIII’s idea was to simply replace the old property deed books with fakes that showed they didn’t own much of the land.

“According to the journal, John’s one concern was getting into the courthouse. The old magistrate, Judge Denman—he must have been in his eighties—had been sitting there, seemingly half asleep, and finally spoke up and told them that he had been down in North Georgia in Adairsville trying to help his great-granddaddy’s family. Everyone thought his mind was wandering, but he continued to tell them that Sherman had burned the Georgia family plantation. The family had a fine old three-story plantation mansion, and they had packed the attic with wheat to help them through the coming hard times. Sherman’s men had the plantation slaves put torches to the house and barns, burning everything—including the hidden wheat. When one of the little girls tried to stop the slaves, an officer struck her in the leg with his rifle butt and broke it. She walked with a limp for the rest of her life. They lost everything. Fortunately, when the carpetbaggers came for the judge, he was still in Georgia. The Yankees missed him. He proudly told the plantations owners that he still had his courthouse keys.”

“I can already see where this is going.”

“He kept detailed notes of this event. I suppose he thought he might need proof once they started reclaiming the land. He even had all present sign the journal. The judge went in during the dark of night and replaced the pages of the deed books of most of the owner's deeds with fakes. He slit the old page edges near the binder and glued the new pages. The new paper had been stained with tea to age it, and the handwriting was varied and sloppy. It was tedious and dangerous work, but the Yankees never questioned the inserts. I guess they were just too busy being vindictive to pay close attention. In the case of Swan Bay, it was easy. The original deed books showed John VIII's patent for the original three-hundred-acre patent near the old house on a single sheet. The other deeds were simply cut from the book and replaced with pages which showed that the remainder of the land around the original parcel was owned by six dead soldiers whose families had been wiped out by the fever.

"He even built fake farmsteads and burned them, saying that the slaves did it. The other owners used the same ruse. The Yankees believed it, and the farms were saved. Once Virginia regained control of the local government, the fake deeds were replaced with the originals."

"You need to write a book. Tell me more about the house. This is fascinating."

"I'll do that when I retire. The house consists of a main block with two dependencies, flankers, as we call them. The flanking dependencies are attached to the main block with enclosed passageways called, in architectural terms, hyphens. There are seven windows across the main front of the center block. The two hyphens are one story, and two large flanking dependencies have two stories, but the lower ceilings give them a secondary appearance.

"So," said David, "do you use the house as a country house?"

"Not anymore. Since Lorraine died, when I go there, I stay in a suite in the old farm office. Mary and Jeffrey Beverly run the farm from a smaller building. We've turned the old office into a fine five-star-type inn for the visiting equestrians. Jeffrey and Mary live in the right flanker. It was originally built as apartments for the single men. They called it a garçonnière. We've remodeled it. The left flanker is Cap'n John's original kitchen. All of the mahogany furniture was crafted by Thomas Chippendale. There are twenty-five original chairs in the dining room and one reproduction. It seems that one night during a dinner party, one gentleman got overly heated during an argument about politics and spilled his red wine, ruining the seat cover. The chair was taken to the workshop the next day, but the oily rags started a fire during the night and burned the workshop. The French silk wall hangings were installed by John V during the 1790 renovations. The ancestors had imported furnishings and household items on their return voyages, which were almost as profitable as the tobacco trips.

"The silver is mostly by Paul Storr of London with a few other eighteenth-century pieces included. Silver was in demand, and because it was small, they packed the spaces between the furniture with it on the return voyages. They made a small fortune on that alone. Am I boring you with all this 18C talk? If so, I'll move on."

"Oh no. We love antique furniture. We especially love the silver. We can't afford the furniture, but we have managed to collect a few small pieces of silver from the London silver vaults."

"Yes, well, y'all must come visit. Do you ride? You can be my guest at the next hunt club ball."

"Yes! Thank you. We would love that."

"I'll have my secretary set it up. You'll love the large sterling silver punch bowl. Capt'n John imported several of them according to the journal. I have one, and there's another one at Westover Plantation across the river.

"We use them both for the hunt club punch. There's a funny story about the Westover bowl. The Episcopal Church, it was Anglican in those days, was on Westover land not far from the house. After Sunday services, the local congregation stopped at the house for a cup or two and a small lunch. They called it a collation. Some of the congregation overstayed their welcome, and finally the wife put a stop to it. She demanded that her husband either move the church or sell the bowl. He moved the church."

"I love it. I can just hear those arguments."

"I had all the silk wall coverings replaced by the same company that made the originals. Cost me a small fortune, but they *are* beautiful. You'll love the sideboards in the dining room. Be sure to look at the sides of those Chippendale sideboards. There are hidden doors near the back that most people miss. There are colorful porcelain urinals inside the cabinets."

David chuckled. "Okay. Now you're just joking with me."

"Nope. I always thought it was an odd old family story, until Lorraine and I toured Fairfax House in York, England. The docent told us the same story. After dinner, the ladies retired across the hall to the withdrawing room—ours is across the hall too—while the men sat around the table smoking and drinking brandy. Rather than miss any of the conversation, they relieved themselves right in the dining room!"

"I can just see Tippy allowing me to take a piss in the middle of our dining room!"

"Lorraine didn't allow it either. There are two Venetian river scene paintings by Canaletto over the fireplaces in the dining room. There is one like it in the dining room in DC, but it is of the River Thames. The Canaletto in my conference room across the hall is a London scene.

"There's a ballroom on the second floor overlooking the river that runs the entire length of the house. We use it as a party space for the horse owners when the mares are in season. In the fall, we host the Princess Anne Hunt Club annual ball."

"Do you ride to hounds there?"

"No. It would be too much trouble to ferry all the horses and dogs across the river." XI conveniently omitted that the DEA facility on the farm would have been a problem. "Most folks are brought over by boat to avoid drinking and driving. We keep as many as we can of the others here overnight. Jeffrey, Mary, and I bunk aboard the sail boat and free up more beds." He laughed.

"Jeffrey and Mary don't have children. They manage the Swan Bay Breeding Center. They are both from old Tidewater, Virginia, families. She organizes all of the social events and is active in the town. She chairs several of the Charles City historic boards and plays the organ at Westover Episcopal Church. They both love horses, so when I stopped growing tobacco, they approached me with a plan for a breeding center. They're well respected in both the local community and the international equestrian world.

"The smaller rooms are furnished in a similar style, but that's about it for us. Let's go down to supper, and you can tell me about your experiences. Do you know the Four Seasons Restaurant?"

"No. When I worked on Wall Street, I heard about it, but for us, it was just too far uptown. But before we go, tell me why you stopped growing tobacco."

"Oh my god, we need another wee dram for this. Just as I graduated from Exeter, the country entered World War II. I enlisted and was quickly promoted to flight instructor. I spent the war years teaching other young men to fly.

"Then, at the end of the war, following in my father's footsteps, I entered Harvard to become a doctor. But during a gross anatomy lab, I began to lose interest. My cadaver was a fifty-year-old female who had died from lung cancer. Once I opened her lungs and saw the effects of smoking, I became disenchanted with both medicine and tobacco. I wasn't squeamish. I'd grown up gutting and dressing deer, ducks, turkeys, and fish. I could wring a chicken's neck and pluck the feathers faster than any of the workers, but I realized that I hated touching sick, whining people. After a while, my instructors finally advised me that I had a lousy bedside manner and told me to find another major.

"Along the way, I had become fascinated with law. I knew enough about medicine that I decided to go to law school and focus on medical issues. I knew soldiers who had returned home with problems I was sure were medical in nature. After World War I, there had been talk about a nerve gas. During Vietnam, soldiers had begun to experience similar problems. I took cases relating to Agent Orange and other biological weapons, losing most of them, but along the way, I had learned so much that I developed a practice that specialized in unearthing hidden secrets large corporations tried to bury.

"One morning—my office was in Richmond at the time because we were still living at Swan Bay—my secretary, Jo, knocked on the door and peered in to tell me my ten o'clock had arrived.

"She opened the door wider, and a striking woman in her mid-fifties entered with her son, who looked to be about twenty-five. Jo introduced her as Mrs. Harriet Wilson and her son, UG, from

Charleston. I later found that UG was an old Huguenot name spelled 'Huger' but pronounced U-G.

"She got right to the point. They were there because her husband, Rene, had died the previous month from lung cancer. The memory of my experience in the lab floated through my mind, and I shuddered.

"She knew from friends that I owned a large ancestral tobacco farm. She paused to observe my reaction. She said that she thought that I might have a conflict of interest, but she assured me that I had been highly recommended by several lawyers in Charleston because of my work with Agent Orange and my knowledge of tobacco. She and her son wanted to sue big tobacco.

"A year later, the trial began in Charleston. The smug defense attorneys wanted to move it on because the tobacco companies didn't want the bad publicity to linger. They didn't believe that a country hick lawyer could beat them. In preparation for the case, I had contacted an expert from Harvard and asked him to testify about the effects of smoking on the lungs, and on the first morning, I called the expert to the stand. After my witness was sworn in, a student from the nearby medical university, dressed in a suit and tie and posing as a legal assistant, entered the courtroom pushing a stainless-steel table covered with a white cloth. Planning ahead, I had asked him to position the cart in front of the judge but in clear sight of the jury. I told the judge that I wanted to enter it as an exhibit. Before the judge could reply, I whipped off the cloth, exposing two pairs of dissected lungs. One set was pink—the other clearly blackened and diseased. The jury gasped, and the lead defense attorney jumped to his feet to object. The judge ordered the table to be removed immediately and glared at me and ordered us into his chambers.

"Once we were behind closed doors, the defense attorney demanded the judge call a mistrial. The judge denied the defense's request but warned me that if I tried another stunt like the one I'd just pulled that he would find me in contempt. Playing the naive country lawyer, I was appropriately contrite. Though I was a country lawyer, I was not in the least naive. I knew that the jury would never unsee those black lungs, and they didn't, eventually awarding the Wilsons with a major sum.

"I knew it wasn't over, however. There would be multiple appeals, including a hearing in front of the South Carolina Supreme Court. I knew too that I had no experience arguing cases before the higher courts, so I invited John MacMurray, a federal judge from across the James River from Swan Bay, to complete a foursome for a round of golf at our club. Over drinks at the nineteenth hole, I mentioned the case. MacMurray chuckled. He knew about my case."

XI sipped his scotch and smiled. "'Well, Judge,' I said, 'if that's true, then you know that the ruling will be appealed. I don't have a lot of experience with appeals, so I'm wondering if you can recommend someone to help me who does.'

"The judge thought for a minute. He told me about a guy named Edward Hardy down in Atlanta. He was young appellate court attorney. The judge thought Edward was a brilliant tactician in the courtroom and that he'd be a good one to help me because his wife was a surgeon.

"That night, I called a friend in Atlanta and found out that Edward Hardy had done his undergraduate work at the University of the South and had taken his law degree from Georgetown, where he'd graduated first in his class. He'd been a clerk in the federal court in Atlanta, and although most of his cases there had involved drugs, Edward's primary legal interest was the rapidly emerging field of environmental law. I thought I had hit the jackpot. I quickly opened a branch office in Atlanta and recruited the young Mr. Hardy to head up the branch. He jumped at the opportunity. During cocktails at the Midnight Sun Restaurant in Atlanta, I learned that the jackpot was even greater than I'd thought. Edward and his wife, Tippy, had been childhood sweethearts."

A sad expression momentarily swept across XI's face as he remembered his own early experiences with his late wife.

"I broached the subject of my upcoming tobacco appeal, and we had begun talking about some of the intricacies of the case at hand when Tippy dropped a bombshell. She told me that Harriet Wilson was her first cousin! When I did a double take, she laughed out loud and remarked that her dad and Harriet's mother were brother and sister. Harriet had inherited two plantations on the Cooper River and most of the commercial real estate on Market Street in Charleston."

"Sounds like another lucky break for the Bishop clan."

"And for the Wilsons too, as it turned out. The case went all the way to the US Supreme Court, and Edward and I prevailed. I won a series of other tobacco-related suits. Edward won a class action in favor of cities that wanted to add the protection of major trees to their zoning ordinances. It was considered a major victory for the environment. By the late 1990s, I had changed the name of the firm to Bishop Hardy. We were leading the nation in the practice of environmental law.

"While the case had worked its way through the courts, my conscience began to nag at me. I had learned too much about the negative effects of tobacco not to act, so I decided to practice what I preached. Despite the fact that it was unprecedented among the large historic farms still in production, I stopped growing tobacco at Swan Bay.

"While Ed and I worked on the cases, my staff at Swan Bay researched the historic flora that would have been there before Cap'n John had arrived. On their recommendation, I decided to replant the native species *Pinus palustris,* more commonly known as longleaf pine. The vast original North American native pine forest, estimated to have covered over ninety million acres, had been severely overfelled during the late eighteenth and nineteenth centuries.

"My fellow landowners were aghast. Yes, the species is highly favored for lumber due to its long straight grain, but it grows slowly and can take 100 to 150 years to reach maturity. They argued that I would not see a return on investment in my lifetime! I knew that, of course, but it didn't stop me. Now enough about me. Let's go eat."

*****

XI led David into the Four Seasons Restaurant. "This is a perfect example of International-Style Midcentury Modern, and I love it. The food's outstanding too. It was designed by a man named Philip

Johnson. He was a Mies van der Rohe wannabe, I think. He was a very wealthy architect with serious Nazi political leanings. The contrast was striking. Mies was a German Catholic who immigrated to America to escape the Nazis, so I think Johnson was an odd choice, but Johnson captured the style and used Mies's furniture throughout. I recommend the Dover Sole. It was swimming in the English Channel yesterday and has been flown in overnight. It will be ceremoniously deboned at the table."

They were shown to a table in the Pool Room, so named because of the large fountain in the center. David looked around and remarked, "As I said, I'm really do love the 18C English style, but this is refreshingly light and spectacular. This stemware is remarkable. This wine glass is interesting."

"Yes, the table settings and stemware were all designed by Garth and Ada Louise Huxtable exclusively for this restaurant."

The waiter poured each a glass of Cade Winery's sauvignon blanc, and the dinner service began.

"I met JB on the soccer field for the first time during our first semester. This fish is delicious. I'm sorry I never got up here."

"JB played a team sport? That's not like him."

"No, and neither did I, but there was strong peer pressure to join a team, so there we were. The coach made everyone run a mile around the track to 'warm up,' but it was actually just to weed out the bad ones. I was second to last off the track, and JB was dead last. We were both doubled over gasping for breath as we stumbled toward the other team members. The coach told both of us to drop and give him twenty pushups. JB looked him straight in the eye and, still gasping, said, 'Only a dumbass fool wastes time doing anything as mindlessly stupid as bloody pushups!' I laughed. Coach ordered us both off of his field and told us not to bother coming back. As we walked away, JB told me he was sorry that he had ruined my chances. I told him that he had allowed us to save face, that I really didn't want to be on the team either and that we would be instant heroes in the eyes of some of the other guys. After that, we became friends. Then I met Kayla. She had a friend named Liz, so Kayla thought we should double date. JB and Liz recognized each other when we all met at the restaurant. They both turned and walked away. Afterward, Kayla and I discovered that JB and Liz were fighting over a study carrel in the library. It was a war of words. Two weeks later, JB admitted to me that he really didn't want the space, but he was 'turned on' by her fierce spirit. He really didn't care where he studied, but now he didn't know how to get into her good graces. Kayla found out that Liz thought that JB was the most handsome guy she had ever met, so we tried again, and this time it worked. They were in love."

"I had no idea it went that far back. So I suppose she went with him on all those weekends to Connecticut?"

"Oh my god. How do you know about that?"

"JB's mother left him a trust fund, but I managed it, so I saw the bills. They were quite steep. What was that about?"

"Well, Washington, Connecticut, was about a six-hour drive south in those days. It was far enough away that the chances of being recognized were small. JB had his Corvette, and Kayla had an old Volvo station wagon. JB arranged to have them both kept at an old garage in town. I couldn't afford the weekends, and Liz was always afraid that, even at that distance, someone might see them checking into the inn. Lots of people love that inn. Liz had her own trust fund, so she and JB paid for everything. JB and I drove down earlier, and the girls drove down arriving after dark. JB always had a suite with a separate but adjoining room with a communicating door to the living room—very Victorian Edwardian house party like. JB paid for the suite, and Liz paid for her own room, which, of course, Kayla and I used. We had room service delivered to the living room, which we split, but JB and Liz were never seen together outside their room. Liz was afraid that if she were caught, it would damage her father's naval career."

"Smart girl. I'm glad y'all had so much fun, and sex! Why didn't he attend the graduation? He went straight to Boston claiming he wanted to buy a house and start his early reading for his law classes."

David blushed. "Ah. Well, that was Liz's idea. She was afraid that if you met her parents during the weekend, someone might let it slip that they were a couple."

"Okay. Sad, but I get it."

David continued, "Liz went to Juilliard, Kayla and I went to Yale, and JB settled into the townhouse in Back Bay on Pinckney Street across from the old Episcopal convent. He knew that the nuns would never talk about Liz's comings and goings from his house. Even so, she arrived after dark on Fridays and left before sunup on Monday. JB and Liz often met at our house in New Haven on weekends just to vary their weekends, and somehow, we all graduated. When we moved to Wharton for grad school, Liz took our house in New Haven and enrolled in Yale's School of Sacred Music, where she excelled. JB enrolled in Harvard's Environmental School. He was an admirer of your firm's stand on environmental issues and thought he might join you."

"I had no idea. He never said. I'm touched." To control his emotions—Bishop boys were trained from birth to control their emotions—he said, "I'm going to the men's room, if you'll excuse me."

When XI returned, the waiter brought another bottle of Cade Estate cabernet sauvignon from the Napa region of Howell Mountain. "I'm not well versed in wines, but this same white will go nicely with our dessert in my opinion. The winery was designed as an environmentally sensitive building, and the vineyards are environmentally managed. They've won national awards for both, and the wine is considered to be exceptional."

"So that brings us to the wedding, and you know all about that."

"Yes, but tell me what was going on in Boston on rehearsal day. I never believed that story. Was JB trying to avoid Liz's mother?"

"Actually, no. His closing on the Pinckney Street house had been held up, and the weather was bad. I joined him at his club for a late lunch and drinks—several drinks. He decided we needed a professional shave, so we did that. The weather was still bad, so more drinks. After the pilot called with the all clear, we spent an hour in rush hour traffic and missed the rehearsal."

"That was a fiasco! JB called me out of the blue to tell me they were to be married. He said the wedding would be in two months, and Liz's mother wanted the National Cathedral. JB and I tried to convince Liz to hold it at Swan Bay, but she wouldn't listen. We didn't have an organ at Swan Bay! She could use the Cadet Chapel at Annapolis since Liz's father was the commandant, but she knew I was on the Cathedral Finance Committee, and she didn't want everyone to have to go over to Annapolis. I agreed to try, but I really had to twist the dean's arm. I met Liz for the first time when they came down to meet the dean, but she spent most of the weekend with the cathedral organist arranging the music. Liz had composed her own recessional, but she finally allowed the cathedral organist to play it. She worked with him for hours on the registration."

"Kayla thought it was more concert than wedding. Communion went on forever."

"The nave altar had to be removed because Mrs. Cochrane referred to it as 'that picnic table.' She insisted that every one of the 750 people commune at the REAL altar using the traditional Rite I liturgy. She wanted the nave platform removed as well, but the dean drew the line there. Mrs. Cochrane had to admit afterward that it made a fine stage for the dresses."

"The reception on your lawn overlooking the Potomac and the city was very fine."

"June 7. Fine weather, but we thought Liz looked a little out of sorts."

"That's because she was two months pregnant."

"Aha!"

"They celebrated too much after JB graduated, and well, they forgot the condom. Liz had always refused birth control for fear it might show up on her medical records and—"

"Her mother would find out."

"Right. JB was livid. He hated children. He insisted on an abortion. They had long ago agreed on no children because their careers would suffer. I was afraid they would split. Kayla offered to take her for an abortion in an effort to save their relationship, but Liz wouldn't do it. JB had a vasectomy instead. There was something about her mother's pregnancy."

"I heard that from the horse's mouth. The Navy OB was not as responsive to Mrs. Cochrane's needs as she wanted, and to hear her tell it, she nearly died during childbirth."

"She held that over Liz's head for her entire life. So after the reception, they flew to London and boarded a Viking ship for a 245-day world cruise for their honeymoon, and John was born at sea.

"They seemed happy in New York. Liz was teaching at Juilliard, and JB enjoyed working in your firm, but Liz said that JB was never close to young John. JB left before dawn every weekday to go to his club for exercise, and he returned after John was asleep. On weekends, they went to Connecticut and left John with his nanny. A real battle erupted when they decided to move to Cali. John was a boarding student in the St. Thomas Fifth Avenue Episcopal Choir School where he was excelling. Liz would go over every afternoon during term to hear him singing Evensong. She always sat in the front row so he could see her. JB wanted to move him to Exeter. He told her that John's voice would break soon, and he'd need to move anyway. He reminded her that Exeter's music department had been good enough for her, but Liz wanted him to be in Colombia, near her. At one point, JB even suggested a school in Switzerland, but Liz knew that was just an excuse to go skiing."

"Damn! I want to flog him! Sorry. That was disrespectful of the dead. Luis found the best school in Colombia, in his opinion. It was in Bogota, and Liz wasn't happy about that, but there wasn't really anything they could agree on in Cali. The Catholics have a fine reputation worldwide as educators, so it was decided. The school had been a monastery, but their numbers were declining, so they upgraded the old monks' cells as dorm rooms for boys. It didn't have a music program, but she held firm that John must be in Colombia. Whew. I'm tired. Thank you for telling me all this."

"Thank you for your candor, XI, but it's time for me to go. I can still get the Acela to New Haven."

"And you for yours, David."

*****

On Thursday, XI left New York from what Amtrak euphemistically still called Penn Station even though most of the station had been brutally demolished years ago. He took the 7:00 a.m. to Washington's

Union Station and ate breakfast in Acela's first-class section as the dregs of New Jersey's industrial areas flashed by. The trip took about three hours. He had two meetings set up. The first was with an old friend who had recently opened a new private school in Alexandria, Virginia, and the later one was with Edward and the director of the Drug Enforcement Agency, Kent Miller. He and Kent had been classmates at Exeter, but this wasn't going to be an easy meeting of the old boys' club.

Margaret Scott-Simmons had been his wife's bridge partner.

"Thanks for meeting with me on such short notice, Margaret. It's been far too long, and I apologize."

"An apology isn't necessary, XI. I'm sorry, though, my time is short today. What may I do for you?"

"Of course. Simply put, I need a new school for my grandson, John. He's living with me now."

"Yes. I was sorry to hear about your loss. Give me a brief synopsis of his curriculum vitae, please."

"He attended Juilliard's Allegro preschool and primary school until he was seven. He then got an early admission to St. Thomas's Choir School in New York. He was a boarding student. His parents moved to Cali, Colombia, where his mother assumed the deanship of the music school at the university. John boarded at a small Catholic monastery turned school in Bogota, Colombia, from age eleven until recently. He is an exceptionally well-trained pianist and organist."

"I see. Impressive. I'm sure you know we are a school for international business. Our students are children of international diplomats, civil servants, and conservative politicians. We are not a boarding school. We also leave the arts to others. We do have a comprehensive physical education program though. But before you just assume, we don't just service the wealthy. If a student is sufficiently motivated but from reduced circumstances, we do have financial aid packages. Is your grandson on track to become a professional musician?"

"Oh no. I have a degree from Harvard law in mind."

"Excellent. His background in Colombia means that he speaks Spanish, and from St. Thomas, he knows Latin, so he will be a real asset here. He may start with the fall semester."

For his next meeting, XI had arranged to meet in the presidential suite of his club. He believed this setting would allow Kent to enter and leave without attracting attention since they were both members.

"Why all the cloak-and-dagger stuff, XI? I prefer the free scotch in your library."

Edward laughed. "We're offering you a quick out, Kent. You're not going to like what we're about to ask you."

"Spit it out so I can run, then, if necessary."

XI blurted out, "My son and daughter-in-law were murdered by Espinis's men. We have proof, and we recovered their bodies, but that's not public information. Our folks in the Ops Center noticed that JB and Liz had not moved in four hours."

"What do you mean 'noticed'? How could they 'notice'?"

"JB, Liz, and John all had GPS trackers embedded under their skin before they left for Colombia. I insisted on that, given the problems with kidnappers in South America."

"Smart move. So I assume someone noticed they were stationary. Then what?"

"My staff alerted me. We watched for another hour, and I asked a small group to fly to Cali and check them out. Maybe some would consider that as ridiculous, but I wanted to be sure. Luis rented a helicopter. My guys picked up the GPS signal and started to lower themselves to the bodies when they attracted the attention of armed men who fired on my guys. My guys were well prepared and managed to kill the armed men. The men were taking cover in a hole in the hillside that my guys decided must be some sort of cave. It was in a small area of jungle next to a very large coca field. The bodies were on the edge of a two-thousand-foot sheer drop to the valley below. We have no idea why they were so near the coca field.

"I became worried for my grandson, so I had the chopper leave the bodies at the Cali airport and fly to Bogota to pick up my grandson. By the time they got to him, he was asleep, and they had to drug him to rescue him, but they just made it. The chopper pilot noticed two trucks running at high speed toward the school. They slammed through the gates, but by then, the chopper was about ten miles out.

The jet had moved to Bogota, so John was loaded aboard, and they flew to Swan Bay."

"Oh my god. I'm so sorry. What can I do to help?"

Edward picked up the discussion. "We know that no jury in Colombia will prosecute Espinis, and our evidence, though conclusive to us, is circumstantial, so we are going to Cali and execute the bastard."

"Oh hell no you're not. Not with DEA men or equipment. You're asking to murder a private citizen in a foreign country. We're not the CIA. This would require presidential approval, and if anyone found out the president agreed to this, he could be impeached. The firestorm would be unending. No. I'm not going to prison over this vendetta. XI, we appreciate the service you are providing for our country. When we three first met in your library and you broached the subject of using Swan Bay as a training center, as I'm sure you remember, I jumped at the chance."

"I seem to recall your saying that between the new administration and the media, the hunter was becoming the hunted, and you needed an out-of-the-way, quiet training center."

"Correct. I do appreciate your position, and we want to continue our relationship, but I'm leaving, and to be clear, this conversation never happened. You do not have government permission for this foolhardy plan. Oh, and if for some stupid reason, you go ahead and are caught, the US government will not come to your rescue. You will be criminals, and our relationship will suddenly and completely cease to exist. Thanks for the drink."

CHAPTER 5

Espinis

Cali, Colombia

Standing on the terrace of his large Spanish Colonial villa high in the mountains east of Cali, watching the sun set over the city below, Jorge El Rosa and his half-sister, Maria, were having an argument as usual, but this one was more serious than most. Their father had amassed a fortune from his large gold mines in the mountains, and when he died, he left the two children in charge. Jorge, known as Espinis—the Thorn—was the COO and the treasurer. He turned the land above the old mines into coca fields, and he oversaw the planting, production, and distribution of the product. He was also the enforcer. Maria, an attorney, was the president and CEO. Maria was the daughter of one of their father's mistresses, and she still used her mother's name, Rodrigues. She was the silent partner. Together they controlled one of the largest drug cartels in South America. He was ruthless and hot-tempered. Anyone who got in his way felt the power of the Thorn and didn't live to tell about it. He kept a small army of enforcers. Maria could be equally ruthless, but she preferred to pretend to be benevolent. No one knew of their connection. She lived in Cali and rarely ever went to his villa. She laundered money for the cartel, and she was visibly charitable. They each had one son. His wife had died giving birth to his only child. His son, however, had died in a mysterious accident at school. Espinis was an average-looking man, but she was a trim dark-haired beauty with impeccable manners and taste.

"God damn it, Jorge! Why in hell did you kill them?"

"They were standing at the mouth of the entrance to the cave in the processing mine. We had no choice, you stupid idiot! You have no idea what it takes to protect this work."

"They had no idea. To them it was probably just a cave. I personally vetted them. I worked hard to get her here. She was the star of my music school. It cost a fortune to pay off the old dean so I could put her in charge. Juilliard fought a wicked fight to keep her. She would have put us on the cultural map in a few more years. I have personally committed to spend millions to improve the Escuela de Musica at the Universidad de Valle. She was one in a million. He was only interested in environmental policy. He worked to help the city rewrite the zoning laws to prevent structural damages from flooding and earthquakes. They were harmless."

"You stupid cow, they were Americanos, and I never trust them. Good riddance. Go buy yourself another piano player."

"And you sent a kill squad to get the boy right in front of the whole school? What harm was he?"

"I know he had something to do with my son's death. I just know it."

"Well, thank God you missed. My son, Paulo, told me that Jorge smoked so much weed at night that he was still stoned at noon! We'll have Americans prowling around now. You've unleashed something I've worked hard to contain."

"Contain? Contain? How did the Americanos know where to find the bodies if they were so well contained? They just swooped in and hauled them away. They managed to kill four of my best guards too. Anyway, you started this. And tell me, why were they so close to my best field?"

"We've been over this before, and you agreed. She had no idea that she already had the job when she interviewed with the board. She told them she wanted to research pre-Colombian music. She believed that Western music written in cold climates was written for reverberant spaces, but the rest of the world relied on repetitive rhythm to sustain the sound of their music. Grass huts are not reverberant. The board salivated at the possibility of more international exposure. They had apparently heard of the village and drove their camper up there to try to make a recording. It's that simple."

"It's done. Shut up. Now you and your worthless son are going to America and take care of this kid."

"Hell no. I don't have time for a wild goose chase. I won't do it. We don't even know what he actually looks like. We need a picture."

"Well, Paulo will go. He has no choice. He owes me for saving his sorry stupid ass, and now it's payback time. Move him out. He can start by looking for tall blond boy organists in all the Catholic churches."

She laughed. "You really have no idea just how big America is, do you? I'll bribe their maid to go into their penthouse and grab a picture. That's the best we can do."

"I don't care. Just do it. When he finds a target, he's to call you, and you'll check it out then call me. Now leave."

"I have promised the board a new organ and a new recital hall. I can't go back on my word now. I'd look like a fool."

"You are a fool. Now that she's dead, you have the perfect out. How much did you promise them?"

"Two hundred million, more or less."

"Christ! You idiot. No piano player is worth that. How much have you already given them?"

"Fifty. And don't you complain. You've got five hundred million in small bills stacked in caves inside the production plant. We won't miss the money."

"Jesus! That's my spare cash in case I need to buy somebody off in a hurry. Oh, wait. I've got an idea. The boy's an organist. Xavier says he's damned good. Build the hall and invite him to give the inaugural recital in honor of his mother. His ego will serve me well. Hell, I might even take out the whole family."

"What are you talking about?"

"He comes here, and after the concert, wham! Or I might just kidnap him and demand two hundred as payment. I'll kill him AND get my money back. Win-win!"

"No. Hell no. I won't do it."

"Okay. Then I'll just go hire a contractor and do it myself. I can get it done for less too."

"No, you can't. You don't know the first thing about concert halls."

"I know about opera. We'll just build an opera house and stick an organ in it."

"You ignorant fool. Don't you remember our trip to Paris and the night at the opera?"

"Of course. How could I ever forget that night. The singing was superb. It brought tears to my eyes!"

"And you remember going to the opera here in our symphony hall the next season?"

"How could I forget? I left at the intermission. Everything was garbled. Those singers were third-rate at best."

"No, those singers were first rate trying to sing in a space that was never intended for opera. Our symphony hall is a copy of the Boston Symphony Hall. It's known as a shoebox, and it's considered perfect for a symphony. Opera and organ concerts should NOT be held in the same room. We'd be the laughingstock of the whole musical world. Opera needs a short reverberation time so that the singers can be clearly heard. The audience sits as close as possible, even stacked up the side walls, to get them closer. The symphony sounds best with a longer reverberation time, but an organ needs a very long reverberation time, essentially like a large stone cathedral. A properly designed opera house, a symphonic hall, and an organ hall are separate spaces. One size will not fit all. The new hall will be tall, narrow, and long."

"Somebody can make it work."

"Yes, maybe, but that's not what I want, and that's not what I promised the board."

"Okay. You win. I don't want us to be embarrassed. I'll call off your son then, for the moment, but go get the picture just in case we need it. There's no need for him to go on a wild goose chase across America, but I'll control the money. Spend your own and I'll pay you back when it's finished. Start immediately. I need my money back, and I want that boy put in the ground. My god. Fifty million will buy any architect in the world! Offer him the promise of an opera house in the same fee."

"Are you going to pay for an opera house?"

"Sure. Just as soon as your organ room is finished. No more design money though."

"I can make it work for now. I'll agree to use my own money for my part, and you can pay me back after it's finished. We'll proceed."

CHAPTER 6

John's Journal

"What's up, my boy? You're in another world."

John jumped.

"Sorry, I didn't mean to startle you."

"Oh, it's okay. I've read Cap'n's journal. I've read some of the others too. Makes some of my problems seem silly, so I decided to try to write one of my own. I realized that my music composition books that were left in the chapel are basically the same thing, so I have included my best work in this journal." He laughed. "It'll drive some future historian crazy, I hope. Mine isn't a dry-as-toast journal, though. I've added dialogue."

XI noticed that it was the first time the boy had laughed since he arrived. "When can I read it?"

"Just let me print you a copy."

"Sit with me while I read. I may have questions."

*****

John Bishop XIII

My earliest memory is of my father yelling at me. I forgot that when my father was at home, I wasn't supposed to play the little toy baby grand piano my Grandmother Cochrane had given me for Christmas. I quickly grabbed it, and I tripped on the rug. The piano slipped out of my hands and broke into pieces. I ran crying to my room. I loved that piano. Mother was not at home for some reason, but my nanny took me into her arms and held me until I stopped crying.

XI cringed when he read of JB's cruel attitude.

Her name was Ines. I called her Ms. Ines. She was one of my mother's students at Juilliard, and she was from Argentina. She lived with us in our apartment in the Carlyle Hotel. My nursery and her room were near the kitchen. My parents' room was beyond the living room. Mother's Bosendorfer concert grand piano occupied one end of the living room, and Ms. Ines was allowed to practice when my father was not at home. Mother's parents bought it for her in Austria from the factory while her father was stationed in Europe. I was told that it had moved all over the world, and sometimes their housing unit was so small they rented another apartment just for her practice room. Ms. Ines and my mother gave me my first piano lessons. When I was four, Mother took me to the Allegro Preschool on her way to Juilliard. The school taught basic music to small children, and I loved it. Ms. Ines had morning classes, so she picked me up after school and took me home. We practiced my lessons, and then she practiced hers. Sometimes, she let me sit in a chair beside the piano. I had to be very still and quiet. Although I didn't understand the words at the time, when she made a mistake, she cursed—in Spanish. She taught Spanish to me, and later, when I was trapped in that hellhole school in Bogota, I learned what those curse words meant, and I used them freely. I could outcurse most of the other boys because I used her dialect and mimicked her fiery temper. Ms. Ines made me take naps until Mother returned in the late afternoons. Ms. Ines cooked supper, and Mother and I played the piano and sang until my bedtime.

I learned to read at school. I learned to sit up straight and breathe properly. I learned to stand still when I sang too. Mother taught me about vowels and consonances, and she made me enunciate my consonances clearly but without exaggeration. One evening, she began the twenty-third psalm. She read a line, and then I repeated it.

"See that T *at the end of the word* want*? Spit it out. No, no, not that much. Like this. Yes, that's right. Now that* l *and* k *in walk, it's*

not 'wok through the valley,' it's 'wall-kuk' Try it. Again. Yes. Good." Then she sang a line, and I sang it. Once she was satisfied, she played a line, and then I played it. I learned to play and sing plainsong without even knowing it. Ms. Ines introduced me to Bach and to Schumann's Kinderwacht. She told me I was a sponge.

I started first grade at Allegro Primary School. My home routine didn't change. My music improved. One day, Ms. Ines was sick, so Mother took me with her. She was giving organ lessons that day. I had never seen or heard an organ, but I was hooked after the first hour! I wanted to play! At the end of the day, she let me. I couldn't reach the pedals, and that made me mad, but she taught me to play legato. "John, you must attack the piano keys but release the organ keys. They play the same music, but in very different ways." Soon, we had a little one manual portiv organ beside the piano. It had five ranks of pipes and had been built to her design by a company near Charlotte, North Carolina. Ms. Ines wouldn't touch it, and she wouldn't let me play it, but Mother and I played it every night.

During summer break, for my sixth birthday, we went on vacation. I couldn't believe my father was going with us. We drove across the Hudson River and flew on a small white jet to Swan Bay. I had never been on a plane or heard of the farm. I was told that it was my ancestral Bishop home. I loved it. There were more trees than in Central Park. I was allowed to run on the front lawn and visit the stables. I had never known such freedom. The people were all very nice. I immediately loved Grandfather Bishop. Mr. Pink, Mr. Jeffrey, and Ms. Mary and Ms. Mamie and all the other people were nice to me. Ms. Mary took Mother and me on the sailboat across the James River to Westover Episcopal Church, where she was the organist. They told me I had been baptized there and that all the Bishops except Capt'n John and John Jr. had been baptized at the font. I learned that Capt'n John had been a warden of the parish and a burgess for Charles City—that was the same as a mayor today. Ms. Mary allowed me to play the organ. She and Mother arranged the music for Sunday service. Mother played one of her compositions as the offertory. Mr. Pink was fun. He took me all over Swan Bay on his ATV. I really loved Mr. Jeffrey and Ms. Mary's new chocolate Lab puppy named Buster. He followed me everywhere. I really wanted a dog, but

Mother was allergic, and she didn't think dogs should be cooped up in Manhattan apartments.

I gave my first recital at the end of the school year. I was six. I played and sang a lullaby Ms. Ines composed for me. It started with dissonant chords—she called them the reluctant child—and ended with a whisper. The words were Spanish, but the program notes had the English translation. My father was out of town. It didn't matter. I hardly ever saw him anyway. He left every morning before dawn and returned after I was in bed. He and Mother went away to Connecticut almost every weekend, leaving me with Ms. Ines.

XI sighed.

A man from St. Thomas's Choir School happened to be at the recital to hear his daughter. He congratulated me, and after talking with my mother, he invited me to audition for the choir school. I was given early acceptance to St. T's, as the boys called it, and I moved into their boarding school. I was homesick the first week, but my house mother was very understanding, and the youngest boys were allowed to go home on the weekends, so I quickly became adjusted to the routine. On Saturdays, I was allowed to attend the Juilliard Preparatory Education program. On nice days, Mother and I walked over to the school through Central Park. I loved choir school. I was in awe of the church. It was big and built of stone with large stained-glass windows up high near the ceiling. I started boarding full time and before long, I was allowed to sing the services. I first studied piano, but when my legs were long enough to reach the organ pedals, I began organ lessons. I couldn't get enough. My mother always came to Evensong and sat on the front row, where I could see her.

When I was eleven, disaster struck. They told me we were going on a trip. When I asked where, they told me it was a surprise. They did not tell me that my mother had accepted a position as dean of La Escuela de Musica, Universidad del Valle in Cali, Colombia. My father opened a law firm in Cali. We moved into a large penthouse apartment near the university. I was pissed. I'd been tricked. I raised hell. Nothing worked. I wanted to know when I could get back to New York and school. No answer. I was only there a week when we took a trip on the white jet to Bogota.

We arrived at the place just before 4:00 p.m. I wanted to know why we were there but got no answer. The place looked like a prison. A well-

kept prison, but even the beautiful flowers couldn't hide the high stucco walls and gates. The afternoon was overcast, but the rain had stopped. The place was virtually empty. No one mentioned school. We were welcomed by Father Xavier. We toured parts of the complex. I was fascinated with the huge dome on top of the Chapel of St. Francis. I later learned that these guys were Franciscans called the Order of Friars Minor. They all wore brown. It was late in the afternoon when we entered the chapel. Mother dipped her fingers into the holy water, genuflected, and crossed herself. I'd never seen her do that before. My father just stood there looking bored. The chapel was dim, but just as we moved down to the front, a cloud must have parted because suddenly there was a bright area high up in the ceiling, that part of the ceiling inside the dome. It was painted blue and gold, and there were clear glass windows all around. Suddenly, a shaft of sunlight came shining through one of the high clear windows, showing shimmering dust particles in the air. To me, the dust motes looked like little angels floating down and flying back to God in the song we sang, the Sanctus, about the seraphim and cherubim surrounding the throne of God, singing, "Holy, holy, holy." These angels weren't singing. At least, if they were, I couldn't hear them. The new shimmering light was hitting the brilliant large gold crucifix just in front of me. The wall behind the crucifix was glowing too. The wall was covered in real gold with little painted statues all over it. The reredos at St. T's was stone and was also covered with stone statues, but they weren't gold. This golden wall was unlike anything I had ever seen. There was a large, mostly dark picture on the golden wall behind the cross. As quickly as the sun had appeared, it disappeared, and the room was dim again. I noticed the stained-glass windows. I just stood and looked at them. The windows were smaller than those at St. T's. Those on the south wall were brighter than those on the north wall, but not as bright as the golden wall had just been. St. Thomas was surrounded by tall buildings that mostly blocked the direct sun, but nothing blocked the sun here. Mother said the windows on the south wall were from the New Testament and were brighter because they told stories about Jesus. The pictures on the north wall were from the Old Testament, and they were dimmer because the sun never really shone from the north, and they were about the world before Jesus came. Father Xavier seemed pleased that I understood. As we turned to leave, I saw the massive organ pipes high up on the back wall. We left the chapel just as the bells in the tower chimed the hour. I instinctively looked up. There were two towers. One of them had large blue clock faces with golden hands. I was fascinated. I knew about bells, but this was the first time I ever actually stopped to listen. We couldn't really stop on the sidewalks of New York. The bells were something I wanted to know more about. We moved on. I liked the gym and the activities areas.

Father Xavier invited us into his private dining room for supper. My curly blond hair and blue eyes seemed to disturb him. It turned out that I was certainly whiter and taller than the other boys in the school. All the other boys had dark skin, dark eyes, and short dark hair. I was given chocolate ice cream for dessert. I loved chocolate ice cream. Ms. Ines used to buy it for me during our walks in Central Park. While I was trying to eat my ice cream, I fell asleep. I learned later that my food had been drugged.

XI gasped.

The other boys arrived about noon the next day, and I discovered that I had been left. This was to be my new school. There was quite a bit of confusion as families moved their sons in and arranged their rooms. As usual, there were tears. My new roommate, Tomas, walked in. Tomas was a second-year boy. He had been assigned to show me the way of life at the school. I was confused and asked Tomas if he had seen my parents.

Tomas said, "No, but there are adults everywhere. It's lunchtime. Maybe they are waiting for you in the refectory."

"You talk funny."

"So do you."

We both laughed.

"I speak English, Latin, and Spanish."

"Well, maybe you can teach me some English."

"It's 'teach you English,' not 'some English,' and we don't begin sentences with 'well.' A well is a hole in the ground used to supply water. But no, I'm leaving as soon as I find my mother and my father. Let's go. I'm hungry."

The refectory was crowded with adults and boys, but I searched in vain. Dejected, I sat down to eat. I walked over to one of the brothers and asked where my parents were. I was told in a dismissive tone to go on with the other students. He said I would see my parents in a few weeks. Disgusted, I returned to my room. I thought about ways to be sent home.

The problems started the next morning. The dorm buildings were simple. Four floors of brick cells, now dorm rooms, opened onto a narrow, open outdoor corridor. Each small room had a window, two beds which were stacked, two chests of drawers, two small desks, and two chairs. There was an overhead fluorescent light fixture, and a small hand sink with two towel rods. The common toilet rooms were in the center of the building on each floor. There was a tile wall with water constantly trickling down which served as a urinal, and behind the wet wall was a row of water closets. Between the water closets, short screens held the toilet paper. There was a large shower room off to the side with seven shower heads. The boys all stripped in their rooms, wrapped their towel around themselves, and walked down the open balcony to the bathroom for their morning shower. I had just hung my towel on a hook and walked up to the urinal wall. Before I had even begun to pee, an older boy walked up beside me, turned, and started peeing on me. The other boys began to laugh and chant, "Jorge, Jorge, Jorge." The older boy was just standing there with his legs spread, peeing and grinning at me.

XI laughed. John had run into the school bully on the first day. He wondered how he would handle it. Bored, John asked, "How do you like it so far, Grandfather?"

"I've just read the part where the bully peed on you. How did you handle that?"

"Ha. Read on. At St. T's, bullying was strictly forbidden, but before I went there, the first and about the only advice my father ever gave me was that, if it happened, to just hit him back. Otherwise, he said, it would never stop."

"That's actually good advice. It will hurt, but you must hurt him back. Okay. I'm going to read on."

"Like that do you, Albo? There's more where it comes from, Albo." Without so much as a change in expression, and with all the strength I could muster, I kneed Jorge in the balls as hard as I could. The idiot was just standing there with his legs wide apart, so I just did it.

Good boy, thought XI.

The other boys gasped. Later, Tomas told me that Jorge was the drug lord Espinis's son, and no one had dared to touch him before. Jorge went down in pain, and as he rolled on the floor, I peed all over him. I simply turned and walked into the shower to wash Jorge's pee off. I went back to my room, brushed my teeth, and got dressed. I went to breakfast. Classes started after breakfast, and I asked each priest and brother when my parents were coming. I had no idea who this "Espinis guy" was.

The next morning, they were waiting on me, except it wasn't pee this time. Two guys grabbed me as I walked in and held me against the wall. There were no other boys in the room. They obviously knew what was coming and had been ordered to stay away. My arms and legs were pinned. Jorge began punching me in the gut. He knocked the breath out of me. I collapsed onto the floor. The other two guys grabbed me and carried me around the wall and stuck my head into the toilet.

Jorge snarled, "From now on, you're mine, Albo."

Oh my god, thought XI.

I knew what an "Albo" was and that it was his way of saying white boy. As Jorge and his buddies left, the other boys came in but said absolutely nothing. Seething, I walked into the shower without saying a word. The other boys were amazed I didn't seem to be crying. I showered and went back to my room to dress. As I walked down the stairs, I noticed the bullies were standing outside the refectory laughing and clowning around while they waited for the doors to open for breakfast. Jorge's back was to me. No one seemed to notice me as I walked up to Jorge. I approached Jorge's back from the left, and using my best soccer kick, suddenly, quickly, and with as much force as possible, turned and used my right leg and foot and took out the back of Jorge's left knee. Jorge went down howling in pain. A brawl broke out. Father Xavier had seen the attack and ran over and grabbed me by the back of the collar. He was dragging me away, but I was fighting him and screaming my best Spanish obscenities. Father had to get one of the brothers to help him control me. They took me into a small office. With the brother watching, Father said, "We do not behave like animals here. You will apologize to Jorge immediately. Brother Francis, go get Jorge."

As the brother left, I said, "No. I will not apologize to him. He started it."

The brother came back in with a grinning but limping Jorge. Jorge had a good idea of what might happen next. Father's beatings were the stuff of legends. Each year the legends had grown stronger as the older boys embellished the stories while retelling them to the new kids.

"Now, apologize to Jorge."

"No! He peed on me."

"Apologize to him now, or face the consequences. This is your last warning."

"No. He should apologize to me."

Father looked at Brother Francis, and while Jorge watched, the brother grabbed me and yanked down my pants and underpants in one swift stroke. Father sat down, and the brother turned me over Father's lap while handing him a wide leather strap. The strap had a wooden handle attached to one end. I was trying to get up, but I was held fast. Jorge was grinning and had almost forgotten about his knee. The first swat was swift and hard. I jumped. That hurt! No one had ever hit me like that before.

XI gasped again. He had to get up and pace. He poured himself another wee dram of Macallan and continued.

"I bet you just got to the paddled part."

"Yes. Let me finish this part."

I didn't cry out. Father hit me again. I still didn't respond. I jumped after each lash, but I only boiled more. Father hit me ten times, and still I did not respond in any way. Jorge seemed amazed. I later learned that no one had ever endured ten lashes without screaming out. Brother Francis stood me up and told me to pull up my pants. My butt was on fire, but I did as I was told.

"Now, are you ready to apologize?"

Without saying a word, I kicked Father in the shin as hard as I could. Then I yelled, "You old bastard. I want to go home. Now!"

"You really called him an old bastard?"

"Yep."

Father told the brother to take me to the penance room. Jorge left in absolute amazement. Did he really want to tell the boys what had happened? They already knew I had not screamed as many of them had done, but this was something entirely new.

The penance room was a small cell on the back of the dorm. A strong padlock held the wooden door to the wall. Strong iron strap hinges creaked as the brother opened the door. There was a slot in the bottom of the door which was covered with a wooden flap. I couldn't reach the one small, dirty high window above the door. There was a small box in the corner that smelled like a toilet. There was no light fixture. A bare, sagging, stained cot without so much as a pillow leaned against one wall. I quickly understood this was serious business. The room was hot and smelled bad. There were bugs and flies buzzing around. I carefully walked over to the cot and laid down on my stomach. There was no chance I would roll over. I managed to sleep until there was a knock on the door. The flap at the bottom opened. Someone slid a cup of watery, barely warm soup of some kind through the slot. I could tell it was almost dark outside. I drank the soup and began to think about my situation. My butt burned like hell. This place was a real hellhole. I wasn't going to be allowed to go home, and I wouldn't take another beating. I needed to come up with a plan. Slowly I formulated an idea. I needed to simply avoid them all, except perhaps Tomas. To hell with all of them. Tomas had not helped me, but for some reason, I liked Tomas. I realized that for some reason, Jorge was someone to leave alone if possible. I would be required to go to class, but I would not participate unless absolutely necessary. Perhaps bad studies would get me sent home. I decided that I wouldn't speak Spanish. I was not one of them. I didn't look like them, and I wouldn't act like them. I would find a way to avoid the toilet room. I would find a way to avoid having to sit with them in the refectory. I felt better now that I had a plan, but my butt really burned.

When the soup appeared the next morning, I told the person my butt was on fire. Later, another brother came in and quietly asked me to show him my butt. The brother gasped. "Oh. You need to come with me. Now." The brother took me to what he called the infirmary. They examined me and applied an ointment to my now infected, welted, and oozing cheeks. I stayed there until Saturday.

On Saturday, I was taken back to see Father Xavier. I was put in a very small room. Father was in a small room too, but there was a small screen between them. Father seemed to be sitting down, but my butt was still a little tender. I just stood there, waiting on Father to do something. Father whispered, "You must now confess your sins, my son."

I started to speak but then said nothing for a moment. I knew the definition of confession but not in the sense Father meant. "Sir, I'm sorry I kicked you and called you a bad name."

"And what about your brother Jorge."

"No, sir. He started it when he peed on me, and he is NOT *my brother."*

"Then go back to your room. You may not receive communion until you make a full, sincere confession."

I knew I didn't want Father's communion if I had to apologize to Jorge first. I had been to communion many times at St. T's, but I was never asked to confess my sins to a priest in private like that, and I wouldn't do it.

XI frowned. He hoped that John hadn't become prejudiced.

As I walked gingerly back to my room, I had an idea. I remembered seeing a running track behind the gym. Several men were running around it. I also remembered there was a nice toilet and shower in the gym. I would start running. I had been on the soccer team and the track team at St. T's, so this would be a piece of cake.

Tomas was waiting for me in the room.

"Did you confess?"

"I don't want to talk about it, but I'll help you with English lessons if you will do something for me."

"What?"

"I'm going to need to avoid Jorge and all of his guys as much as possible. I'm not afraid of them, but Father has taken Jorge's side for some reason. Father refuses to listen to me. I will not take another beating from Jorge or from Father."

"Oh, your fights with Jorge and your beating from Father have become a new legend. My father told me Jorge's father runs the largest drug cartel in all of Cali, and maybe even the whole world. Do not ever even whisper about it. I'm very serious. My father said Jorge's father is a very mean man, but his family gives a lot of money to the school. My father told me to stay away from Jorge at all times. Did you really never cry? The older boys can't believe it, and the new boys think you are Superman."

"What's a drug cartel?"

"They make cocaine. They sell it all over the world."

I didn't know what cocaine was, and I wasn't interested in Jorge's father. "No. I didn't cry, and I'm never going to cry about anything. Here's what I need you to do. I'm going to wake up early and go running behind the gym. I will pack my clothes and shower in the gym. I'll show up for breakfast, but if any of the boys ask why I'm not showering with them, just tell them I have to keep meeting with Father in the mornings until I confess, and I'm never going to confess!"

"I can do it. Now let's start the lessons."

Later that night, I asked Tomas how long we would stay in school.

Tomas said we would all go home after midnight Mass on Christmas Eve.

All the parents attended the Mass and then took the boys home.

"Do I have to go to Mass?"

Tomas looked surprised but said, "After breakfast on Sunday, we go to the chapel for Mass. Everyone is there."

"I don't want to be in the same room with Father Xavier."

"You don't have a choice. He won't hurt you in the chapel."

The next morning, the bells began ringing wildly. They sounded differently than they normally did. I ran out onto the balcony and saw that they were swinging. I liked the sound better because it was fuller and more sonorous. Tomas yelled, "Hurry up, John. There's a priest at the front door who takes names of everyone who is tardy. Father can be very strict with punishment for boys who aren't in their seats for Sunday Mass when the bells stop ringing."

I didn't want that again. Tomas sensed my reluctance and said, "Don't worry. Jorge is always late. He won't sit near us. Our pews will be full. His guys sit on the side aisle by the wall near the back anyway. Sometimes, he runs in just in time for the homily. Jorge can do anything he likes around here, and no one dares question him. Now come on! I'm not going to get punished for being late because I was trying to drag your scarred butt in there!"

The morning light bathed the chapel in warmth. The golden wall was glowing, but not as bright as it had been on my first day. I didn't know that the afternoon light was more direct than the morning light. I soon learned that this chapel was properly oriented east-west, but St. T's wasn't because of the street grid of New York. There were candles everywhere. I sat beside Tomas. The chapel was filled with students and people I hadn't seen before. I turned to ask Tomas a question, and Tomas quickly put his finger to his lips. I noticed the people were absolutely silent. Tomas knelt to pray, and I followed his example, but I didn't know what to say to God except I wanted my parents to come get me.

A little bell rang somewhere. Everyone stood, and suddenly, the organ sounded forth with a fine sound. It was everywhere, bouncing off the walls and ceiling, rattling the glass, and I loved it. The priests all wore beautiful green robes covered in gold, but there was no choir in procession. I thought it odd. Various priests began moving about and reading and praying in Latin. The singing was coming from the back, but it was very bad. I barely recognized the psalm. Father Xavier climbed into the high pulpit and started his homily in Spanish. I vaguely listened. I had no real interest in anything he might say. He was a minion of hell as far as I was concerned. His style was pompous and sometimes bombastic and condescending. He was talking about obeying the priests, and then he started talking about hell for bad boys. I decided this place was like hell, but I was going to find a way out as soon as I could. Father finished and sat down.

Then there was more singing coming from behind me around the organ. I tried to look, but Tomas quickly grabbed me and made me turn back around. The singers were not all in time with the organ, and many of them were off pitch. I actually cringed at some of the old men's flatted notes, and the sharp high notes of the boys were just as bad. Still, the space helped them. I counted about six seconds of reverberation. That would make a herd of bellowing donkeys sound better. When it mercifully ended, Father Xavier and two other priests went up to the golden wall. Father sang off-key in Latin, and it was hard to hear him, but so far, there was nothing I hadn't seen hundreds of times before. Row by row, the boys got up and walked toward Father, but they didn't kneel. I couldn't see exactly what they were doing. It didn't matter.

When it was my turn, Father put out his hands, stopped me, and said, "No. You will not receive the body of Christ until you make a full, proper confession!"

Some of the boys were giggling, and even though the choir was singing again, I could hear whispers of "Gringo" coming from some of the boys. I turned to walk back. I thought about running but decided against it. Instead, I held my head up and walked toward the back doors. I was leaving and had no intention of ever coming back.

Quietly I hissed to myself, "This place is hell. It's my new home."

The brother who took names was standing in the back and, sensing my intent, blocked the doors. I, without thinking, turned and quickly climbed the stairs. I found myself in the choir gallery below the organ pipes. Up here, they sounded worse than they had downstairs. The men were on the back row. I walked down a few steps and stood beside one of the boys. I looked over at the music and realized the words were Latin. I didn't know the music, but apparently, neither did this boy. I started singing the words in a rather loud voice. I had no problem sight-reading the notes. At least my timing and intonation were correct. The organ console was down two rows in front of me. The organist was sitting facing the choir, and he was trying to direct with his right arm, but the choir took very little notice of his efforts.

The organist looked around the music rack, spotted me, and smiled. He pointed at me and made a come here motion with his finger. I was afraid. I was sure I would be punished again for breaking some rule. Cautiously I approached the console. There were three rows of keys. I watched with delight as the organist's hands and feet flew over the keys and pedals. This guy played like my mother, but two other guys pushed and pulled the knobs and turned pages. I had learned to help our organist with turning pages, but we rarely needed assistants to change the stops. Father was improvising. How did these guys know what to do next? When the music stopped, the organist asked me some questions.

"What is your name, my young angelic-looking fellow?"

"I'm John Bishop, sir."

"Where did you learn to sing and read music?"

"My mother taught me. She also taught me to play the organ and piano. When I was seven, I started studying at St. Thomas Choir School in New York City."

"How nice. Would you play something for me, please?" I asked him what he wanted to hear.

"Slide on over here and play whatever you like."

The two console assistants moved away, and Father slid over on the bench to give me some room.

"What will you play for us?"

"Johann Sebastian Bach's 'Sheep May Safely Graze.'"

I pushed some of the stop knobs in and pulled others out and played. He told me that I played really well and that my technique was correct. He asked if I ever improvised.

"Yes, sir. My mother taught me that the music is already in the organ. I just need to let it out properly. She said Michelangelo had said the same thing about the blocks of marble he carved into sculptures. She showed me pictures of his sculpture on her computer."

One of the assistants quietly muttered in French, assuming John wouldn't understand, "Le enfant prodige."

The other one muttered, "Si."

"John, I want you to introduce me to your mother the next time she comes for a visit."

"Yes, sir. I hope she comes soon, but she's very busy."

"John, my name is Father Arturo. Would you like to take organ lessons from me and join my choir? I will teach you the French style of improvisation and introduce you to French music and the Catholic Mass. St. Thomas is an Anglican Church, so our services are different. This instrument was designed to play French music."

"Yes, sir, I would like to take the lessons, but the choir doesn't sing very well."

He sighed. "Out of the mouths of babes." The assistants laughed. "Yes, you are correct, but as payment for the lessons, perhaps you can train the boys to sing. How long were you in school in New York?"

"Four years. I will try, sir, but I don't think some of them can learn to sing."

"Well, perhaps, but let me worry about that. You just teach them as you were taught. Choir practice is every afternoon at 3:00 p.m. The choir room is just behind the chapel."

"But, sir, that's when I must do chores. I'm on permanent cleaning duties until I confess."

"Well, I'll fix it. The boys who sing in the choir or serve at Mass don't have chores."

I liked the sound of that! It would minimize more of my exposure to the other boys. I would have to come into the chapel, but being up here was much better than being down there, even with the horrible singing. Maybe I could change that too. I also decided if I could play the organ when the choir went down to communion. I could avoid Father Xavier completely. Perhaps he wouldn't even notice. I wouldn't be as visible with my back to the altar.

On Monday, my new routine started to take shape. I slipped out of the dorm at sunrise. I had packed a small bag the night before. Running was easy. Having been on the track team taught me to pace myself and avoid injuries. I quickly showered and walked quietly into the refectory for breakfast. I still had not worked out a plan to avoid the boys at mealtime, but as I slid my tray down the line to let the serving boys slop food onto my plate, I decided to ask if I could work in the kitchen. I thought I might be allowed to eat in there. After breakfast, I approached the cook. I was told yes.

"The boys in the kitchen are local charity boys who work for their education, but I know about you, boy. Everyone does, so as an act of penance, you can clean the pots and pans and eat with the charity boys. I will also use you on the cooking line. You will prep the vegetables, and if you're lucky, you can learn to cook. Come in thirty minutes early."

I liked this idea because no one could see the pot-washing sink from the refectory, and I might need to learn to cook too. The food was bad—too salty—but maybe I could learn to prepare my own. I would need to adjust my running schedule, but it wouldn't be a problem. That left classroom time, study time, and evening dorm time. Classroom time couldn't be avoided, but as I left the choir loft on that first Sunday, I had noticed a small door near the back of the organ pipes. I looked inside to see a spiral stair. I thought the stair might lead up to the bells, so I decided that I could slip up there to study. Most of my plan was coming together, but there was still the issue of the time in the dorm before lights out.

At 3:00 p.m., I attended my first choir practice. Father Arturo introduced me and asked me to begin the class. I didn't realize it, but the boys knew me. I had apparently become something of a hero. The old men didn't like me, but I was determined to win them over. I asked the choir to stand up.

"We'll be practicing from a standing position from now on. Place your feet comfortably apart and relax your shoulders. You're not to stand at attention like soldiers." The old men groaned and immediately sat down. I ignored them. "Now, breathe in through your nose. Only breathe

through your mouth for short, quick breaths. Let it out slowly. Now just stand there and relax while we begin." I sat down at the piano and played a note. "Sing 'ah.'"

This was going to take real work. At the end of the practice session, Father met with me. "You are better than you led me to believe. The boys love you. Keep it up. It's working."

Some of the boys got it, and some didn't. I continued to ignore the men, but on Wednesday, I told them that I needed to work with the boys, and they could be excused until Saturday practice in the chapel. They shuffled out. I asked the boys who were struggling to come, one by one, to the piano. I played a note, sang it, played it again, and asked the boy to sing it with me. Slowly I began to raise their understanding and ability. One boy, Juan, simply couldn't sing. I decided to make him my assistant. He was to hand out and collect the music folders. He said he wanted to learn to play the piano, so we sat down and started a lesson. He caught on quickly, so I asked him to play the notes while the boys practiced their vocal warm-ups. I had my back to him and quickly learned that he couldn't hear my commands. I persuaded Father A to take him for a hearing test. Juan came in a few days later with hearing aids and a big smile on his face.

Father Arturo was a well-trained classical organist. He was French, and he told me that he had studied organ with the great French organist Marie Clair Alain. She had studied with some of the great French organists of her time. He had been her pupil at the Paris Conservatory before he studied for Holy Orders. He had the great fortune to have been able to play some of the great French organs built by Aristide Cavaillé-Coll. Unfortunately, his choral conducting skills were minimal. During his early years, he had never directed a choir. I quickly determined who would learn to sing and who would not. The service music slowly got better. Latin was still a problem, so they all had to memorize each work. It was painful. At least Father could pronounce and explain the words.

True to his word, Father started the organ lessons. After a long talk with Father Xavier, he persuaded Father Xavier to let him have me. I think Father Xavier was glad to get me into something more out of the way. The first few lessons involved crawling inside the organ chamber and getting to know the workings. Father explained the instrument to me.

"This instrument came from France. It was built by the famed organ builder Cavaille-Coll. It had been in a large Jesuit monastery near the Swiss border, but when World War II broke out and France fell, the monks there removed the organ, the medieval stained glass, the bells, the gold altar, the crucifix, and the altar painting for safekeeping. One of the postulants for Holy Orders, Georg Rose, had an uncle who owned a bank just across the border in Basel, Switzerland. He persuaded the monks to store their valuables there. Georg was German. He finally left the monastery to fight for his homeland. After the war, Georg had moved to Bogota for the warmer climate and reentered the monastery. The Germans had bombed the French monastery thinking the Allies were going to use the tower as a sniper location. After the war, the monastery was not rebuilt. Georg received permission from the Minister General to allow the fittings to be moved to this chapel."

Father added that he had been persuaded to move to Bogota and take on the music program. "You and I are fortunate to be able to play such a fine instrument."

Father began to stimulate my imagination by playing music of different French composers and styles. He was trying to teach me the basics of taste as he perceived it. We began to criticize various works, and I began to improvise. I copied the works of others and began to play my own compositions. They were elementary at first, but they began to show promise. My extempore improvisations, as Father called them, in the French tradition were improving. Father occasionally began to let me play the offertory. Father moved on to explain the relationship of the architecture, the music, and the words of the Mass.

"Do you remember our talk about a litany?"

"Yes. I've sung the Great Litany on the first Sunday in Lent many times. You said we'll start practicing the Jehan Alain Litanies in a few months."

He had told me that a litany was actually the repetition of a single prayer.

"Yes, but your Great Litany is a little different. Have you heard people recite the Rosary? That's a litany. Alain's is wickedly difficult. We'll take it measure by measure."

I wasn't bothered by the idea of its difficulty, but behind my back, I could hear the console assistants sniggering. My sight-reading abilities quickly shut them up.

"Good. The architecture does the same thing. The arches repeat whether they are round as ours are or pointed as the gothic ones are. They are seemingly endless. Each arch is a litany: a repeated prayer. Large ones, small ones, onward they go, forward, backward, up and up, spring across and intersecting in the middle of the ceiling, but each is the same structure, and they support each other until finally, they all reach the altar—our golden wall. That wall contains representations of saints and angels to remind us of all those who have gone before us who join us at each Mass. Together we all are reunited in the Mass by surrounding the altar."

"Are you familiar with the structure of the Mass?"

I said yes. He asked me to tell him what I knew. I began explaining the structure of the Mass and the relationship of music to the liturgy. I discussed the standard parts of Kyrie, Gloria, Credo, Sanctus, and Agnus Dei. I said that different composers create different musical settings to the same words much the same way that different artists paint the same scenes but in different ways.

"The music is not simply selected at random either. The church year is divided into parts we call seasons."

"Yes, I know about the liturgical year."

"Good. Then let's move on."

"Father, I think you should compose a simple, elegant, but traditional setting of the Mass for the choir, perhaps in Spanish since their Latin is so bad. We could stand a weaker singer between two stronger ones, and with a strong, simple melody leading them, they would improve. You could simplify the tenor and bass parts to reduce the moans of the men."

As he laughed, he exclaimed, "Great idea, but after I've composed the melody, I want you to add depth to the organ interludes to compensate for the simplicity. Nothing too elaborate you understand. We can pull this off, and Father Xavier won't even notice. He's tone-deaf anyway."

The choir improved, and I was becoming a French-style organist. I solved my evening dorm issue by getting permission to practice after the brothers were in bed. I was alone in the chapel. I wrote the compositions out as I worked through them. It was tedious. I would quietly return to the dorm after the others were asleep. Some nights when I stayed too long, I simply slept on one of the choir pews. As far as the other boys were concerned, I had mostly vanished. Father Xavier was happy because the problem had gone away. He didn't really care how or why. Had it not been for my classes, no one would have missed me. I enjoyed being left alone.

In the late fall, we began work on the music for the Christmas Eve Mass. The choir members liked working with me. I made them laugh. They really worked hard on the Christmas music. Father had allowed me to select the choral music for the service. I kept it simple to allow the boys to sing at their best level. The pieces were really just my variations on a few Christmas carols. Everyone loves Christmas carols. Mother had written that she and Father were off to ski in Switzerland for Christmas. Luis would pick me up, and I would spend Christmas break with his family. I was mad as hell, so I wrote her back and told her not to bother. I told her I wanted to stay in school, where I could practice without interruption.

I grew to understand the religion classes. I learned to appreciate the Catholic faith and the Mass, but I hated the Colombian and world history classes. I made good grades just to spite the bastards. I excelled at Spanish, Latin, and math, and I liked biology and chemistry. I was amused at old Father Ignatus who taught art history. Father had a strong German accent, and he absolutely hated modern art. He took every opportunity to rant about the degenerate scratchings, blobs, and ugly architecture, as he called them. He repeatedly used the German words Gott verdammt *and* kacke. *I looked them up and laughed. I added these German curse words to the Spanish ones Ms. Ines had used. I decided I liked modern art and architecture since I hated Father Ignatus, so I began to study them on my own. I began to love French Impressionism simply because Father hated it so much. I learned about the German Bauhaus school of design using machine precision technology as an art form, and I could recognize the architects, their buildings, and their furniture designs. Mies van der Rohe became my favorite. I decided that he was a classical, minimalist, modernist who used the ancient Greek proportional system in his work. Sleek building detailing and polished stainless-steel and leather furniture appealed to me. It seemed classically logical to me. Father drilled us in the philosophy of the Counter-Reformation. He loved the earthy art that taught morals by using visual examples the peasants could understand. His was a German Catholic mindset trapped in the modern German Protestant world. We learned that the Catholics formed the Counter-Reformation after the Council of Trent and that the rise of the Baroque was a counterpoint to Martin Luther and the protestants. The protestants destroyed the art in the old churches under the concept of purifying the buildings to allow all attention to be focused on the Word rather than icons. After the Council of Trent gave the Catholics permission to step up the use of art as a teaching tool, their churches were filled with art on every available surface. This exuberance spilled over into sculpture, architecture, music, and writing. The word* baroque *is derived from the word for a lumpy pearl. It refers to the excessive curves of Baroque art forms as opposed to the perfection of Renaissance art forms. Baroque says more is better. The modernist concept of less is more was foreign to the old conservative priest.*

"Wait. The Council of Trent was a meeting that allowed art to flourish? I've never heard that."

"The Counter-Reformation was an attempt to hold the hearts and minds of the people to the teachings of the Roman Church. It was an attempt at modernizing the churches without changing the basics. The art simply used scenes from everyday life as a way to reach the people with things they understood rather than using otherworldly forms of distant saints and angels as teaching tools as Gothic art did. Also remember, Gothic religious art was based on dead people."

"Fascinating. I'll need some time to think about this idea."

Father A, as I began to call him, told me that Father X—I secretly loved calling him X for nonexistent—had called him into his study. "Some of the boys are making ridiculous claims that they are hearing banshees and demons singing in the chapel late at night. What's that about?"

Father A told me he said, "It's our problem child. I've given him permission to practice after Compline. It keeps him busy, and his grades don't seem to be affected." Father A also decided to tell Father X that the reason I wouldn't go to confession was because I was an Anglican, not a Catholic. Father X understood and told Father A to just have me play during the communion and not to come down with the choir. That was fine, because I had already figured that out, but now I wasn't afraid that I would get beaten again.

Father X told him, "Well, tell him to tone it down. These boys need their sleep."

Late one night, Father A climbed up to the gallery. I was in full concentration mode with my eyes closed. There were sounds coming from the organ that Father A didn't know were possible! When I stopped, I was startled to see Father.

"What are you playing? I've never heard the reeds growl that way."

"It's my new composition about my family."

"What do you call it?"

"Last week, we studied Ovid and the pre-Christian Roman religion. I call this piece 'Parentalia.'"

"Ah. The Roman festival of ancestral days—dies parentales. You wrote that in a week?"

"Yes. My father told me that we were Scots, so after learning about the old Romans, I began studying Scottish history, trying to understand my ancestors. It's what I imagine my Scottish ancestors were like. That was the first section I call 'My Fathers.'"

"So that's why it's so distant yet masculine. The reeds sound a little like a bagpipe drone and that high mixture—horrible combination."

"That's what I am trying to find. A bagpipe has nine diatonic notes. I've used the reeds and made them growl by closing all of the swell boxes to reduce the volume, but the notation is my own. The next section will be called 'My Mothers.' Would you like to hear it?"

"Absolutely. I want to hear as much as you've finished. May I join you on the bench?"

"Yes, but since the assistants aren't available at night, I need to pause to make changes. The next section is based on the sound of my mother's singing."

Because I had scribbled the stop changes onto my score, Father stood and moved from side to side, changing the stops for me. He was enthralled as the alto sound continued and ultimately became slightly louder as more stops were added, ending in a harmonic litany.

"That's the end of the movement. The next movement is called 'Birth,' but maybe I'll call it 'Dies Natalis' instead."

I began by using the softest stops on the organ to imitate a distant, almost vibrating sound as if within the womb, but still in dissonant, almost harsh notes, and gradually worked into something that sounded like birds, finally arriving at a point that Father recognized as a complete litany based on the earlier beginning.

"The last section was called 'Hope,' but now I'll call it 'Lemuria' to stay with the Latin, or maybe Regenerate. I'm trying to reconcile my feelings about my family."

It began with a similar dissonance and atonality, but it ended with a trumpet fanfare the likes of which Father had never heard. It was not that it was loud but that it was so impossibly fast.

When I finished, Father just sat there spellbound. "I simply don't know what to say, John. This work is so very dark and dissonant, yet you reconcile each section into something positive and, dare I say, hopeful. It's outstanding!"

"It's just scribbles at this point, but I'm happy with the finished work."

"All this in a week. You're right. This is scribbling, but what amazing scribbles. You must put it to paper in a proper format, and be sure to provide those tonal preferences for each section. You'll want other organists to know your intent."

"Do you think anyone else will want to play it?"

"Oh my god, yes. I want to send the final work to several of my friends. It's wickedly difficult. I didn't know our old girl here could be played as fast as that fanfare, but it will make organists want to rise to the challenge! You must be certain to protect this book with the original thoughts. Don't ever lose it. How did you decide to write this?"

"It just comes into my mind at odd times. I don't know. Tomas thinks I'm probably crazy."

"But your tonal combinations don't always follow our traditions. May I suggest a few minor changes?"

"No, thank you. They follow the sounds in my head. I don't feel bound to the old ways. Our old girl, as you call her, has millions of combinations of sounds, so why stick with the old ways for everything?

Actually, according to my math studies, her forty stops times two—on, off—can produce millions of combinations we've never dreamed of, so why limit our work?"

"For the simple reason that some of the combinations don't sound good, that's why. Somehow, though, this composition you've written manages to work. I suppose that if you are composing in a new modern style, you do need some freedom to select new sounds, and no, you are anything but crazy. This same process happens with artists. They see something in their heads too.

"Now I want you to do a little research on an Englishman named John Donne. He was an Anglican priest, actually the dean of St. Paul's Anglican Cathedral in London, but he wrote a poem entitled, 'No Man Is an Island.' It begins,

> ***No man is an island,***
> ***Entire of itself,***
> ***Everyman is a piece of a continent,***
> ***A part of the main.***

"I want you to study it and some of his other writings and write me a composition based on his idea, and no darkness this time. This is to be a bright, hopeful work."

*****

My parents spent the summers living in a small camping trailer in remote villages in the Andes. Mother was writing a book about pre-Columbian music, so she refused to take an instrument because she didn't want to influence the people. Apparently many of the villagers had never had much contact with the modern world. I went once, but I hated the idea of a summer in the bug-infested jungle with no instrument at all, so I refused to go again. She and my father crept through the jungle trying to record the singing of the natives without being seen. I told her that was crazy, but she insisted that it was the only way to get authentic sounds that weren't part of a performance.

"My god, John. Do you think that's what they were doing that got them killed?"

"I don't know. We never discussed it again. She was determined to do it her way."

"They were found at the bottom of a very large coca field."

"I doubt they knew what coca looked like."

"That's possible. JB hardly knew what tobacco looked like. He never took any interest in the crop here, but it makes me wonder if they just stumbled into danger." XI sighed. "I guess we'll never know. Let me continue to read."

They sent me to Swan Bay in Virginia for the summer. I loved it and the people, but there were no schools near the farm, so I had to go back at the start of school. I spent a few weekends in Cali, but I felt like an outsider, an inconvenience. Over the fall break of my second year in that hellhole prison, something new happened.

XI was beginning to understand the hellhole comments.

Just after the other boys left for fall break, a man showed up with a truck full of computer equipment. My curiosity caused me to ask if I could help unload the truck. The computer man, Julio, was more than happy to let me do as much of the work as possible. The new computer lab was located on the back of the classroom building on the third floor. There was no elevator, so I just carried everything up the stairs. I had to open the larger boxes and take those parts up separately. I opened everything according to Julio's directions and set up the lab. By the time I had connected all the equipment, I had asked hundreds of questions and had a good understanding of exactly what each piece did and how it all interacted.

"Sir, will you teach me how the programs work?"

Julio introduced me to coding Basic language. I quickly grasped the logic of the program. After all, Father A and I discussed Bach's use of ciphers during our theory sessions. In my mind, computer coding was just another form of math. I had no problem with the idea of the binary and hexadecimal codes either. Binary coding is 0-1, on-off—just like the organ stop knobs and keys. I just thought of this class as a continuation of the math classes. Math is its own precise language, but this was something new.

I quickly sensed that his guy was very lazy. He started giving me assignments that seemed odd to me. It was almost like I was writing code for his programs so that he could claim deniability.

"Since there are no other students here, let's move on to the language, C, John. It is a more powerful, function-based language."

I quickly moved on to C++. This was even more powerful than C. The boys returned from summer vacation. It never occurred to them that I had never left the school. Only Tomas knew. He hadn't told the other boys for fear the teasing and bullying would start all over again. Unfortunately Jorge was in my computer section. I managed to sit as far away as possible.

"Hey, Julio!" Jorge yelled. "Teach me to find porn."

Julio had never mentioned to me that he would be the instructor, but now it all started to make sense. That's why the guy didn't leave once the installation was finished. Since none of the brothers had ever stopped by to see the work, they obviously weren't going to teach. Julio finally did have to get one of the priests to stop by on a regular basis to keep Jorge in line. The other boys slowly started to learn. I was careful to never show my expertise to the other boys. Julio was spending quite a bit of time with me, but the other boys thought it was because I was having a difficult time with it.

During the second semester, Jorge yelled out, "Julio, we want to learn to be hackers. We're tired of Java, man."

Jorge just wanted to learn to hack porn sites without having to pay. This piqued Julio's curiosity. He decided it might be a good diversion. He was an expert hacker himself. Julio started by giving us a basic background in security. He could only scratch the surface because mastering this would take years. He also stressed every keystroke we entered could be discovered by someone. He told us about laws against hacking and the prison times we would surely face. He used his own work to show us how to research our prey and how to write and run programs to break passwords. This was advanced work for young boys. Most simply couldn't grasp it, but Jorge and I absorbed it all. I began to see a pattern in all of Julio's example programs. The logic was all the same, and the architectural structure never varied much. I again assumed the guy was smart but lazy. Julio continued to push me as quickly as he could. I was on fire. Other than my music, this was the only other good thing about this prison.

For some reason, Julio didn't show one day. He had left instructions, but Jorge took the opportunity to boast. Jorge just couldn't help himself.

"Julio writes all of the programs and manages my father's computer network. There was probably some problem more important than a bunch of kids. One of the idiots probably pushed the wrong button or something."

Jorge boasted that his father had paid for the entire lab from the wealth he made running a drug cartel. I quickly put it all together. Suddenly, I became afraid, terrified actually. I didn't know much about cartels or drugs, but I knew about Espinis from Tomas. I did not want to become involved with this man or his business. I pretended not to listen. I simply got up and walked out, saying I was going to study. That night, in my dorm room, I decided I would need to pretend to slow down and have trouble grasping the lessons. I wanted to learn as much as possible, but I no longer wanted Julio to think I was interested. I went to class, but I deliberately made mistakes. My programs were full of forced errors. I just said I couldn't understand. I appeared to struggle. Julio saw I was trying, but he didn't understand the problem. Julio lost interest. He turned his attention to Jorge instead. I had sufficiently covered myself, but I had actually run many trial hacks. I got just to the point of breaching the firewalls and stopped. I knew I could get through, but I didn't want the attention. Besides, this hellhole was prison enough. I could only imagine what a Colombian prison was like.

The next morning, I went to the track to run. I wasn't regular. Some days, I was tired and just didn't get up. If it were raining, I might go into the gym and work out with the equipment. After all, my only goal was to avoid the bullies in the toilet. I had not slept well the night before. When I stopped, the coach walked up.

"Come over here, John, and let's talk."

I had no idea the coach even knew my name.

"John, have you ever played football?"

"Yes, sir, but we call it soccer. I played on the teams at my previous schools."

"I want you to come to practice. Your running ability, your size, and your training might be just what our team needs."

I had watched a few of the games, and I was interested. Neither Jorge nor his buddies were on the team. "When do you practice?"

"Wednesdays and Fridays at three. Our games are usually on Saturdays and Sunday afternoons."

"That's my study time, but I can work it in."

"Great. Come to the gym on Wednesday. I know you aren't very regular in your workouts. Will that be a problem with your practice? The team members depend on each other."

"Oh no, sir. I really don't have a reason to be regular in my exercise, I just like it."

"Fine. See you Wednesday. Don't be late."

While we were playing our main opponent, I managed to score the winning goal. Suddenly I became a hero. I didn't really know how to handle this new development.

Without really meaning to, my life in my hellhole of a prison had taken on a structure much like the monastic patterns I had been taught in religion classes. Of course, I didn't fast or observe the daily offices. I certainly didn't pray or read scripture, but I went about quietly with my head down and avoided as much contact with anyone as possible. On my free afternoons, I climbed up to the belfry to study. I loved it up there. I quickly found a spot in a room above the bells where the bells were less loud. The views out over the city were very nice. I returned every afternoon to the kitchen for supper, and then I began my organ work.

Father A had introduced me to other great French Romantic composers who, in Father's opinion, were perfect for the chapel organ. We spent long hours discussing music theory and stylistic differences of various periods of music. I sometimes said outrageous things just to wind the old guy up, but he really was the only person with whom I could have an intelligent conversation. I learned the works of Jehan Alain, Jean Langlais, Marcel Dupre, Widor, and many others. I came to love the works of Langlais, for some reason. Father asked me to find a suitable French Noel for Christmas. Instead, I played Langlais's "La Nativite" for the Christmas Eve Mass offertory. It is actually a very quiet, short, poetic work, but to me, it evokes thoughts of the infant Christ child sleeping in the manger. I could almost hear Mary rocking and humming to her baby. I hadn't told Father it was coming. The old man was moved to tears.

While doing research in the computer lab, I stumbled onto some online organ recordings. They were from a museum at Harvard. I researched it and discovered the organ was by a Dutch company, and the organist was a Brit named E. Power Biggs. The music was by Bach, and I loved it.

One morning, while I was running, as I approached the far turn on the track, Jorge sprang out of the woods. The morning was overcast, and the sun was struggling to rise through the fog. There was a deep ravine down there with an uncleared jungle. The trees had grown right up to the track. No one else was around. The coach never arrived this early because he was at another one of the daily offices in the chapel.

"Found you, gringo! You're mine now!"

Screaming wouldn't have done any good. Jorge grabbed me and started forcing me into the ravine. I struggled. Jorge was walking backward, pulling me deeper into the jungle. We were about halfway down the steep slope, deep into the jungle, when Jorge suddenly tripped on a root and stumbled backward. I broke free, and as he tried to grab me to regain his balance, I pushed him away with as much force as I could muster. Jorge fell backward and hit his head on a boulder. He appeared to be out cold, but even in the dim light, I saw blood coming from Jorge's head. I ran! The rain had started coming down in sheets. I decided it was early enough that I could slip back into my dorm room. Now, my irregular workout schedule might just work in my favor. I had not been seen. I took off my wet clothes and quietly crawled into bed. When Tomas's alarm went off thirty minutes later, he was not surprised to see me in bed. I was terrified. I was short of breath. What could I say when Jorge turned up? I simply went about my daily routine, but I was sick with fear. I didn't have a plan for this! I went into the scullery to start washing the pots, but suddenly my bowels turned to water. I barely made it to the toilet. Sitting there, I began to pray. I finally confessed, but using the confession I had learned at St. T's, not in Father X's way.

Almighty and most merciful Father, we have erred and strayed from thy ways like lost

> ***sheep, we have followed too much the devices and desires of our own hearts, we have offended against thy holy laws, we have left undone those things which we ought to have done, and we have done those things which we ought not to have done.***

I started to sob uncontrollably. It was hard to continue.

> ***But Thou O Lord, have mercy upon us, spare thou those who Confess their faults, restore thou those who are penitent, according to thy promises declared unto mankind in Christ Jesus our Lord; and grant O most merciful Father, for his sake, that we may hereafter live a godly, righteous, and sober life. To the glory of thy Holy Name. Amen.***

I suddenly realized that there was no one there to give me absolution. I felt doomed.

XI shifted in his seat away from John's eyes because he was in tears as he read this.

Jorge didn't show up for breakfast, which seemed to be a little odd to his buddies because he never missed a meal. When he didn't show up for his morning classes, the guys started to talk. After he missed lunch, they visited Father X. Exasperated, Father sent the brothers out to find Jorge. Father assumed he was up to no good. In the late afternoon, they discovered his body. The police were called. Later they reported that he had three joints in his pocket. The toxicology report showed drugs in his system. They ruled the cause of death as accidental. They concluded he had gone into the ravine to get high. His buddies said nothing. Espinis was outraged and demanded a more thorough investigation. I was still absolutely terrified. I stayed in my routine, but I was still sick with fear. I couldn't really eat much, and I sometimes had to run to the toilet. I said nothing.

Three days later, a funeral Mass was said for Jorge. I nearly collapsed when Father X said to me, "Sing Gounod's 'Ave Maria' as a solo for the offertory at the funeral."

Even though my treble voice had changed, I was the best baritone in the choir. A baritone was not perfect for this piece, but Father said, "No. Consider this your act of contrition for this lost child. You will offer this song to God. That is an order."

Not wanting to throw any suspicion on myself, I agreed. I was still worried Espinis somehow knew. I nearly threw up when I entered the chapel for the service. The service was full of more pomp than I had ever seen. The archbishop gave the homily. Everyone seemed to be showing off for the drug lord. The chapel was overflowing. I wondered how many drug-dealing murderers were in the chapel. I sang, but I was afraid I was drawing too much attention to myself. Afterward, Father A smiled at me and motioned for me to come to the console. When I sat down, Father handed me the score for Franck's "Panis Angelicus."

"Play this as they move the casket out."

"But I've never ever seen this."

"You've got a few minutes. Look it over. I'll be your assistant. You can do it."

I quickly read through the piece. "But this is a choral score, not an organ score. You play it. It's not appropriate for this situation."

"Father Xavier told me to make you play it. Jorge's father specifically asked for it. Just do it."

I looked at the text. "The bread of angels becomes the bread of humankind." Hmmmm, I thought, for these guys? The last line was the killer. "O marvelous thing! The poor one, the servant, and the humble all partake of the Lord." I thought I had never seen a more inappropriate text for a room full of killers and dope dealers.

"But this chapel is full of murderers and drug dealers, Father. I don't want to do it. I've done too much already!"

"Have you not learned anything about God while you've been here, John? We're all made in his image. He loves us unconditionally—warts and all."

"But..."

"No buts. God will be the only judge of us all. You and I aren't called to judge people. Our job is to love our neighbor. Someone's life may be changed by your music today. Now sit here and play it as an angel of God and change a life."

"Okay, Father. I can do this. I don't need you or the console assistants for this one."

I had an idea. I wasn't fully convinced by Father A's theology. I would need to be quick. The Mass was ending.

They left, but Father stood at the top of the stair obviously blocking any idea of my leaving. I grabbed the book from the top of the console and quickly opened it to Psalm 59, "Eripe me de inimicis." We had studied it just last week. It reads, "Deliver me from mine enemies, O God; defend me from them that rise up against me." Yep, perfect, I decided. That would do it. I checked the mirror while the retiring procession was forming. Father A was giving me a "start now" sign, but I still waited. I didn't want the Franck to start too soon. When the crucifer started down the aisle, I began playing the melody of the Franck "Panis Angelicus." That's what I had been ordered to do. My timing was very good because I was just ending the melody as Father X, the bishop, and the archbishop, always the last in line, passed out of sight under the gallery. Father A started down the stair. I then began my transition. I moved extempore into the psalm but in the same key and mood as the Franck. My improvisation used as many of the reeds as possible, and I made the organ roar through the middle of the psalm for the verse, "Put them down O Lord our defense." When I finished with the last line, "Unto thee O my Strength, will I sing; for you, O God thou art my refuge and my merciful God." I had the strings whispering a prayer. I turned the organ off and walked down. Father was just smiling, almost laughing, at me. He gave me the thumbs-up. He knew exactly what I had done. As I passed by, I surprised him by handing him an autographed score entitled, "Nemo Insula est"—no one is an island—and it read, "Dedicated to Father Arturio."

The next week was quiet until that night when the men came for me.

XI just sat there. He knew he had his work cut out for him if he were going to save this boy, but his first thoughts returned to justice. His red swollen eyes betrayed his forced smile.

John stammered, "Grandfather, I'm terrified. I thought the men were sent by Espinis. I thought I would be tortured and killed." He blurted out, "I-I murdered Jorge!"

"No, no, no, my boy. No. Self-defense is not murder. Come here." XI hugged him. "What you did was justified. No court anywhere would convict you of murder. Now put that thought out of your mind. We'll never speak of it again. Agreed?"

John wasn't sure, but he agreed.

"This is good work. I like the dialogue. You must try to write a little every day. Now, let's go find Mamie. She has some real chocolate ice cream."

CHAPTER 7

Justice

"Let's take our ice cream out onto the porch, John. We need to have a serious talk."

"Okay with me."

"There are some things you need to know about Swan Bay's recent history. I know Pink told you that the barns in the woods beyond the airstrip are rented and therefore out of bounds, and that's true, but what he couldn't say is that they are rented to the US Drug Enforcement Agency—the DEA."

"Sounds like James Bond stuff."

"No, not exactly. We operate a training center and a small staff of agents on our own payroll to supplement the feds. The training center is a national center. It's not well-known. In fact, almost no one knows about it, but it's not a secret. We just stay away from the press and certain members of Congress. My agents make raids along the interstate highway and along the Chesapeake waterfront. Any money we confiscate goes to the DEA, and then a portion is returned to us as payment. We are what's known as a private contractor, but all federal DEA agents come here to train. They are flown in and out but never told exactly where they are. Capt'n John's old worker's cabins have been moved over there and refitted as living quarters for them while they are here. It's all legal. We just keep it quiet. As you might soon guess, if you haven't already, the Breeding Center is very important, but it's not my main interest. I leave it entirely up to Jeffrey and Mary. I ride horses, but that's about it."

"A front?"

"Actually it came first as a way to utilize the old barns, but now, yes. The Ops Center comes first in my priorities."

"Can I see it? It sounds interesting."

"Not yet. I'm working on getting you cleared to enter. Maybe in a few weeks. And speaking of money, you should have gathered by now that we have money. The Breeding Center is profitable, the Training Center is profitable, and my law practice is profitable, and you, young sir, are very wealthy for a boy your age. Both your parents had trust funds which you've now inherited. You'll soon get a black platinum American Express card on my account. I manage your assets because you're too young for your own account. In addition, when you inherit my trust, which includes this farm, you will be very wealthy indeed. Look at this number written here. Memorize it and never forget it. You, my partner, Edward, and I are the only ones who have it. Edward is my executor."

"What's this number for?"

"It's a numbered account for the Bank of Switzerland. Our ancestors have kept their profits there forever. Captain John never shipped all his profits to America. He never trusted the local currency, and everyone since then has continued the practice. He first kept the money in the Bank of England, but his descendants moved it to Germany when the Revolutionary War broke out. It was finally all moved to Switzerland. We have our own vault beneath a street in Zurich. It's all legal. We have paid the taxes. When the US government started collecting taxes, my grandfather cut a deal with the US Treasury Department. He opened the journals and accounts for their inspection. The accountants worked out the numbers. I'll take you to the bank someday."

"Wow. I can't spend that much money per month!"

"No, of course not. The excess will be reinvested by our accountants. You'll meet with them soon. There are all sorts of tax issues, so you don't need to worry about any of that. Now, I've got to fly to New York for a meeting tomorrow morning. Keep writing."

"Before you go, may I ask about the accident involving my grandmother?"

XI sighed. "Yes." He told him the entire story.

*****

Jeffrey had called a red alert meeting. All twenty members of the team were called in. They met in their SCIF (Sensitive Compartmented Information Facility). It blocks electronic transmissions, so they could talk freely without fear of being monitored by outsiders. This type of meeting was common. XI was stuck in New York waiting on the weather to clear. He was curious, though, about the reason for the meeting because he and Jeffrey hadn't talked for several weeks. Jeffrey began by stating clearly that anyone who volunteered was on his own and would not be protected by the government. He tersely told them that a team would go to Cali and eliminate Espinis. When hands went up, everyone had volunteered. Many of them were ex-military and had been on combat missions. The others were ready for a chance to prove themselves. As was their practice, they started with a PowerPoint presentation of the facts. Afterward, They immediately began arguing about weapons.

"Okay. We all agreed on Russian AK-47s, but they will only be used as a last resort. They won't look American to anyone investigating, but this operation needs to be as stealthy as possible to avoid a firefight. The suppressed Glock will work better."

They agreed on Glocks, but the argument then began between the G41 Gen4s, and the G21 Gen4s.

"The G21s are new but small and lightweight, Jeffrey. We need the flexibility since we don't really know what we're going to find."

Finally, Jeffrey agreed to let each man chose. After all, it was their life at stake. They agreed on the GL-0004S-5 24-7 sound suppressor.

"We like the in-scope white dot rather than a red dot for the low-light night environment, Jeffrey. The dot is inside the scope and it's highly accurate. It doesn't alert anyone standing near the target because there's no red dot on his forehead."

One of the team members remarked, "I really don't want to kill unnecessarily. Can we just tranquilize the guards and only kill Espinis? Only kill a guard if your own lives are in danger?"

Another argument began. Finally the vets arranged for animal tranquilizer guns. They would carry extra syringes just in case they needed more time. All agreed that while the guards were accessories, they only knew that Espinis had given the orders. Next, they argued about the guard dogs. The satellite photos showed four German Shepherds. Several of the team members, including both of the vets, argued strenuously the dogs had been bred to kill and could never be rehabilitated. "We want the dogs put down as quickly and as quietly as possible."

There were too many dog lovers on the team. The farm has a kennel of hunting dogs they all loved, and most of them had personal pets as well. The dogs roamed the airfield to drive the birds away. Their dogs were family. They argued the dogs should be tranquilized. Finally, they agreed to use hamburger meat laced with as much sedative as possible. This would mean carrying an extra cooler.

One of the guys quipped, "Better label the cooler. Some of the boys are so dumb they will probably forget and eat the meat."

The nervous laughter served to calm everyone down a little, and the vets reluctantly agreed to the concept. The vets added, "We'll mix the food since we understand the drugs better than anyone in the room."

Next, they argued about leaving the compound gates open when they left to let the dogs roam free when they woke up. No one wanted to save the dogs just to let them starve. The Vets wouldn't budge on this one. They would not agree to unleash them on any unsuspecting person who happened to pass by. This was a stalemate until the stable girl who mucked the horse stalls simply reminded them, "Since the photos show the servants feeding the dogs, there won't be a problem. The poor servants haven't done anything wrong, so why kill or tranquilize them? Go in on their night off. They'll take care of the dogs in the morning when they return."

They had just acquired new GoPro cameras, and they wanted to use them on this mission. Then they argued between the head-strap mount and the chest-mount harness.

Jeffrey argued, "The chest-mounted unit might get in the way. Use the head mount, but practice using it before you go."

Even though it was larger, they settled on the black GoPro Hero5. It was longer but thinner than the other models. The techies wanted the cloud upload and the Raw + WDR photos. They had already programmed them to send the video to the company satellite rather than the cloud. The cloud wasn't secure to their standards.

Next, it was the date and the weather. They pulled up the weather satellite and looked at Cali. "Jeffrey, we don't care if it's raining. In fact, we prefer it for cover, but on a clear night, we certainly don't want a bright moon. We'll need to go in between the DEA satellite passes though. We don't want to be seen on those."

Fortunately, the new moon would rise next week, so that and the servant's night off became their target date, rain or no rain. Their custom boots didn't squeak on wet surfaces, so those would be used along with helmets and Kevlar vests. There was grumbling. The vests would be hot as hell in the Colombian heat and humidity, but they weren't stupid people. There were a thousand other details to be ironed out, including who did what. Finally they turned to transportation. It was to be a small team on the ground, so the jet would be needed, but all the markings would be removed, and a fake tail registration number would be applied.

Jeffrey had an idea. "We'll disguise a large panel truck as a standard parcel delivery truck to transport everything to the house. There's an old abandoned house about a quarter mile below the mansion, so the truck will stop there, and the team will advance on foot."

Everyone thought it was a good idea. No one would suspect a truck delivering goodies. Even if they did, the driver could say this was a new route for him and he was lost. He would be armed anyway. Just as the planning session was about to wrap, XI walked in. He was tired, but he wanted a summary briefing. Before Jeffrey got the first sentence out though, XI stopped him.

"Gentlemen, I understand your motives. God knows, I want to see the bastard eliminated, but let me state clearly, I will not sanction an assassination. We have no legal standing, and if we are caught, not only will we all go to prison, I may lose most or all of my assets, most surely those associated with this property. I won't risk that, and I will not have a murder on my conscience. I appreciate that many of you have killed for our country, and I know that was righteous, but this won't work."

The planning session concluded at 9:00 p.m., and Jeffrey dragged himself to his apartment in the manor house for a scotch, his supper, a shower, and bed. Mary was talking to him while he enjoyed his drink.

"I came home about five this afternoon to find John sitting in the ballroom playing his mother's piano. He had picked up my score of Beethoven's Sonata No. 8 in C minor, Opus 13, 'Pathetique.'"

"That piano's his now. Is he any good?"

"Good? My god, the boy's technique is better than mine. He played with such feeling. I was almost overcome. When he finished, I sat down on the bench beside him. He apologized for disturbing me. He's practiced here before, but the child is a genius, Jeffrey."

"XI told me John had been tortured and bullied while he was in school in Bogota. He was basically kept a prisoner. He avoided the bullies by staying in the chapel or choir room practicing for hours every day."

"He needs some real care. Why don't I take him with me tomorrow to Williamsburg? I'll also take him to Westover Church and let him play the organ."

"Good idea. Why don't you take the boat? Would you take him down to the Jamestown site and show him around too?"

"Sure. That would be fun. I need to go down there and check on the work anyway. Attendance is alarmingly low. We have been trying to find new ways to attract people. American history isn't a popular subject in schools now."

John jumped at the chance to go out in the boat. Mary had grown up on the river and knew it like the back of her hand. Their forty-five-foot Morgan sailboat was named *Swan IV*.

"The winds are light, so we're using the diesel engine. Jack, the rector of Westover Church, has a meeting this morning, so the plan changed, and we're going to the Jamestown site first."

Mary was on the board of Preservation Virginia, and she chaired the archaeology committee. She showed him the dig, and he was impressed. They spent most of the morning viewing the grounds and taking the two behind-the-scene tours. He was allowed behind the ropes to walk the very ground the founders and Capt'n John had trod. They didn't have time to visit the collections. They would have to wait for another visit. He knew he would be back. She bought him a Jamestown T-shirt in the shop. Watching him try on T-shirts gave her a sense he was still growing. They also suddenly realized he didn't have any money. They took the boat back to the marina near Charles City. She called Jack and agreed they would have lunch together on the boat before going to the church.

Jack suggested, "You must come play it some Sunday."

Mary suggested Evensong next week. John had a sudden flashback of his mother. He was quiet on the return journey back. Mary didn't understand why, so in an effort to break the spell, she raised the sails and let him take the helm. There was an adequate breeze. It took him a little while, but he got the feel of it.

"Do you know anything about Capt'n John's boat? What happened to it?"

"The simple answer is that the Yankees burned it during the Civil War."

*****

In Colombia, one of the other cartels had had a similar idea as the Ops team. A hot, sweaty group of cartel soldiers were packed in a truck parked behind the abandoned house near Espinis's estate. They all got out, grateful for the little breeze. The temperature had actually dropped a few degrees because rain had started. They made their way to the villa. The dogs started barking. Using silencers, the barking quickly stopped. The rain was steady now, so the guards standing under the overhang of the main house roof by the front door didn't bother to check on the dogs. Those dogs were always going after some animal. Two snipers raised their silenced guns. Both guards went down. Two techies climbed the gate and bypassed the alarms and opened the gates. The team moved in. Two more of the team flanked the front door. Two others went toward the kitchen door.

The remainder of Espinis's guards were eating pie. They all fell before they had time to react. Security was lax. That surprised the attackers. They didn't know Espinis had convinced himself that no one would dare attack his home. The path was clear. Espinis was facing away from the door, working on his computer in his library. The volume was turned up as he listened to an opera. The kill shot was from the right and just behind his ear. He toppled over sideways out of his chair. The whole affair was over in less than fifteen minutes. They had never had as clean an operation. They were ready to set the fire bombs as planned. The timers were set to go off just after dawn to avoid a bright fire in the sky. A rising sun over the Andes would help to cover the fire, but hopefully, the rain would continue, and the low-level clouds would cover the smoke.

The leader stopped them. "Wait a minute."

"What is it, Captain? We need to move now."

"Get the truck up here. We're going to be delayed a little."

"Yes, sir. What do you see?"

"Look at those paintings. I'm no art expert, but I think they're old European masters. Get Juan in here. He knows all about this. Look at those old ornate gold frames. Start taking them down. Search the house quickly. Grab every picture you see."

They began removing pictures and running with them to the truck. "You know," remarked Juan, "that might be Nazi loot! Espinis is too young to have been in the war, but he might have gotten them from someone who was. I'm glad someone had the presence of mind to grab them."

Juan was the cartel accountant and also had a degree in European history.

"Yes, I agree, but I want my guys out of here."

Juan was looking at the computer. He scrolled down and saw a total of $25,500,495,875.25.

"Jesus! Look at that!"

The soldiers had heard the discussion and walked over to the screen. "I hate to burst your bubble, but you do realize that this amount is probably a small part of his profits?"

"We'll keep looking, then, but the other amounts are not on this computer. Where can we find the rest?"

"I suspect the money is literally spread out everywhere. We'll never find it all."

With a few quick keyboard strokes, Juan transferred all the money into the cartel's Cayman Islands alternate cash account. They used it often as a quick transfer account to avoid anyone from tracing confiscated funds. The others turned away and began looking for more loot. Juan found a little book beside the computer and quickly stuck it in his pocket. He transferred all the files onto a USB stick and carefully closed the computer. He found the server, transferred the files onto a second stick just in case, shut it down, unplugged it, and took it with him. He then picked up a MacBook Pro on the desk and transferred the files onto a third stick. He was careful not to close it to avoid losing the log in info. He carried them to the truck. He decided the large oriental rug on the living room floor was too fine to burn, so he had three guys load it onto the truck too.

One of the guys yelled, "Juan, you gotta come down here and see this! Hurry!"

Juan ran to see an open vault door. Inside were more stacks of gold bars than he had ever seen. There were glass cases of jewelry, silver, and gold objects. "Christ A'mighty! Y'all have an hour to load as much gold as you can."

Juan looked at the jewelry and selected some of the better pieces. His pockets were stuffed. He thought it might be stolen loot. He spied a set of old church communion silver. It was nearly black with age, but he quickly picked up a paten and saw that it was engraved, Grace Church Charleston. There were matching chalices, patens, a ciborium, a large flagon, and three large alms basins. All were inscribed. All carried a hallmark. Being a good Catholic, he recognized the communion silver, but the English inscriptions didn't make sense in Cali.

It took two trips to move the heavy gold to the abandoned house. They set the fires and quickly left. They were running late. Dawn was only thirty minutes away. No one in Cali saw the flames or smoke due to the weather. When the servants arrived later in the morning, they took one look and ran.

*****

XI had again asked Mary to take John somewhere for the day to try to get him to relax, so this time, they took the ferry across the James River and went back to Williamsburg for the day. XI thought John needed a better understanding of American history and how he fit into the James River continuum. John needed to exchange some of the clothes he had purchased because they really didn't fit. After touring the sights, they had an early supper at the Fat Canary Restaurant on Duke of Gloucester Street. John had his first pork chop, and it was served with baked apples and a small goat cheese souffle.

Two days later, several of the remaining ops team members were in the center canteen at five o'clock drinking a beer and turned on the news to check the ball scores.

"Look at this, guys! Where's XI?"

"He and Luis are in the manor house getting their scotch."

"Call him. He needs to see this!"

XI and Luis couldn't believe their eyes. Reporters were broadcasting live from Colombia. At 3:15 p.m., a magnitude 9 earthquake hit near Cali. The destruction was massive. In the Andes, whole villages were feared to have been wiped out. Luis's wife called. She wanted him to come home. Bogota had felt the tremors, and the kids were afraid. He quickly flew home.

The next week he returned with surprising news. At the village near the place where JB and Liz had been killed, the old people, the children, and a few pregnant women survived, but those in the coca fields perished in an instant. Clearing the jungle for cultivation had destroyed the root system of the trees that stabilized the mountainside. A massive landslide had wiped away the coca fields. His most surprising news was that JB and Liz had stumbled onto Espinis's main processing lab. The quake had exposed the lab underneath the fields. The entrance was right where they had been shot.

"That's why they were killed, XI. They stumbled into the hornet's nest."

One of the computer techs quickly positioned the satellite and brought up images of the area. Luis quickly began a briefing. "There was nothing left but the bare rock of the mountainside. The roof of the lab had buckled and slid down the mountain. We're looking at the interior because the roof is simply gone. We now know that the cocaine was shipped by the rail line on the eastern side of the mountain. Apparently this was one of Espinis's father's old gold mines. The railroad officials believe the railroad tunnel collapsed, and the tankers exploded into a fireball. Because the train entrances were blocked by debris, the fireball rushed back down into the lab and roasted everything there. Rescue workers determined that Espinis had stored his cash in cavernous rooms that opened off of the main tunnel. The rooms had been squared off to more easily stack the bundles of money. The caverns were packed solid. The burning gas and oil ignited the upper stacks of cash. The cash smoldered, but ultimately, it all was reduced to ash. No one will ever know the amount. Everyone, of course, denies any knowledge of the existence of this place."

"The hell you say. The railroad officials knew."

"We'll never prove that."

"Roller, let's look at Espinis's villa for a minute."

The villa's roof had collapsed on top of the burning body. The roof structure burned away, leaving his remains on top of the pile as if he had been roasted like a pig. The images showed the gruesome details. The dogs, and later the jungle animals, had feasted for days. The wild animals pulled the limbs away. Gnawed bones of Espinis and his guards were strewn across the site. Espinis was gone. The cartel was in ruins.

Luis was amazed. "The whole area is still impassable. I doubt anyone knows he's dead yet. There's no communication, and the roads are covered with fallen trees and debris all over the mountains. The only reason we know about the village and processing plant is the railroad sent a helicopter and film crew to survey the tracks. A rival cartel killed Espinis and looted the place."

"Well, Luis, their operation has gone better than anyone could have hoped for. Someone has removed the thorn and burned the rosebush."

While the others celebrated with more beer, Luis quietly asked XI to step outside. "While I was at home, a good friend, well, a former good friend, as it is now, named Juan asked to see me. He wanted to meet privately so we arranged to stay in the church after Mass. He told me a sad tale that, unfortunately, isn't uncommon in today's world. It seems that a few years ago, a middle-aged lady came into his office—Juan is a well-respected accountant who is also the parish treasurer—and asked his advice on helping her put her accounts in order. She claimed to have inherited a very large estate and had no mind for numbers. He agreed. As time passed, he began to suspect something, but by then, he was in too far and couldn't get out. He had become the de facto accountant for a large cartel, and the woman was the wife of the head. Juan was laundering a vast amount of money."

"What did he want from you? I hope to God you haven't gotten involved with a cartel too!"

"XI, I hope you know me better than that! The cartel has put him in charge of getting rid of the stolen art and valuables that they can't easily convert into cash. They also gave him ten million dollars as his part of the raid. He doesn't want it and has no idea of how he can get rid of either the goods or the money. He believes that the artwork pieces are old masters and may even be Jewish property stolen during WWII. Espinis's father was rumored to have been an escaped Nazi. As proof, he has given me photographic copies of the art and jewelry. He also wants me to help get asylum somewhere for his family. I am hoping that Mary can research these pieces and offer some help."

"This is risky. I hope no one else knows about this. I suggest you move your entire family here for an extended vacation while we try to sort this out. This is one hell of a risky mess, Luis, but I'll talk with Mary."

Mary was enlisted to research the art and other objects. Mary had taken three days, but working on Luis's hunch, she had discovered a small group of art historians at the Holocaust Memorial in Berlin who were trying to track artwork the Nazis had stolen.

"By US and British accounts, approximately one hundred thousand objects are still in the vaults of Swiss banks, but the Swiss will not admit to anything."

XI bristled at this. He had vaults of his own. His were all legal, but this was new information to him.

"All of the works are indeed old masters. Some of the former Jewish owners are known from old documents and photographs. How these things wound up in Colombia is a mystery, but Luis's speculation that Espinis had either purchased them from cash-strapped Nazis who had escaped Europe after the war or that his father had moved them out of Europe seems plausible."

"Thanks, Mary. I don't doubt this information at all. I'm going to call New York and find a rabbi. Several of our attorneys are Jewish."

Luis and XI flew to New York, and by the end of the day, they had a plan. Everything was stored in a warehouse in Bogota. "Get Juan to thoroughly wipe this all down to remove fingerprints and DNA. A Jewish group based in Argentina will fly in, load it all in a truck, and fly it to Berlin. People there will be expecting it."

"They'll think it's a bomb, XI."

"No, 'my rabbi'"—he made air quotation marks—"will assure them."

"That'll work, and it'll be a very kind gesture. XI, I'm grateful. Juan doesn't want to have anything to do with stolen art, and he can't go to the authorities or even an art expert, so the sooner he gets this stuff out of there, the better. We'll let the museum sort it out. This has gotten very complicated. What about the money, the ten million?"

"The simple solution, in my opinion, is for Juan to add his ill-gained profit to the ten and tell the cartel that the amount is the proceeds from the sale of the loot. Just give them their damned money back. The world will think Espinis died in the earthquake and fire. Everything was burned."

"I think that's brilliant. I don't yet know what to do with the jewelry. Can you determine if any of it's prewar European? If so, I'll send it too."

"Mary's already done it, and you're correct. All of it's prewar, and some of it is extremely valuable."

"Okay. Consider it done."

"What about the Charleston Church plate? How it got to Cali, Colombia, is anybody's guess."

"As for the Charleston silver, yes, Mary says it was stolen, but not from Charleston. Everyone thought the Yankee Army under General Sherman was going to march south and burn Charleston, so Grace Church sent their silver to a bank in the State Capital, Columbia, South Carolina. Sherman didn't march to Charleston but instead marched through Columbia. Most of the city burned, and this silver vanished. Pink said this story has circulated in his family for years. His paternal ancestor was the Rev. Dr. Charles Cotesworth Pinckney, and he had been rector of Grace Church, Episcopal, during the Civil War. He says the story is absolutely true."

"Well, well. Won't they be surprised. Use the same anonymous technique. Mary and Ms. Mamie want to polish it first. We'll send it back to Charleston. I'll tell Pink and swear him to keep it to himself."

"What about asylum for Juan?"

"I don't know yet. I'll keep working, but we need a better angle."

*****

Mary also realized John was going through another stage of puberty and was growing rapidly. She convinced XI to send him to an endocrinologist. After more tests and a full-body scan, the doctor said there was nothing abnormal to worry about. Over the course of the summer, John had grown to a six-foot, six-inch broad-shouldered, trim, fit young man. His slim fingers now spanned an octave and four notes. He had started practicing his scales again on the ballroom piano using Mary's old *Scale and Arpeggio Manual for Piano*. His feet were larger, and his legs were longer, but he managed to practice the pedal scales on the Westover Church organ. The staff started avoiding the house during his practice hours, but no one complained. They all laughed and said it could only be because of Ms. Mamie's cooking. He was all muscle and no fat, but he didn't look like a body-builder. He looked more like a swimmer. With his curly blond hair and watery blue eyes, he could have been a movie star.

*****

In Cali, a new disaster had been developing.

"I can't get a call through to Espinis. It's been weeks. I'm worried."

"You're his sister, Maria. Women worry. The cell towers in that area are still down. He'll call. Money is piling up here, and you know how he hates that. We lost the production lab. Maybe he's gone up there."

"No. Someone would have called. The bank won't tell me anything, and that's strange. They say their computers are still down. I don't believe them. I'm going up to the villa.

"Take Paulo and some armed men with you. Don't go alone, but let me warn you, the money seems to be gone. Find his book with the account number in it. We're sunk without that."

"I know the Cayman account number. His vault is full of gold, but the cash was in the mountain. We can survive without the cash."

She was shocked at the total destruction. She wailed and was inconsolable for a time. The men found the sculls, but not much else, and there were bullets rolling around in the sculls.

"This is murder. Pure murder. Was it another cartel?"

"It must have happened before the earthquake. We'll find the servants and find out what they know, but look at this. It's an empty chewing gum wrapper. It was in the bushes by the driveway. The writing is in English. The Americanos use this brand."

Growling and jumping to a wrong conclusion, she yelled, "Americanos. Revenge! They want revenge, I'll give them revenge! Paulo, go find that blond boy and kill him. I'm going to the Caymans and get my money."

*****

XI heard screams coming from John's cabin. It was only 11:00 p.m., but John had gone to bed early. XI rushed in to find the boy fighting something in his sleep. Shaking him awake, he asked, "Is it Espinis?"

"Yes. I keep having the same nightmare. He got me."

"You know he didn't, and he never will. Now go back to sleep."

"How do you know? He's still out there."

"I'll explain it all in the morning, but believe me, you're safe. He'll never get you. Your clearance had arrived. Tomorrow after breakfast, I'll take you to the Ops Center, and then you'll understand."

When they arrived at the center, Jeffrey, Luis, and Pink were waiting. Roller, a young trim black woman, wheeled herself in, and XI introduced her.

"John, Roller runs our IT Department. She's a computer genius. I found her being wasted in a menial job, so I hired her. She had been a naval weapons officer. When her ship was hit by a rogue wave during a violent storm, it knocked her down, and she broke her back when she landed on a companionway doorsill. That's why she's in the wheelchair."

"Roller, huh? Great name."

"Yep. I made it up myself before anyone could take pity on me."

"I know a little about computers too. Show me around."

"She can show it to you later. Come into our SCIF. You need to watch some video."

"What's a scif?"

"Sorry. It is an acronym and stands for Sensitive Compartmented Information Facility. Basically, no one can intercept our conversations in this room." XI spent the next hour explaining the entire sequence of events leading up to the fire and earthquake. John sat there motionless. When XI finished, John simply said without any emotion in his voice, "Okay. I'm glad he's gone. Now maybe I'll sleep better. If you don't mind, I need to go see Ms. Mamie. I'm starved."

"Just one more thing. After breakfast I want you to come back and work with Roller and Luis. A friend of Luis's, a man named Juan, gave Luis a little book and a couple of flash drives from Espinis's computers. They're password protected, and no one in the cartel can break the passwords. Luis thought you might try."

"That sounds like fun, Grandfather."

*****

Roller tried to unlock the passwords and failed. "Let me try."

Roller quipped, "Believe me, you can't do it. I've tried everything."

"Then what can it hurt?"

Roller realized that she was watching a boy after her own heart. It took him thirty minutes, but when he cracked it, XI asked, "How did you know to do this?"

"Remember my journal? Our computer teacher, Julio, worked for Espinis, and Espinis paid for our lab. This guy ran Espinis's system and wrote all of the cartel programs. The lazy bastard used his own programs as lessons. Look at these passwords. They are all variations of each other."

"Damn," exclaimed XI.

John first started trying to read the little book, while Roller copied and printed all the computer files. He couldn't understand it until he tried to read it out loud. He began to realize it was similar to the language some of the Colombian mountain boys spoke among themselves when they didn't want anyone else to understand, but he had never seen it written. There were a few words he couldn't quite understand. He and Luis tried to sound those out, and as they sounded them out in context, they started to make sense. The book contained the history of Espinis's family—in great detail.

"Espinis's vanity is all here. What an ego. He really did think he was too powerful to be touched."

Roller was amazed at the speed of his translation.

With Luis's help, John started paraphrasing out loud. "The history begins with El Rosa's father, Georg Rose. '*He was German but was sent out of the country to a monastery in a small village in France near the Swiss border. Georg discovered his pregnant girlfriend had a second lover and, in a fit of jealous rage, brutally murdered them both. His family sent him away and hid him. He was supposed to be a postulant for Holy Orders, but Georg was just biding his time until he could escape.*

When World War II broke out and France fell, the monks feared their fine ancient'—what's this word, Luis?"

"Romanesque, I think."

"Oh, of course. It's just like the school chapel—'*Romanesque chapel was at risk. Georg helped the monks dismantle the fine organ, the priceless medieval stained glass, the altar, and the bells. Those fittings were carefully inventoried. Plans and details of the layout of the organ and detailed sketches of the windows and the altar were packed with all of the parts. Each window panel was numbered to aid in future resetting.*'"

"Look! Those drawings are right here!"

"'*All of this, along with the large gold crucifix, and a large'*—is that word *Car-a-vag-gio*?"

"I don't know, John. I'm no art expert. Sound it out again, please, but as a single word. Okay, yes, that's what it sounds like to me."

"Maybe that is the painting behind the crucifix. It's very dark, nearly black, and it only becomes really visible in the late afternoon when the sun is shining directly on it."

"Bingo. Continue."

"'*Caravaggio paintings were shipped to Switzerland and stored in a bank vault in Basel. Georg traveled with the trucks, oversaw the placement in the vaults, and signed for it all. He returned to the monastery. He then decided to enlist in Hitler's army.*'"

"What an ass!" injected Luis.

"'*After he bragged about his knowledge of transporting goods, Georg was placed in a team to oversee the confiscation of Jewish art, jewelry, and gold. Georg had been hoping for a position away from the front, but this was even better. He and his team traveled through the occupied countries and enjoyed themselves. They were ruthless and developed a sense of knowing exactly where to find treasure. Georg oversaw the transportation of much of this into Swiss bank vaults. He kept very good records.*'"

"Aha!" exclaimed XI.

"'*As the Allies advanced into France, the Germans feared the Allies had occupied the old monastery dome and towers. They were wrong, but by the time they realized it, the chapel had been reduced to rubble.*'"

"What a waste."

"'*At the end of the war, Georg put on a clerical collar and began moving through monasteries toward the Atlantic coast. He was traveling with a fellow Nazi friend*—I can't decipher this name—*who was Father Xavier's father.*'"

"Shit! No wonder. This explains a lot of my hellish problems already!"

"How many times must I tell you not to use profanity, boy!"

"Sorry, Grandfather. I'll try."

"'*Using the bank account numbers, Georg withdrew a few gold bars to finance their trip to South America. Once there, Georg moved into the monastery in Bogota and entered as a postulant. He had changed his name to Jorge El Rosa—his mother's maiden name. He learned through the priests there that his old monastery would not be rebuilt. He wrote to the superior general and asked if the old fittings might be moved to the Bogota Chapel. He told the Jesuit authorities that while the chapel was a fine building of the same size and style, it lacked the proper details, and these fittings would make the liturgy even more meaningful.*'"

"That's not quite the same story that Father Xavier and Father Arturo told everyone. They even fooled the superior general, and probably the bishop and archbishop," snapped Luis. "Everything there is stolen goods. I'll take a copy with me and get to the bottom of this!"

He kept paraphrasing.

"'*After five years, El Rosa told the Fathers that he couldn't continue in the monastery. He had actually decided the Nazi hunters weren't looking for him, and by then he had quietly removed thirty of the best old master paintings and hundreds of gold bars from the vaults in Switzerland. He began mining Colombian gold. The most productive mine was under the old village. He married and had a son. The son, Jorge, nicknamed Espinis, and Father Xavier had grown up together.*'"

"Can this get any worse?" asked XI.

"According to this, the lab y'all were looking for while I was in the hellhole school was in the damned mountain right under my parents' noses just like the video showed. This is proof. One of the computer files contained an accounting of all the money he had white-washed through the monastery. Espinis was financing the education of nearly one-third of all of the boys there. They were all sons of the cartel members and would be required to work off this money once they graduated. Damn. What a story. No wonder most of the other boys ignored me. They were basically slaves."

"This time, I'll let the swearing go because you are correct. This answers everything."

They opened another file. "Hot damn!" Roller exclaimed from her wheelchair. "Look at this. My god. This is a detailed map of the drug routes. We have the names and contact info of all of the runners, stash houses, and dealers. This was current as of three weeks ago. I'll bet some of the ships they loaded just before the quake are still en route."

"Oh yes!" XI exclaimed. "We'll wipe them all out. This is too big for our little group. I'll call Kent and get the DEA on it ASAP. This involves every major port and city in America. We'll take Baltimore. They can have the rest. Every DEA office in America will be very happy. We can legally make a fortune with this intel. John, I think you've earned yourself a place on the Ops computer team."

*****

John spent the rest of the summer at Swan Bay. He spent his mornings in the center coding new programs. He didn't really like the confinement of the windowless space, so he spent as many afternoons as possible learning to drive one of the old breeding center's stick shift trucks and driving around the plantation. Somehow, the breeding center didn't appeal to him. He was not old enough to have a driver's license, but Jeffrey needed to keep him busy. Even though he had a security clearance, there were times Jeffrey didn't want him to be in the center. Besides, XI wouldn't have time to teach him to drive, and DC is not a place where teenagers need to practice their driving skills. He also had an ulterior motive for having him learn the use of a clutch. He couldn't hurt the old truck. It was only used to haul manure anyway. XI had been keeping JB's 1957 canary-yellow and white Chevrolet Corvette convertible in mint condition. The car had a four-speed manual transmission, 283-cubic-inch engine with 220 horsepower. JB bought it while he was in school and only drove it on weekends. Today, it would probably sell for about $125,000. When Jeffrey was convinced John could manage the clutch, he took him over to a storage building and opened the barn doors. The boys had washed and polished it.

"Man. What a car! She's beautiful."

Jeffrey explained it had been his father's, but now as soon as he was old enough to get a driver's license, he could have it. For now, of course, he could only drive it around the farm.

"The only modification from the original is the seat belts your father added."

John looked it over, opened the door, and jumped in the driver's seat.

Jeffrey hopped into the passenger seat, explained the layout, and handed John the key, warning him, "She's very powerful. Take it easy at first."

"I'll treat her like my little baby."

They slowly drove off and were gone for two hours.

After lunch on July Fourth, XI told him that he would continue his studies. "You're going to move to Potomac House and be ready for school immediately. By tradition, you really should be going to New Hampshire, but I suspect you've had your belly full of boarding school."

CHAPTER 8

DC

John rode with XI in the 1959 MG sports car from Swan Bay into town. XI drove too fast, but John didn't complain. He was glad he was buckled in. Then they hit the DC traffic. It seemed the whole town had decided to come home from the holidays at the same time. At least it forced XI to slow down. When they finally drove into the grounds at Potomac House, John immediately noticed the similarity to the house at Swan Bay. He commented on it to XI.

"Yes. You are perceptive. It is a scaled-down version. The three of us didn't need another large house. Leave your bags in the car for now. The staff will get them. I'm going to let you have your pick of accommodations. Let me show you around first."

They entered the central hall, and as he had said, it was smaller, but it was still grand. John began to wonder if everyone in America lived in houses like this. He noticed the walls were painted the same shade as the silk in the manor house. XI casually remarked he had gotten the silk in the Swan Bay house reproduced by a mill in France, but it was just cost prohibitive to run enough for this house too. The dining room was to the left. John noticed the fireplace was similar to the two in the plantation house dining room. This one had a similar painting, but of a different river. XI explained that it was by the same artist, the Italian Canaletto, but this scene was of the River Thames in London. John noticed that the sideboard to the right of the fireplace was similar to the two at Swan Bay.

"Yes, it is exactly the same and even has the original chamber pot you will never use!"

John laughed.

He continued, "The breakfront on the other side of the fireplace is by Chippendale too. Capt'n John imported household goods after he had made the tobacco runs. According to the journals, we had a warehouse full of this furniture, but most of it was sold to keep the plantation running after the tobacco recession. This piece had been damaged. All these glass panes had gotten broken, so it just remained. It is a beauty, though, even with the replacement glass. It is a 1764 George III mahogany breakfront bookcase. It has a double broken swan's neck pediment. That may actually be why it was never sold. The center section is flanked by two conforming but slightly smaller wings separated from the center by hand-carved pilasters. The bottom door panels are surrounded by raised hand-carved egg and dart roping. It is eleven feet long and eight feet, six inches high. It will not fit just anywhere. The silver displayed on the shelves is eighteenth-century English hand chased sterling. Some of it was made by Paul Storr in his London shop. The rest was made by Jones of Birmingham. Capt'n John made a small fortune importing silver. The pieces were small, the demand was high, and it could be packed in between larger pieces."

John didn't know much about furniture, but he knew, even with his minimalist, modernist, classical tendencies, these two pieces must be important.

"How can it be moved?"

"It breaks down into eight pieces. Then it's easy."

The dining room table and chairs were reproductions.

"Ms. Mamie told me the chairs in the dining room at Swan Bay were originally a set of twenty-six, but one of them had burned in a fire. Do you know how it happened?"

"Sadly, it's true. The story is this. During a heated political argument over the coming American Revolution, one of the chair seats had gotten stained when a guest knocked over a decanter of claret. The chair had been taken to the workshop on the plantation to be cleaned. The workers left the rags they had soaked with solvents laying around. They spontaneously combusted in the middle of the night. Fortunately, the workshop was the only building burned, but it was a total loss."

They passed back into the hall.

"The two paintings across from the stairs are of John VIII and his new bride, Violet, by an American artist named John Singer Sargent. They must always hang side by side because the backdrop is of them as they were leaving St. Gile's Cathedral, Edinburgh, after their wedding. The entire family and most of the house servants made the trip across the Atlantic for the wedding. They stayed at Ochiltree Castle. At that time, the castle was the home of Captain James Stewart. He was related to our ancestor Charteris Hew Lady Elizabeth Ramsay. Our ancestor Capt'n John was Sir William and Lady Elizabeth's second son. The first Bishop in Britain is mentioned in the Doomsday Book. The Bishop shield is still visible over the castle entrance at Ochiltree."

They walked across the hall and through to a small parlor boasting a portrait by Gainesborough over the mantel. They walked through a small paneled dining room. It had a portrait by Reynolds over the mantel. XI led him into a hyphen, which served as a bar, and into a large two-story library. The paneling and shelving were made of dark walnut from Swan Bay. XI told John he was welcome to read anything.

"When we are at home and not busy, which will probably be rare, we will spend our evenings in this room by the fire. Your father loved this room. Unfortunately, it was probably the only thing about this property other than the swimming pool he did like. He said he felt smothered in town."

John instantly understood, and he became more convinced when they looked at the bedroom suites on the second floor. They were just a little too close together. They passed back through the house into the other hyphen. It served as a butler's pantry. They walked into a large, warm, inviting kitchen. XI introduced Maybell, his cook, to John. Douglas, her husband, and XI's maid, Annabelle, were sitting at a small table having afternoon tea. Douglas stood and shook John's hand.

"Please join us."

XI introduced John to the maid. "Douglas is my chief of staff. He runs this place. He keeps all the household accounts and occasionally acts as butler. He runs all the errands I simply don't have the time to do. He keeps this place shipshape and running like a fine watch. Not that you will find out anytime soon, but Douglas here makes the finest mint julep in Virginia. He will help you with your needs too, but if I hear you are abusing the privilege, you will be in deep trouble."

"Young John and I will get along just fine, XI. We'll have a good time shopping for his new wardrobe."

"The school has a relaxed dress code, but he'll need something better than these casual clothes. Go see Joel over in the mall. He will need a sports jacket or two, perhaps a cashmere blue blazer could be one of them, and something tweedy for next fall."

John didn't like the sound of tweedy. He already knew tweedy wouldn't happen.

"He'll need a few suits and dress shirts and ties, and get him a dark cashmere topcoat. Oh, and get him a dinner jacket and a tux while you're at it, and for God's sake, buy some decent shoes. He can't be seen in this town in those boat shoes he wears."

"We'll head out tomorrow."

XI and John declined the tea. They headed out to walk the grounds. Every inch was landscaped to perfection. They walked down to the river, and on the way back up to the house, XI showed him the pool and pool house. They were mostly hidden in the landscaping.

"John, you may live here, or you may take one of the bedrooms upstairs. The pool is heated by solar panels on the other side of the pool house. The pool boy comes on Wednesday afternoons, and the gardener is around and about at odd times, but no one else will bother you out here. Your father stayed here on the rare times he bothered to grace us with his presence. There is a matching garden house symmetrically placed behind the landscaping on the other side of the lawn. It has been completely renovated, and Douglas and

Maybell live there, but you are not to wander over there unless they invite you."

John went in. It was spacious with a vaulted ceiling, a fireplace, and wet bar in the main room. There was a smaller room he could use as a bedroom. Across the main room from the bedroom was a full bath with a small wood-paneled sauna inside.

"May I change the furnishings?"

"Of course. Do anything you want as long as you don't destroy the building."

"Then, I'll be happy to stay here. I want to put the little organ in here too."

At ten the next morning, John and Douglas walked into the store, and Douglas introduced him to Joel.

"Good to meet you, John. You look more like XI than you do JB, though. You don't have your father's build at all, do you? What are you? About six feet, five inches? Your father wasn't that tall."

Quickly changing the subject, Douglas told Joel what John would need. Joel took measurements.

"You'll need custom shirts. No one makes an off-the-rack shirt to fit you. I suggest our Reserve Collection of shirts in our wash-and-wear fabrics."

"The maid will love you for that," said Douglas.

"Great. Then we will also get khaki and navy-blue slacks that are wash-and-wear. All the guys your age are wearing them. You'll need gray linen and gray wool pairs too. Let's look at shirt fabrics. I suggest oxford cloth with button-down collars. You won't need to keep up with collar stays. I suggest this blue and this white and these stripes."

John liked the clean look of the oxford cloth. They worked their way through the list until they came to the white dinner jacket.

"Not loving it at all. What other options do you suggest?"

Joel agreed. The white was too stark with his hair and coloring. John selected an off-white linen fabric. Joel called it ecru. John was happy. While being fitted for the tux, John didn't really like the selections for the bow ties and cummerbunds.

"Can't I be a just little individualistic here, guys?"

Douglas had an idea. "Buy the black set for now. I know exactly what you need."

John bought twelve shirts, twelve pairs of slacks, several suits, shoes, a topcoat, a tux, the dinner jacket, and the black-tie set.

John proudly said, "I'll pay."

He pulled out his new black metallic AmEx Centurion card. John suddenly realized he had no idea how to use the card.

Joel kindly said, "Here, let me help you with that. These new chips can be tricky."

Going through the mall, John spied something he liked in a jewelry store window. It was a set of 24k gold cufflinks and shirt studs which looked like finely crafted birds. They had been cast from the designs of a wood-carver in South Carolina. The birds reminded him of Swan Bay, so he bought those using his newly discovered technique with the credit card. Douglas led him into a Scottish shop. John was attracted to some brightly colored Scottish cashmere sweaters. He bought those. Then Douglas introduced him to an entirely new experience: Scottish tartans. Douglas showed him a book of registered Scottish tartans and turned to a Ramsay tartan.

"John, if you like this, I want us to keep it a surprise from XI. I'll tell you when the time is right. I'll help you dress too. Studs and cufflinks are tricky. You can wear your father's tartan kilt, but you'll need a new Prince Charlie shirt, jacket, and waistcoat. That's why I told you to buy the black-tie set. You'll need these shoes and socks too."

John remarked, "I want to look at that book of tartans again. This is fascinating stuff, but where's the Bishop tartan?"

"XI told me that there isn't an ancient one. The family has always worn a Ramsay. There are five different Ramsay tartans. XI and JB wore different ones."

As he looked through the book, he spotted a Ramsay blue and black tartan. It had white vertical and horizontal stripes.

"Douglas, look at this. I want a new kilt and a full set of accessories and a throw blanket in this pattern too! Oh, this red is my ancestral grandmother's tartan—Ramsay of Dalhousie. I want a set of this too."

It had been an exceedingly expensive morning. On the drive home, John asked, "Did you work here when my father was a boy? What was he like?"

"One, yes, and two, I don't really know. Your grandmother discovered Maybell. Maybell was the cook at a shelter for pregnant girls, and your grandmother was a sponsor. In those days we black folk just thought of these white women as 'rich do-gooders' trying to soothe their consciences, but there was something about your grandmother that was different. Maybell liked her immediately, and your grandmother thought of Maybell as a young Mamie. Maybell left the shelter to work for your family at a much better salary. We were both twenty-five at the time. XI sent her to cooking school in France. That had always been one of her dreams. Your grandparents never met a stranger, and they threw some fine parties before the accident. I had just left the Air Force, and I didn't know what I wanted to do. I had been assigned to the Officer's Club at Andrews Air Force Base, so all I knew how to do was run a club. XI asked me to run the house and be their occasional butler here in DC and at Swan Bay. At first, I didn't like the idea of working on a farm, but once we went down there and met everybody, we were treated like one of the family. After your grandmother died, well, XI just sorta existed, and we took care of his needs. JB was always at school. He hardly ever came home after his mother died. He went to the farm a few times, but I never really knew him."

They ate lunch at the little table in the kitchen. XI was at the office. They ate French onion soup. Maybell was simmering a pot roast with fresh herbs and vegetables on a back burner of the six-burner Viking gas stove. It was for supper. She ladled enough pot liquor out to make four large ramekins of soup for the three of them and the maid. She crumbled four large slices of Gruyère cheese and sprinkled them over the soup. She added slices of French bread on top before she placed the ramekins in the broiler. For XI, she had put a full bottle of his 1998 Marcoux Chateauneuf du Pape red wine into the simmering pot with the roast. The soup was delicious. John knew he was either going to need to start swimming laps in the pool or find a place to run or both if he wanted to fit into all the new clothes.

That afternoon, after a swim, he turned his attention to the pool house. He decided to remove everything except the rugs. He was pleased to find he had high-speed internet access, Wi-Fi, and cable TV. He purchased two Sony XBR Z9D 100-inch series 4K ultra HD TVs. One was for the sitting room, and the other was for the bedroom. He then purchased a powerful MacBook Pro laptop computer and Wi-Fi printer. It would also print from his iPhone and iPad. It dawned on him to hack into the Bogota school's server and retrieve all his organ compositions. It was easy. Once he had them all, he simply erased the old files. He then started searching midcentury modern furniture. He spotted Eames lounge chairs immediately, but he didn't like the look of the new leather. It looked plastic compared to those he had seen while studying the style in school. He scrolled on down and found a site called eBay. He found four antique Eames chairs and two ottomans. The shells were the original Rosewood, and the aged black leather looked very comfortable. He set up an account and bought them. He found a large oval Saarinen pedestal table with four matching chairs and two Bertoia barstools with wire chrome bases and black leather seat pads for the bar. There was still a large space on one side of the room.

XI walked in a few days later. "Our New York office in the Seagram's Building has this style of furniture. You need something large over there. I suggest that you move your mother's piano into here."

"But Mary loves to play that piano."

"Then buy her a new one, but don't tell her it is hers. She would never accept it. I agree the ballroom needs a piano. Send her to Vienna and ask her to oversee the final voicing for you since she knows the acoustics of the room better than you. You don't have time to go. School starts next week. I've arranged for you to attend a fine business school that's run by an old friend of your grandmother's. It's not an arts school, but I don't think you need more music at the moment. This place will be good for you, and it's just a quick commute from here with very little traffic."

John enrolled in the Arlington International Studies School. XI had also gotten the soccer coach to let John try out for the team.

John wasn't too sure about that. He looked at computer science but decided he was already beyond them. He would need to talk with Roller and find something else. He would need to find a place to practice the organ. Roller sent him a text. She suggested he enroll in a night program at a tech school and learn as much as he could about computer hardware and repair. He agreed and very quickly located a local school specializing in electronic engineering with a specialty in computer hardware design and repair. He enrolled. He also located an Episcopal Church in town that had a Flentrop organ, so he volunteered to be a sub, and he was allowed practice time. He also found a fine Schoenstein Organ in town and quickly got permission to practice there as well. He was going to be a busy guy. His fears about a new school were abating somewhat. His studies were going well. He was exempt from the languages courses, but he took German as a way to study something different.

In his English lit course, he discovered the works of Shakespeare. He was fascinated with the old Scot, *Macbeth*, but he really enjoyed *Romeo and Juliet.* He enjoyed dissecting the structure of the plays because he found his favorite structural idea—counterpoint. His discussions with Father Arturo were coming back.

*****

While sitting on a bench in the locker room taking his street shoes off, John spotted him immediately. How could he not? Thomas Kalhan Jr. had the disgusting habit of walking around the locker room naked, talking with the team members. John noticed that when Thomas found one of the guys sitting on a bench, he would walk up to the guy and get into the guy's face.

John would need to find a way to avoid that! Thomas spotted him.

"Hey, you, dirty blond mop. This is a closed locker room. Leave." As he walked toward him, John immediately stood. John was more than a head taller than Thomas, causing Thomas to look up.

"I'm John Bishop. I'm a new team member."

"Oh yeah. Coach said something about a newbie. Go over there and get your gear and sit down and listen. You won't get any field time this year. Maybe next year if you're lucky. We have a first-rate soccer team already."

John had seen their record. It left room for improvement. John knew he wasn't an Olympic-quality athlete, but he knew he could hold his own with this group, and he was subconsciously beginning to retreat. He had found the school bully, and he didn't want another round of trouble. John quickly understood though, given his size, he could handle Thomas if he had to.

"I'm the captain of this team. I'm the son of US Senator Thomas Kalhan Sr."

John quickly learned that it was true because Thomas repeated it in almost every conversation.

The team took the field, and John was immediately benched. John watched and learned. The guys were good, but he spotted room for improvement. Thomas wasn't the best player. When practice ended and the guys ran off to the locker room, the coach asked John to take a few laps around the track. That was easy. He had continued to run with the Ops team on the plantation dirt roads. Coach liked what he saw. John had stamina. At the next practice, Coach began running John into the scrimmages for a few minutes. Thomas was not happy. John began to get more field time, and without much effort, he was able to outperform Thomas. John sensed he was causing a problem, but he decided, to hell with it. He liked playing. The other team members began to like John too. He wasn't a braggart. Thomas seethed. During the first match of the season, John scored a goal. They went on to win by one score, and he had secured his place.

On the way into the locker room, Thomas ran up to him and said, "Don't hit the showers yet. Have a seat and cool down. Coach will be in to talk with you after he finishes his meeting with the athletic director."

John had no intention of sitting down. He never sat in that locker room. He only put his feet on the bench to put on his socks and tie his shoes.

John was beginning to get tired of waiting. He had other things to do. All the team had showered, dressed, and left, but Naked Thomas, as they called him behind his back, was still strutting around in all his glory. Thomas finally yelled at John and told him to go on and shower. The coach was still in the meeting. John stripped, wrapped his towel around his waist, and walked to the shower. When he had finished, he quickly dressed in a pair of clean soccer shorts and a T-shirt. The locker room seemed to be empty. It was very quiet. He stepped over the bench and away from his locker, turned to prop his foot on the bench, and bent down to tie his shoe. He sensed movement behind him. He turned around, and there was Naked Thomas. This time, there were two other guys with him. These guys were not soccer players. They were wearing football jerseys of the local high school team. Thomas was standing there in a pseudo military stance with his legs spread and both hands behind his back. The two big guys grabbed John's arms. Big mistake. They neglected his legs.

"So, newbie, you thought you could just waltz in here and take over my team, did you? Well, I'm going to correct that idea right now."

Thomas flashed his right hand from behind his back, and in one move, he opened a switchblade knife and stabbed John behind his left knee. John screamed and instinctively kneed Thomas in the balls with his right knee as hard as he could. Thomas went down. The shock caused the other two goons to relax their hold just enough for John to get his arms free. He bashed their heads together as hard as he could. They went down. They were knocked out. John grabbed his iPhone and called 911 to report the assault. He then called Douglas, who was waiting in the car on the street. He told Douglas he had been stabbed and was bleeding. Douglas jumped the curb and drove over the soccer field to pick him up. The knife was still in his leg. Somehow, he had the presence of mind to not touch it. He hobbled to the car, but he was still bleeding. Douglas drove like a bat out of hell. He left ruts in the playing field where he peeled out, but that was someone else's problem. Fortunately, the hospital was close, and he knew the shortcuts. Rush hour gridlock hadn't set in, so for DC, traffic was light. The carpet in the station wagon was ruined, but that was minor. XI would probably sell the damned thing now anyway. Douglas knew the spurts were arterial. He had quickly used his belt as a tourniquet. When they arrived at the George Washington University Hospital Trauma Center, John felt as though he would pass out. Douglas helped him up to the admissions desk. He was quickly admitted into a cubicle, and a nurse came in to get the background information. She quickly triaged the situation. John was in real trouble. She got the trauma doctor. He called for the portable x-ray machine while he tried to stop the bleeding. Fortunately, Thomas had missed cutting the ligament, but he had sliced the muscle and nicked the bone. Small bone fragments were seen on the images. The blood flow was coming from the artery. John needed surgery, stat. He called for a surgical team.

As John was being wheeled into surgery, three ambulances arrived. There were cops everywhere. Within thirty minutes, the waiting room became crowded. Even the head of school and the coach were there. Everyone wanted information. The trauma doctor could only tell them John had been stabbed, two boys were unconscious with possible concussions, and they thought Thomas possibly had severe testicular trauma. The senator didn't like the sound of that! He had been called away from the floor of the Senate, and he demanded more answers. Immediately! Everyone assumed it was not their son's fault. Everyone except XI, Douglas, the head of school, and the coach decided the new boy had started it. The coach had a very good sense of what might have happened. Douglas suggested they go for a cup of coffee. When they were away from the others, he told them what John had told him and the trauma doctor. The coach knew that the two football players and Thomas were good buddies, so he had no doubt who had started it. A few hours later, the trauma doctor found them and asked to speak to XI. XI told him he wanted all his friends to hear the conversation.

"Your grandson is very lucky. Whoever put the tourniquet on his leg slowed the bleeding and saved his life, but it is a good thing he didn't wait on an ambulance. Another few minutes and he might have bled out. We removed the knife during surgery. Fortunately, no one tried to pull it out. It helped by putting pressure on the artery too. It went in vertically. Otherwise, the damage would have been much worse. I gave the knife to the police."

The doctor continued, "John told me the story, and for what it's worth, I relayed it to the police. As you know, the senator is a very powerful man. He has demanded John be arrested for assault. The cops told him one guy couldn't have possibly started a fight against those three guys, but the senator insisted John had planned the whole thing ahead of time. It was premeditated. He told them his son didn't own a switchblade. John has been arrested. He will be handcuffed to his hospital bed."

"That son of a bitch. We'll just see about that." XI stormed off to call an attorney.

The head of school and the coach excused themselves to go find the senator and the other parents.

John woke up about 1:00 a.m. and was disoriented. Bags of fluids and blood hung in a rack over his head and coursed down into his body. Every member of the Ops team had donated blood for John. Someone on the other side of a curtain was yelling and cursing. The nurse came in to shut him up. She checked on John after she had sedated the other guy.

"Where am I?"

"You are in the hospital. You've just had surgery on your knee, but you will recover. There are people here who want to see you."

John was in a semiprivate room. Patients must either be very important or infectious to get a private room in this hospital. He suddenly realized he was cuffed to the bed. The police walked in followed by a man in a suit who identified himself as his attorney.

"Why am I chained to this bed? Take it off!"

"John, you have been arrested for premediated assault with a deadly weapon."

"But I didn't start it. They attacked me!"

"John, don't say another word. I'm working to get you off."

"But—"

"Not one more word!"

John stopped talking, and the cop read him his rights. Damn. *Not again!* he thought. Once the cops left, XI and Douglas walked in and asked how he was feeling. John wanted to know everything. They told him. He told them what he had told the doctor downstairs. XI said once the knife was processed, all the evidence would support his story. He told him to relax and focus on getting better. The doctor came in and explained to John just how lucky he was. He told him he would need rehab.

"For how long?"

The doctor evaded the question by simply stating that everyone was different. The next morning the staff transferred him to a wheelchair, telling him it was only a temporary move. Roller wheeled herself through the door. "Well, well. Just look at you sitting there eye to eye with me. How are you doing?"

"I'm not going to play soccer anymore. I might have trouble with the organ pedals."

"Oh hell no. I'm not going to let you sit there feeling sorry for your white ass. You're going to be up walking by the end of the week. I'm going with you to rehab right now. I know your therapist. We have history, and he will hurt you if you don't obey him, buddy. Come on, move it."

On the way down to rehab, she said, "I hear you got them good, John. The two goons have mild concussions, but they have thick skulls. Probably nothing football wouldn't have done to them eventually, unless it already has. That boy Thomas? It was severe blunt testicular trauma. Serves him right, if you ask me, but he'll be all right. The nurses told me he's all numbed up, and he's a pain in their asses. Of course, he's on a posh wing in a private room." She noticed John was cuffed to the chair.

That afternoon, Douglas came in. "How you holding up? You gave me a hell of a scare, boy!"

"I don't know. My head is fuzzy. That rehab guy tortured me. I'm sore."

Douglas frowned. "That's just the pain meds. We'll get you off them today so's you don't end up like your grandmother."

"I don't want that! Grandfather told me the story, sir."

"John, don't call me sir. I work for you."

"My mother taught me to respect my elders, sir, and besides, you saved my life. I can't ever disrespect you."

"Let's agree to a compromise then."

"Well, maybe we can agree that you're forever my best friend."

"Great, but just call me Douglas. After your grandmother died, it was like all the air had suddenly been sucked out of the house. JB flew back to school the same afternoon. He spent his summers on Cape Cod in a house he and his friends rented. Occasionally the two would meet at the farm, but as time passed, they saw less and less of each other. XI spent most of his time in New York after that, so the house was like a silent tomb. You've brought life back. XI seems happier now than before the funeral. She was the glue that held everything together. Now, I want to talk to you. Do you know what an alpha dog is?"

"No, s—ah, no."

"Well, it's time you learned because you're an alpha dog for sure. Some guys just have it naturally. Male alpha dogs always lead the pack. I think it comes from our tribal instinct, but I'm no expert. It seems to work like this. When you were in that highly respectable choir school, you were one of the soloists. The other boys looked up to you, and everyone was polite, but when you went to Colombia, they weren't polite, and you threatened the existing alpha dog. You also got a taste of racism. That's not fun, is it? In the school here, you also threatened the alpha dog."

"I didn't mean to threaten those guys. They were bullies."

"But that's often what bullies are. In the service, we were trained to understand that only rank gave anyone authority. Out in the world, it's the bullies who use force to keep their position. It works in the animal world. There can never be two bulls in a pasture. Two stags will fight to the death. Two roosters will fight to the death too. You and Jorge fought to the death, but for you, it was self-defense."

"What can I do? I don't need to control anyone, man or woman."

"With your size now, I think those days are over, but you need to always be on guard. After this little talk, you'll know what to look for."

John was released into his grandfather's custody. The senator had yelled and screamed at the judge, so the judge retaliated by letting John go home. He wasn't allowed to leave the area. The area did not include Swan Bay. The senator demanded his son was innocent despite the fingerprints on the blade. The senator demanded a speedy trial, citing his busy schedule. Congress was in recess, and he needed this cleared up immediately. XI agreed, because he knew the outcome. The senator was a banker, not a trial attorney. The case was turned over to the DA's office for trial. There were all sorts of legal time-killing maneuvers John didn't understand. Douglas told him that was the way lawyers ran up their billable hours. Finally, the trial began.

The DA called John, Douglas, the trauma doctor, the trauma nurse, the orthopedic surgeon, the rehab therapist, and the vascular surgeon to testify. John was impressed with the responses. He especially liked the trauma nurse. She lit into the DA like a banshee for having the audacity to even question her experience and abilities. The judge cautioned her twice for her foul language. The three attackers were portrayed as saints. They had never been in trouble with the law, which translated to "never got caught." The goons testified, and they all lied. Their stories were all fabricated. They testified they had defended themselves from this unholy terror who attacked them out of the blue. The two football players didn't even know John. They testified they had just stopped by to congratulate Thomas on a great win.

John's attorney began. There were DNA results shown on the screen. They showed the earlier DNA results, and they even compared them to the new results. Thomas's and one of the goon's DNA were both on the handle. There were scans, x-rays, lab results, and medical reports. He got one of the goons to admit the knife was his. His fingerprints, as well as Thomas's, were on the handle. They were stupid jocks. During a break, John asked how they could get away with the lies. He said they hadn't.

"John, whenever someone lies on the stand or in a deposition, they usually have a tell."

Tomas and two of his friends had been teaching John to play poker in their dorm room in Bogota, so John had a good understanding of what poker faces and tells were.

"Did you see them look away from the jury when they lied? Did you see the ticks and the fidgeting? Thomas rubbed his right eye every time. The jury saw it all, so it isn't just your word against theirs. The evidence is conclusive to support your presentation of the facts."

During a break, a teenaged black guy and a DC police officer walked in and sat down behind John. The police officer whispered into the attorney's ear. John recognized the boy. His name was Richard Stone. He was a player on the soccer team. John didn't really know him, personally, but he was one of the good players.

"Your Honor, may we approach?"

The Judge motioned with his hand.

"Your Honor, we have a new surprise witness. He has just come forward with his father." He motioned to Officer Stone.

The defense protested, but the judge ordered the attorneys into his chambers. A few minutes later, the lawyers returned to the courtroom, and Richard and his father were led into chambers by the bailiff. Thirty minutes later, they all returned to the courtroom. The judge said he would allow the boy to testify. The DA protested he hadn't had time to depose this boy. The judge gave them twenty-four hours, and not one minute more. The media had been covering the whole trial. They were running for the doors with this latest potential bombshell. They smelled blood. It was all over the evening news with the local talking TV bobbleheads speculating about what this would mean to a powerful senator's son. It was in the newspaper the next morning.

The story was all over the internet.

Richard took the stand just after lunch the following day. The attorney had worked long into the night with him. He was well prepared. Richard said he had left his house keys in his locker and had returned to get them. No one saw him because the entrance door and his locker were on the next row over. He heard a noise. He had peeked around the lockers to see what was happening. He peeked around the lockers just as the football players grabbed John. He told the court verbatim what Thomas had said. He saw the knife in Thomas's hand, and he saw the stabbing. He wished he had come to John's defense, but it just happened too fast. He saw John take Thomas out, and in the commotion, he ran. He just ran. He said it had been eating at him ever since because he didn't even try to help. His head was down in shame. He told the court he was a minority student and had a scholarship. His parents, even though they both worked two jobs, couldn't afford to send him to school there without financial help. He heard about the trial on TV. At breakfast on the morning they walked into the courtroom, he finally confessed to his father. His father took an emergency leave day to get him to court. The DA had no questions. The DA gave a forceful closing, but he had lost the fight. Even the senator looked defeated. The judge instructed the jury. The jury returned an hour later with the verdict. Guilty. All three were guilty. The three were led out of the courtroom by the bailiff. Their mothers were in tears, but John didn't show any emotion. He still faced a hard rehab. He was still walking with a cane. John went over to Richard and thanked him for coming forward. Later as they ate supper, XI quietly told John that he was going to pay for the remainder of Richard's tuition and would send him to the university of his choice. XI had already sent a letter of guarantee to the head of school. He only asked for absolute anonymity.

The sentencing phase started two weeks later. Thomas was sentenced to prison with the maximum time for premeditated assault with a deadly weapon. The football player who furnished the knife got a slightly shorter sentence, but he went to prison too. They would not be allowed to be in the same prison. The other guy got five years' probation and was expelled from school. The judge forced him into a DC public school with one thousand hours of community service in a program of the judge's approval. He was not allowed to leave DC without the court's permission. Those three wouldn't be going to Harvard or anywhere else for years. There would be no scholarships. John wanted to quit school. Two schools, three attacks. He wanted to retreat to Swan Bay and rehab his knee. He knew that he would never play sports again, but his main concern was the organ pedals. That had to work. XI wouldn't hear of it. He promised to find another school next fall. John tried as hard as possible with the rehab, and he swam for hours in the pool. He went to bed exhausted every night. XI took pity on him and rewarded his hard work by letting him go to Swan Bay for the summer. On the day he was to leave, word came that Thomas was dead. Apparently his bragging about his powerful father getting him an early release was too much. He was found dead in a storage room with a shiv in his jugular. John needed to get out of town and away from the media as quickly as possible.

*****

"I've had an idea, Madre."

Maria knew Paulo, and she knew about his dumb ideas. "Speak up. I can hardly hear you. What now?"

"Is that better?"

"Yes, much."

"I searched for John Bishop on the internet. There are thousands of them."

She laughed. "Why am I not surprised. What else?"

"Since we don't have a middle initial or name, I started with A John Bishop to Z John Bishop, and then from John A Bishop to John Z Bishop using his age as a parameter."

"Interesting. What did you find?"

"Nothing, that is until I removed the age limit and then I started over. When I finally got to John X Bishop, I made a typo and a John Bishop X popped up."

"That's odd. What did you do next?"

"Well, as you said, it was odd, but this was an obit for a guy who owned a large tobacco farm in Virginia. It listed his survivor as John Bishop XI, so I began to wonder if these might be Roman numerals."

"You think there were eleven men named John Bishop? No one would do that."

"Well, if JB is a nickname for John Bishop, then he would have been number twelve, and the kid would have been thirteen."

"I find that hard to believe, but now that you mention it, I do seem to recall that when I was researching Liz, her husband had the letters XII after his name. I thought that was some sort of honorific title. Good work. Now what?"

"More research. XI is the senior partner in the firm Bishop Hardy in New York City, so I'll go there and snoop around."

"No. Absolutely not. Lawyers will not respond to snoopers. If you're on the right track, they will be ready for you, and you will have put them on high alert."

"Okay. I'll go to DC and check out XI's house. If I don't find anything, I'll try to find the farm. I think looking for a blond Catholic organist is a waste of my time."

"Do all of the above. Hurry up. It's been months. I've nearly run out of money. Finishing that damned recital hall has bankrupted me. The cartel money is gone. I want you to broaden your search, but do it quickly. Don't stay too long in one place. These rich people call the cops in a hurry. Check the house early and then again in the afternoon and only for one or two days. Don't just sit there all day."

CHAPTER 9

Atlanta

Jeffrey, Mary, and John were having supper in the small dining room when XI walked in.

"I'm going to go have a wee dram. Anyone want to join me? I'm flying to Atlanta tomorrow to meet with Edward."

"Oh, Atlanta. I recently read an article about an exhibit in a museum there on French Impressionism. I would really like to see it. May I tag along, please?"

"What do you know about that?"

"I studied it extensively. It's my favorite period."

"Yes, you may go with me, but we've got thirty or so paintings by those artists in storage here still in the original shipping crates. They've never been opened. When we cleared out the attics and storage rooms to install the new heating and cooling equipment, I built a new storage barn to house all of the family artifacts we couldn't display. Eberhart designed and built it to museum standards."

"Please tell me you're joking."

"No joke. John IX, my grandfather, studied medicine in Paris and drank wine with those guys. Well, he bought the wine for them. He spent free weekends traveling across France, bought their paintings, and shipped them home. Neither his mother nor, later, his wife would let him hang them in the house. They thought the paintings were vulgar and unsophisticated. We have his journals showing when he bought each piece, a description, the price, the shipping instructions, the customs paperwork, and everything else that might be needed to authenticate the pieces. They've never been seen in public, and the art world doesn't know about them. There are two bronze sculptures in the storage barn also. One is by...I think the name was Rodin. I can't remember the name of the other one though, but I think it was Moore. The Rodin is of a nude, and the Moore is something very abstract, so as you can imagine, they are still in the crates too. If you like them, perhaps we can get them out and ask Mary to oversee their authentication with an expert. After I added your mother's parents' belongings, and your father's few belongings, I began to realize the barn was too small. I was going to give the artwork to one of the museums. Your other grandparents had a large collection of Navy presentation silver. It seems every time he changed commands, or got promoted, he was given a piece of engraved silver. That stuff is in our storage too."

"Yes, please. I want it all, but for now, let's head for Atlanta."

The jet landed at Dekalb-Peachtree Airport. Private planes used it because of the massive air traffic at Hartsfield-Jackson International. It was also situated between Interstate 85 and Peachtree Road, which was much closer to town. One of Edward's messengers was waiting. He led them to a new electric I-Pace Jaguar SUV. Because the attorneys were internationally known for their environmental standards, Jaguar sent them this experimental model to test on American freeways and country roads.

The office was in midtown in a new high rise on Seventeenth Street. The firm was instrumental in obtaining all the permits necessary to turn an old steel mill into a new mixed-use development. These old sites were known as brown fields, and the permitting process was wicked. The office building earned a Leadership in Energy and Environmental Design (LEED) Platinum Award from the US Green Building Council for its energy efficiency.

After the driver dropped XI off at the office, he drove John down to the High Museum. John was not prepared for the modern sculptural design of the building. He spent an hour just looking at the building before he even started on the paintings. He spent the day there. He called XI when the museum was about to close. They picked him up on the way uptown to their hotel in a part of town known as Buckhead. He was told the gridlocked street they were on was named Peachtree Street, and it became Peachtree Road farther out. As they were driving up Peachtree Road, a large, handsome, cream-colored, cross-shaped Gothic-style stone church with a tall central stone tower sat on the top of the hill. John asked about it. Edward said it was the Episcopal Cathedral of St. Philip, and he and his family were parishioners. Edward and the messenger waited while they checked into XI's usual hotel suite, then they drove to Edward's house.

Edward's house was on West Paces Ferry Road, near a large country club. The winding tree-lined road was situated along beautiful rolling hills north of downtown. All the houses were either very large mansions or slightly smaller ones, but they all sat on large tree-covered lots. John couldn't quite place the style of the Hardys' house, but it was huge. They pulled into a circular driveway which led to a semidetached two-story garage. The garage was set at an angle to the front of the house. The large garage doors weren't really visible from the street. They walked across a brick-paved walk set in a manicured lawn to a low front porch and then into the foyer. A stair rose through the center of the foyer. On the right, large sliding pocket doors opened into a living room. The living room ran along the side of the house, and the dining room was on the opposite side of the foyer. The family room opened through matching symmetrically placed pocket doors behind the stairs. The family room ran the full length of the house. A large kitchen was open to the family room. The house was simply divided between a more formal street side and an informal garden side. The floors were made of antique heart pine. They walked into the family room. It was paneled in a wood which John later learned was called pecky cypress. The pecky part was from bug and insect holes. Apparently it was a very rare, highly prized wood. Edward introduced him to his wife, Tippy, and his son, Charlie. Charlie and John were the same age, and they bonded within seconds. They could pass as fraternal twins, but Charlie had short black hair, whereas John's was blond and curly. Charlie invited

John out to his room. They walked out through the large French doors on the back of the family room into a large screened porch. They left the porch and walked across a stone terrace. Behind the kitchen was an outdoor kitchen. They walked down a flight of stairs, across a flat manicured lawn with a soccer net at one end, down more steps, through a gate set within trees and shrubs, and found a hidden pool and pool house. Charlie's room, as he called it, was beside the pool. It was similar to John's place at Potomac House, except it was one large room with two baths with showers. It was filled with sports and workout equipment, but there was a seating area in front of a fireplace, and there was a seventy-five-inch TV over the fireplace. He had two single beds against one wall. Books and sports equipment covered every chair except one. One bed was piled with clothes. There was a wet bar in front of the bathroom doors. There was a drum set and four timpani with an assortment of sticks and mallets and music stands. Sheet music was scattered around on the floor.

"Y'all are having supper with us. While the adults are having cocktails and burning our steaks on the grill, why don't we go for a swim?"

"That sounds great. I need to exercise my knee. I've been standing all day, and it throbs. Problem is, I don't have a swimsuit."

"No problem. You'll fit into one of mine." He pulled out three from the pile on the bed. "Pick one." He ran out and jumped into the pool while John changed.

"What's wrong with your knee?"

After he jumped into the pool, he told Charlie the story.

"I hate bullies worse than anything," Charlie snarled, "and the locker rooms are always full of them. Dad has always said the only way to deal with one is to hit him back harder."

"Yep. That's my philosophy too."

The adults were sitting on the terrace enjoying the early evening fall air. Tippy sipped a dry gin martini, while Edward and XI sipped their favorite single malt scotch. They nibbled on her tiny cheese biscuits that were topped with pecan halves from Swan Bay's grove.

XI remarked, "The boys seem to have hit it off rather well."

Tippy responded, "Yes, but Charlie never met a stranger. He's our family ambassador. In a new social situation, he just walks right up to someone and starts a conversation. He's really just like a lovable, goofy puppy, but he's academically very gifted, if I may brag just a bit."

"I wish John had that social skill. He's very reserved and a bit socially awkward. I suppose that's from his time in boarding schools. We Bishops have always paid someone else to raise our boys, and I've recently learned that my son had no clue as to how to be a father. I'm sorry to say he learned that from me. John was the only non-Hispanic boy in his Colombian school, and he was bullied. He certainly learned about racial bias there. Somehow, when we were picking that school, the racial problem never occurred to us. He was also bullied in his new school in Arlington. He does know how to take up for himself, though. If he had seriously hurt those boys in his last school, the legal outcome might have been very different."

"Oh, I doubt that, XI. I followed the case very closely," added Edward. "It was a slam dunk. I assure you that sordid case is truly closed. But I must say, Charlie has always been very even-tempered. We've never had a minute's problem with that. His weakness seems to be girls. They want to own him."

Tippy thought to herself, *You don't know the half of it, sweetie. I'm glad I'm not seriously buzzed at this moment. I might spill the beans.*

"I don't know anything about John's relationships with girls. If he's anything like his parents though, he's going to be hot to trot."

They all laughed. Tippy responded, "If he's around Charlie for long, you might find out."

"I wish the distance between them weren't so great. To make matters worse, I've now got to find him another school, and it can't be another boarding school."

The guys swam for an hour and a half until they were called to supper. The dining terrace was surrounded on three sides with a stand of trees. They were Japanese maple trees, just like those at Potomac House. There were smaller, rather sculptural Japanese maples growing in large pots on the edges of the terrace.

"Edward, I like the small maples."

Edward pointed to one and said, "It's called *Acer palmatum dissectum.* It's Tippy's favorite because the delicate leaves turned a rich golden color in the fall." It sat in front of two others he said turned red in the fall.

Supper consisted of six-ounce filets of beef Edward had cooked in the outdoor kitchen. Tippy came out with a large green salad, sourdough bread, butter, olive oil, loaded baked potatoes, and corn on the cob. John was starving. Tippy was very trim, and her short hair was the color of Charlie's. He looked like her. She was gracious and witty, but John sensed she could be a take-charge kind of person in an instant. The conversation seemed to focus on John. They had many questions. It was apparent Edward hadn't told them much. John finally said, "Please, enough about me. Tell me about you."

Charlie laughed. "It's a game we play when we have dinner with someone we've never met. We can't help it."

Tippy excused herself and returned to the kitchen to prepare a tray of coffee and dessert. Charlie went with her to help. The dessert was a Huguenot torte. It was delicious. John complimented her. She said XI had given her the shelled pecans from Swan Bay. Edward said she was descended from an old French Protestant South Carolina family who had escaped Catholic France to avoid religious persecution.

"I know something about persecution myself."

Ignoring John's comment, Charlie said, "The torte is from an old family recipe. She combined tart cooking apples and chopped pecans with some other stuff to make them. Mom's are better than Grandmother's."

Tippy gave him one of those Southern uh-huh looks. This one meant, *You're lying.*

XI pushed away from the table, saying, "This has been wonderful, Tippy, but we need to get back to the hotel. We have an early flight tomorrow. I have a lunch meeting in DC."

Charlie responded, "I wish John could stay a few more days. We could go to a Braves game tomorrow night."

Edward said, "That's a great idea, XI."

John liked it too, but not wanting to seem to be too eager, he protested, "Guys, maybe another time. I've been told it is very wasteful to fly the empty jet one way."

"XI, I like this guy more and more. I've got a solution. Charlie and I are flying to Boston on Monday. He wants to visit MIT, and John can go with us. We could stop off at Swan Bay on the way back and drop him off." Suddenly John remembered the organ in the museum at Harvard. "Grandfather, do you know someone at Harvard who might give me permission to play the organ in the museum?"

"Probably, but there are many museums. Do you know the name?"

"Yes, it is the Busch Reisinger Museum."

"I'll make a call, but the answer is yes."

"Let's run you back to the hotel, XI, and we'll pick up John's bag."

"Do you really play the organ?" asked Charlie. "I'm a percussionist in the Atlanta Symphony Youth Orchestra. Maybe we can play together sometime."

"I saw drums in your pool house."

"Yeah, but they're too big to drag around. I practice out there so I don't drive my folks crazy. I don't have to move them in and out to concerts either. I let the symphony move theirs."

Edward said rather dryly, "Charlie's philosophy is never do for yourself what someone else will do for you."

"Exactly," retorted Charlie.

John quickly changed the subject. "What are you planning to study at MIT?"

"Computer science."

John got a simultaneous "drop it" look from XI and Edward, but Charlie was on a roll. "Are you into computers?"

"Yes, but my real interest is music." He deflected without lying. Grandfather and Edward were relieved for the moment, but they knew it wouldn't last long. Edward was going to need to have a quiet talk with Charlie.

Tippy asked John what his future plans might be.

"Medicine. Either genetics, sports medicine, or orthopedic surgery."

XI looked shocked. "I've never heard that before, but it is in your genes, I suppose. My father was a surgeon."

Edward commented, "Not music?"

"No, sir. Musicians don't make much money, and I don't want to always answer to know-it-all priests and unmusical parishioners."

Tippy laughed. "Doctors don't make much anymore either. I'm an orthopedic surgeon myself. We'll take you over to Emory tomorrow, and I'll show you around."

Edward added, "She's also on the board of the Shepherd Center here. It is a highly ranked rehab hospital for people with spinal cord injuries, brain injuries, and other related conditions. It's just down Peachtree. We'll stop by there tomorrow too."

"I'll need to try to start paving the way for you at Harvard for your medical studies."

"Boston would be too cold in the winter for me."

"Oh no, you don't, boy. You're going to Harvard."

"Charlie already has a full scholarship to Georgia Tech here, but he just wants to be sure before he commits."

"I've heard about Swan Bay." Charlie was trying discreetly for an invitation.

"Edward, I'd really like to show him around if you have time."

"We'll see how the day goes," he responded.

They started early. They went out to a place called Sandy Springs to visit Charlie's school. It was near their house. John was told it was the largest Episcopal school in America. He could believe it. It was part of a large suburban parish, which was actually on campus. The parish church was a modern structure with two fine organs. They had lunch in a new diner on Piedmont Road, which looked like an old stainless-steel railroad passenger car. They went to the Shepherd Center. John thought of Roller. He wondered if there were a center in DC as good as this. They went to Emory and toured the school of medicine and Tippy's department at the hospital.

On Monday, a storm was moving in, and it was a bumpy flight. They took an Uber to MIT. John really wanted to look at their computer center. He was very impressed. It was one of the best. The storm passed south of Boston, so it was a nice day. They took an Uber over to the museum. XI had made the connection.

Edward asked, "What are you going to play?"

"I brought a few scores by Bach and a Buxtehude score I haven't played called Toccata in D minor."

They went up to the organ. He played the Bach first, because he wanted the museum director to know he really did know what he was doing. Then he tackled the Buxtehude.

"I really don't know much about music, John, but it sounds great to me."

"I'm in heaven. I could stay here a week. I want one of these organs!"

They landed at Swan Bay at noon the next day. John put the top down on the Corvette and took Charlie for a ride. Neither one of them had a driver's license yet, but the time was near. They came back, and John wanted to take him out on the four-wheeler, but Edward said there would be another time. Jeffrey and John drove them to the plane.

*****

During a meeting the following week where they discussed the Colombian raid, XI remarked, "Okay, Jeffrey, you and I need to go to Atlanta and talk with Edward. I can't explain all of this by myself."

They flew to Atlanta the next morning and met Edward at his office. It took three hours. Edward was pleased. The files that John had translated had allowed the DEA and the Ops team to destroy Espinis's drug routes in America starting at the ports of entry. The two top men in the United States had been arrested along with several of the underlings. The files showed two direct routes. One from the Pacific into Los Angeles and one across the Caribbean to Miami with several other ports of entry, including Baltimore and Charleston. Espinis had his own shipping line, and his drugs were hidden in cargo containers surrounded by coffee. They spilled enough coffee in the containers to confuse most of the drug dogs. They had acted quickly before the supply had stopped. The US Coast Guard had been alerted and had confiscated the ships en route. When the massive confiscated funds had been divided, their Ops Center's profits were huge. Their meeting with Edward concerned investing the profits.

"I'm confident this chapter is closed, guys. We'll hear no more about Espinis. Good work."

When Jeffrey excused himself to go to the toilet, Edward then said something completely out of the blue and took XI by surprise. "XI, Tippy and I have been talking ever since you and John were here. We have discussed this with Charlie, and he is excited. With your permission, we would like it very much if John could move into our house and go to school with Charlie. If you agree, I will talk with the parish rector and headmaster at the school. In complete confidence, I'll tell them as much of John's situation as I can without compromising anything."

"Edward, I'm at a loss for words, but it would actually solve a huge problem I've been struggling with. Let's all go to lunch and let me think through this."

After lunch, XI said, "Yes. Let me talk with John."

XI and Jeffrey flew back to Swan Bay. XI told him about the move while they were sipping their afternoon scotch. When they landed, XI asked John to meet him on the porch of the cabin.

"John, something has come up that will be a great opportunity for you, in my opinion. I simply have not found a suitable school here, because I've been struggling with another issue concerning your safety. I'm worried that one of the guys might come after you again in a few years when you least expect it. Let's face it, son, you do stand out in a crowd."

"What do you have in mind? I don't think about my safety out here."

"Edward, Tippy, and Charlie have asked me to allow you to move to Atlanta, go to school with Charlie, and live with them. I want you to choose a new identity, something like we might use in the Witness Protection Program."

"How will we explain my new name?"

"The best possible way is to be completely honest and upfront with them. Edward has already told Tippy, and she understands. They are the only people you met there, so I think if Charlie can agree, it will work."

"Charlie will."

John walked into breakfast in the small dining room the next morning where XI was reading the paper.

"I think I have a name. Charteris Hew Ramsay. I'll sign everything C. Hew Ramsay. Just call me Hew."

"Hew. I like it. It keeps our family connections, but no one else will ever make the connection. Good job. The great English Archbishop of Canterbury, the Most Reverend and Right Honorable Thomas Cranmer coined a word he first used in the 1549 Book of Common Prayer: *regenerate*. I'm fouling the religious context here, but you must be reborn in Atlanta."

John, now Hew, laughed. He rode back to DC with XI. As usual, XI drove too fast. Hew packed his few belongings. He would miss the furniture and his piano, but one day, maybe...Douglas drove him to the airport, and he flew to Atlanta. He left as John Bishop XIII, and he arrived as Charteris Hew Ramsay. Charlie was ecstatic. He thought of Hew as the brother he had always wanted. Twins? Well, maybe fraternal. He thought that was funny. Charlie had no problem with the name change. It never came up again.

School started. Hew wasn't concerned this time because he would never play soccer or any other game again, and he certainly would never go near a locker room. His courses mirrored Charlie's. On a whim, he took more German, while Charlie took Spanish. He thought it would help him understand Bach better. When the other kids asked Hew where he had come from, he just honestly said DC. Hew decided to take computer science with Charlie because he thought it might help in the future. Charlie was amazed at how quickly Hew advanced in the course. One incident in the English lit class caused him a bit of trouble. They had been reading Shakespeare's plays. When it came time for their quiz, the teacher walked in and wrote on the board, "Discuss the structure of any one of the plays." Hew was surprised because they had never discussed the structure of a play. He thought for a few minutes and took a chance. He compared the structure of Romeo and Juliet to a fugue. He used Bach's fugue in E flat, BWV 552 commonly called St. Anne, because he thought that the teacher, being a good Episcopalian, might relate to the subject, which was similar to William Croft's great Anglican hymn tune "St. Anne."

"Oh God our help in ages past."

He also said that the primary artistic structure of the Baroque period was counterpoint and added a discussion on the A-B-A, tower, nave, tower form of Baroque church west facades. He submitted his paper and walked out. The next day, everyone got their papers back except Hew. When he asked, he was told to stay after class. The teacher accused him of cheating and asked him how he knew in advance. Hew was pissed. He simply recited his art history studies and his music studies. The teacher remarked that this was the thesis of his dissertation, and he had never considered the connection. Hew aced that course. All was going well except for one problem. Charlie had a jealous girlfriend, and she didn't like Hew.

If Charlie didn't answer a text as quickly as she wanted, or if he didn't answer his phone, she started dropping by his house to check on him. She thought he spent too much time with Hew. She would not agree to find a girl for Hew because she had no intention of going on double dates. She simply lied and told Charlie she didn't like to play matchmaker for anyone. Charlie quickly became annoyed. It came to a rather sudden conclusion. Charlie and Hew were in the pool one afternoon, while Tippy was preparing supper. The girl rang the doorbell and demanded that Tippy tell her where Charlie was. Tippy sent her packing with instructions to never contact Charlie again, but she knew young girls. Tippy needed to find a diversion for Charlie, and perhaps one out of town.

Edward called her at her office the next day. "XI called this morning. He wants Hew and Charlie to come to Swan Bay for the weekend."

He explained what XI had in mind, and he assured her the boys would not be in danger at any time, so she agreed. This might just work right into her own plan. During dinner, Edward asked the boys if they would like to get away for the weekend. They both jumped at the chance.

"Where?"

"Swan Bay."

Charlie was glad to go back there. He thought the trip might just help with his girl problem. He would leave his phone at home, and she wouldn't be able to find him. Maybe she would get the message. Edward picked them up from school on Friday afternoon. The three of them arrived in time for supper. Hew had been telling Charlie about Ms. Mamie's cooking, and he was correct.

After supper, Jeffrey took them down into the Ops Center. Charlie was awestruck.

"Son, it is time I told you a secret." Edward explained the workings of the center and introduced Charlie to the team. Charlie thought it looked like a nuclear sub down there.

"It's just like the sub in the movie *Hunt for Red October*."

They moved into the SCIF, and Jeffrey opened their briefing. "Guys, we have been asked to try to develop a new way to infiltrate a US drug problem, and the DEA really doesn't have the proper age staff to set it up. We think we and you do. Drugs on college campuses are totally out of control. The so-called party schools are the worst because the students are anesthetized to the problem. Most of them are so liberal they think it's no worse than alcohol. Their parents have no idea the problem is right under their noses or that they are financing most of it. Recently, a young person over in Charleston was murdered over a drug deal right across the street from the campus. We have reports of girls selling sex for drugs late at night in the lush gardens of houses in town there. Many of the houses are second homes, and the lawn services or pool boys are the only people who go into those beautiful gardens, and they are there during daylight."

He pulled up images of the city. The boys were impressed with the beauty. He pulled up a map showing the college campus.

"Note these buildings. They are the dorms. Do you notice anything unusual?"

Charlie spotted it immediately. "How many students go there?"

"About eleven thousand."

"So almost everyone lives off campus?"

"Exactly, and here's where they live. This area is known as Harleston Village. It's full of apartments within large old houses, and over here is what they call the East Side. The buildings are run-down over here, so the neighbors are less controlling. The houses have been slums for over a hundred years. These firetraps don't seem to be on the city's radar. The owners rent them for as much money as possible without spending any money to repair them. Some houses still have unvented gas space heaters. Some don't even have air-conditioning. The students bring their own window units and plug them in to inadequate wiring. The students sometimes pile up in the old run-down houses where the landlord has rented out every room as a dorm room except the kitchen and bath. Two or three kids share a single room to cut costs. This helps them with drug and beer money."

Hew jumped. "We're going to college?"

"No. Not on your life. You will stay in high school. Roller is going back to college. She doesn't need much of a cover story. She already has several degrees, so the workload will be a breeze. That will free up her time to be 'sociable.' She will enter as a freshman and find a way to pledge a very popular sorority. She will be set up in a posh apartment suitable for off-campus parties, and the DEA will supply her with a suitable young female agent for a roommate/bodyguard. She will become a party girl with cash to flash around. No one will suspect a girl in a wheelchair of being anything other than a girl with a rich daddy who feels sorry for his daughter who got thrown from a horse while riding and broke her back."

"What will you study, computer science?" Hew laughed.

"No. I'll major in English. I have a degree in it too I'm going to have a good time, boys." Roller laughed.

"Yes, Roller, that's the plan, but keep in mind those beautiful sea islands and white sandy beaches were major booze and heroin import centers during prohibition in the 1920s and even today. You may get invited to parties with the newly arrived tech set in town once you become known. You will start hosting parties. Your apartment will be equipped with the latest video surveillance hidden cameras. We'll try to catch the deals in progress, but we won't know until we try.

We won't arrest them there. We'll follow the dealers. There are many new start-up companies employing newly graduated bright people in town. They are our targets too. Invite them to parties, but be careful. They are in the same computer business as you."

"So what's our part?" questioned Hew. "Roller will be having all the fun."

"We want you two to do something you both love too. You're going to write code and develop a way to join their social media sites. The DEA can't do that, but we think you guys can. Roller will collect as many contacts and friends as she can. She will be seen at as many parties as possible, and she will feed the data back to you, but we want you to feed her anything you find. Charlie, you know all of the young social lingo and buzz words. Hew, write a program targeting any word which might lead to a dealer or drug party. We want to know everything about these kids, and God knows they post it all. If you uncover anything, the DEA will alert the local cops. The college administration will be told of this sting, but frankly, we don't expect much of it happens on campus with the possible exception of word-of-mouth contacts. We want text messages for sure from anyone that you target."

"Wait," said Charlie. "Even I know that's illegal."

"That's why y'all need to find a legal way. Hew knows how to stay under the radar, but if you don't want to be in, just say the word. There will be no hard feelings. This business is not for everyone. If this works, it will expand to all of the college campuses. One other thing. You will not, under any circumstances, work on this on your personal computers, in your school lab, on ANY public site, or Wi-Fi. You will NOT work on this in our house. You may discuss your theories, but absolutely any computer work will happen here on the weekends on stand-alone machines. Not even one keystroke. Hew will tell you we have netted hundreds of millions of dollars because he spotted an architectural pattern, as he calls it, in the repetitions of one lazy programmer. You may never show any of this on a résumé or CV. You may never at any time in the future use even a snippet of anything developed here. Am I crystal clear on that?"

They both agreed and were thrilled at the possibility of spending weekends at the farm. Hew would ask Mary to add another bed to his cabin for Charlie. This was going to be a blast.

"One other thing. Make up a story to tell your friends in case they want to know why you're not available on weekends. Don't go to some exotic place. Just be taking weekend college advanced placement courses at Clemson or someplace."

Roller said, "Let's get started. I need to get to campus."

Hew thought the quickest way to hack text messages would be to get into the federal court computers and enter some warrants for the cell phones. Charlie said he could probably get some forms from his dad's office.

"Okay, guys," snapped Roller. "The first words out of your mouth, Charlie, was to do something illegal off this campus. Get your head in the game right now!"

They got the message. This was serious. Still, Hew thought Charlie might be on to something. Hew went off to read a few articles online. He seemed to remember something about the CIA or somebody having developed a program to get around the cell phone companies' locks. He found the articles, and he had a new direction. Finally, though, he had to admit defeat. The computers just weren't big or powerful enough to hack through the massive servers at the other companies. Jeffrey simply would not pay for the equipment updates since any funds they confiscated would be too small to cover the costs. Hew had to admit defeat.

The college student sting was ready, and Edward had determined that it was all legal. They had named it Black Cougar. The college mascot name was the Cougars. She had come up with the play on their name herself. She was not a sexual cougar, but she was a drug cougar, and young guys were her primary target. Roller left for her new semester as a college party girl in Charleston. She was an instant hit in Charleston. She had a beautiful off-campus apartment with views of the harbor. It didn't take long for the word to spread she had the best party house in town. The medium-rise building was mostly owned by people who lived out of town, and many of them were party people themselves. With her looks, personality, and wads of cash, it didn't take her long to start mining the college and young professional crowds. No one suspected her, because she was one of them. She always refused taking their drugs, claiming the drugs she was already taking for her spinal injuries wouldn't react well with the party drugs. She began sending back information. By the third weekend of her semester, Charlie's program had identified a target. Jeffrey called the DEA's director, and the DEA notified the city police with information from a "confidential, but highly credible source." The police set up surveillance and, in the process, not only netted a group of college-age boys but also uncovered a working pharmaceutical plant right inside one of the old mansions in one of the best parts of the city. Jeffrey decided that since the Black Cougar scheme didn't require any illegal activity on their part, the program could be given to the DEA. Jeffrey wanted Roller back at Swan Bay, and he worked out a plan. The DEA started recruiting young agents to work the campuses.

Using Roller's cover with legal pain meds as their cover, they selected bright students from meager backgrounds with physical handicaps. They would not otherwise be able to afford a college education. The new agents were given full scholarships, nice off-campus apartments, and wads of cash to flash around. The Ops team gathered to celebrate. The Black Cougar scheme was producing fine results. They let both boys have a beer to celebrate. Charlie loved the beer. Hew hated the taste. With their work completed, the boys flew back to Atlanta the next morning. Charlie's girl had moved on to another target. As they were sitting at dinner with Edward and Tippy, Charlie told his mother the girlfriend problem was history.

Hew said, "I want to date, but I've been trying to figure these girls out. I just can't understand them."

Edward and Tippy laughed, and Edward knocked his wineglass over. "Hew, no male in the entire history of the human race has ever figured it out. You are looking for logic. Quit that and just jump into the deep end, son. Follow your heart."

"But use your big head, Hew, not your little one," added Tippy. Charlie looked shocked. Tippy told him to grow up. Charlie didn't know she knew his sexual history.

Edward continued the lesson. "You're trying to wade in by way of the kiddie pool." Everyone laughed again. Exasperated, Hew got up and started cleaning up the spilled wine.

Hew got an email from the Canon for Music at the Cathedral of St. Philip. He wanted to meet Hew. Charlie was scheduled to be the crucifer at the eleven fifteen service on Sunday, so Hew set up the meeting following the service. Dr. Withersby had heard about Hew from the choirmaster at Hew's school, where Hew practiced the organ. He wanted to ask Hew if he might be interested in being a console assistant. Hew agreed and asked if he might also be allowed to use the organ for practice. Dr. Withersby agreed and told Hew the staff would look at the upcoming schedule and find a time slot for him.

XI invited the Hardys to spend Christmas at Swan Bay for a traditional festival. They agreed. Christmas break was only two weeks away.

*****

Edward's secretary buzzed his desk. "Edward, there is a man whose name I think is Douglas on the phone for you. It is hard to tell because of his sobbing, but he said it's urgent."

Edward grabbed the phone. "Douglas? Slow down, Douglas. Take a deep breath. Tell me what's going on."

Edward hung up the phone in shock. There had been a terrible accident. His partner and best friend was dead. He called Jeffrey. Jeffrey hadn't heard, but he would get the details from the state police immediately and call him back.

"Call my cell. I've got to go find Hew right now."

Edward picked up his desk receiver while he scrolled through his contacts, looking for the school number. He had another thought and called the parish rector instead. The rector had just walked into his office, and Edward told him about the death. Edward asked to meet with him as soon as possible. The rector told him to come now, and he would send for Hew.

Edward arrived about thirty minutes later. Hew was in the rector's office, and when he saw Edward's expression, he thought something bad had happened to Charlie or Tippy. Hew just sat there. The rector offered a heartfelt prayer, but Hew was numb. Hew and Edward left immediately. On the drive to the house, Jeffrey called.

"Apparently XI was driving too fast, hit a deer, and lost control of the car."

XI's casket was lying in repose in the small front parlor of the house just as all the generations of his ancestors had been. As was the family tradition, the simple pine box was draped with a large flag of Scotland with a sash of his newly authorized Bishop tartan laid across it longways. When Hew saw it, he went back to the cabin and brought his sash of black and blue Ramsay tartan. He placed it over the Bishop tartan, forming a cross. The coffin was made from an old-growth pine tree which had been hit by lightning. The rings in the tree showed the tree was old when Capt'n John arrived.

Everyone gathered in the hall. All the Ops team, Ms. Mamie and her family, the staff from the Potomac House, the Hardys, and the director of the DEA were there. The director brought the condolences of the president. All the members of the hunt club were there. Some were outside because the hall wasn't large enough. Jack was resplendent in a white cope. He had brought a processional cross and a tunicle which matched the cope for Charlie. They were waiting on Douglas and Hew. Douglas walked in, and Hew followed. Hew was wearing his Father's Ramsay kilt and his new Prince Charlie waistcoat and kit for the first time.

Jeffrey was surprised when he saw it and said, "Wait. I have something you might like, Hew. I'll be right back."

Jeffrey ran upstairs and picked up a new sporran. Someone had hit a fox on the highway, and Mary saw the body soon after it had happened. She sent one of the guys to pick it up. They did it all the time. They had a real problem with animals in the road. Last year, someone hit a ten-point buck. She had it taken to the local taxidermist, who had decided to preserve the entire deer because it was such a beauty. Some senator had paid him a hefty price for it. Jeffrey handed the sporran to Douglas, and Douglas replaced the old black mink sporran with the new farm fox. The red fox head and fur complimented the red and black in the kilt. Mary and Jeffrey's chocolate Lab, Buster, had been hiding under the hall table. When he saw the fox head, he lunged. Hew naturally dropped his hands to cover himself and jumped backward. Luckily, Jeffrey saw it happening and stepped in front of the dog and hauled him into the small dining room and closed the door. There were howls of laughter from the group. That helped to break the somber mood.

The undertakers rolled the casket out into the hall. Mary, Ms. Mamie, and Maybell reverently removed the tartans and the Scottish flag and replaced them with Westover Church's antique white pall. Jack, Westover's rector, stepped to the head of the casket and with a fine clear tenor voice began singing the ancient, familiar lines from Croft's 1724 "Funeral Sentences." He followed the text in Capt'n John's 1559 *Book of Common Prayer*, which began, "I am the resurrection and the life…"

When he had finished, Mac, one of the Ops members standing outside, began playing his bagpipes. Charlie took the cross, and Mac followed. The team of Army honor guard members formed behind Mac. The pallbearers formed up behind the honor guard. Edward, Jeffrey, Douglas, Pink, Luis, and Sam, one of the stable boys, took the pine handles on the sides of the casket. Hew took his place at the head of the casket. Edward took the foot. Jack followed. The procession began the long walk up the hill to the family cemetery. The white pall was replaced with an American flag. There were three large green tents with chairs. Fortunately, the day was bright and relatively warm for late December. Pink and Roller read the lessons. Jeffrey read the twenty-third psalm. Jack read the Gospel, the prayers, and the Committal. When Jack concluded, somewhere in the distance, one of the guards played Taps on a trumpet. The honor guard presented the flag to Hew. Hew stood for the presentation. Just as Hew was about to turn to his friends, Mac started playing the bagpipes again. Hew recognized the first five notes. He had not heard the song since he was six. He suddenly recalled hearing his father sing it while his mother played it. Hew waited until the piper had finished the first verse, and when he realized there would be a repeat, Hew began to sing.

"Amazing Grace, how sweet the sound, that saved a wretch like me."

The piper stopped at the end of the verse, but Hew continued solo. When Hew began the fifth verse—"When we've been there ten thousand years"—with his pure, clean baritone voice rising toward the sky, the piper joined in. The only person not crying was Hew. They were piped back to the house to a livelier tune. The time for mourning was over, but as they walked, Hew thought about the song "Amazing Grace." To him, it was about repentance, forgiveness, and hope.

Regeneration. He thought just maybe, as XI had said, it was time for him to begin to regenerate. They were eating lunch in the ballroom. There were too many people for the dining room. Ms. Mamie and Maybell had outdone themselves. By midafternoon, everyone was into the scotch and sipping Douglas's famous mint juleps from the silver punch bowl telling stories about XI.

Hew approached Edward. "If you don't mind, I'm ready to go home."

*****

After they arrived back in Atlanta, Tippy handed Hew a letter postmarked in New Haven but forwarded from the New York office. The letter was an invitation to a memorial concert. The organ faculties at Juilliard and Yale's Institute of Sacred Music were holding a memorial service for Liz in New Haven. Edward, Tippy, Charlie, Jeffrey, Mary, and Hew flew up for the day. Members of the two faculties performed various works on several of Yale's organs. Everyone simply walked from venue to venue for the different performances. The National Cathedral organist finished the concert by playing Liz's wedding composition on the 197 rank 12,617 pipe organ in Woolsey Hall. Hew had no idea the composition existed. During the reception, the dean of Juilliard and members of Yale's organ faculty presented Hew with his mother's annotated original. Hew asked permission to play it on the large Skinner organ. They had no idea he could play. As he sat down, Hew noticed a score for Dupré's Cortege et Litanie laying on the bench. The National Cathedral organist acted as his console assistant. He finished sight-reading his mother's work and then picked up the Dupré. He drew a few stops, searching for the sound he wanted. It wasn't perfect, but he didn't have time to explore. Noticing the odd combination, the cathedral organist stepped up to assist. Hew simply waved him away. After he finished, the room was silent. Finally, the dean said, "Hew, I've never heard Dupré's piece expressed that way before on an organ. What led you to those stops?"

"That's as close as I could come to reproducing it as I last heard my mother play it. I'm sorry if it was wrong." Hew didn't add that his mother had given him a wineglass and a wooden spoon to help them. She simply showed him the notes which imitated chapel bells and told him to strike the wineglass whenever he saw those notes. After a few strikes, he quit. She asked why he stopped. He said the wineglass sounded the wrong note. His father said he was obviously his mother's child. It was the last time he had heard them both laugh. Today he performed his own memorial concert for his parents.

"Hew, did you know Dupré originally wrote it in 1922 for eleven instruments as an incidental piece for a play?"

"No. So you mean I transcribed a transcription?" They all laughed, but everyone was astounded.

"Hew, are you considering taking a degree in music? If so, I want you to visit me first."

"No, sir. I'm going to study medicine."

Mary heard the dean mutter as he walked away, "Medicine? What a waste." She laughed.

*****

"I wasted a week surveilling Bishop's house, Madre. The place is dead. The only people I saw were the pool service guy and the gardener."

"Hispanic?"

"No. I can't talk to them or bribe them either."

"I checked all of the Catholic churches in the area. You won't believe the number. I looked closer at those that had Spanish-language

Masses. I found two blond males, but they were too old. I wasted too much time there. I tried the Virginia farm. The house can't be seen from the highway, and the place is well guarded. Something goes on there. It's not just a tobacco farm. I rented a boat and spied from the river. The house is huge, but I was spotted, so I left. They have a very long runway too. I saw a small white jet take off from there."

"Hmmm. A private jet. Now we know they have money. I wonder if I paid for it. Where will you go next?"

"I'm going to New Jersey and then into New England."

CHAPTER 10

A New Home

The jet left New Haven, and by the time they were at cruising altitude, everyone except Edward and Hew were asleep. Edward was sitting at the table drinking a late-night "wee dram," morosely staring out the window. Hew poured himself a wee dram and joined him at the table.

"Hew, now listen—"

"For God's sake. We're thousands of feet above the law here, and after these last few days, I deserve it."

Edward saw his point.

Hew sighed. "I wanted to learn to fly when I first arrived at Swan Bay, but Grandfather said absolutely not. He even said I was never to fly in anything without two engines and two pilots."

"Hew, do you know why there was an Army honor guard at XI's burial?"

"No. I just assumed it was for his service to the DEA."

"XI was a pilot instructor in the Army Air Corps before World War II. He was an ace pilot and a tough-as-hell instructor. He told me that after one of the flight school graduations, one of his students walked up to thank him but also asked why he had been so tough. He replied he knew many of his boys would never return, but he didn't want their deaths to have been the result of poor training. The president of the United States arranged for the honor guard, and XI certainly deserved it. Your father was also a pilot. XI didn't think you wanted to learn to fly. When you first visited Swan Bay, you were terrified of the crop duster."

Hew was quiet for a while as he sipped his drink. "Yeah, well, I grew up, you know.

"Edward, I spoke with Douglas while he was helping me into my kilt. I assured him the Potomac staff was fine, and I asked if he and Maybell would consider moving to Atlanta and work with me. He said they had already discussed it, and they would. They want to live in a warmer climate. I don't know exactly how I'll use them, but I thanked him and told them to just relax while I found a house. You and Mary have been better to me than I deserve, but when I graduate, I need to find something closer to Emory."

"Have you heard from Emory?"

"Yes. I have been accepted into premed."

"Congratulations. Charlie is going to accept the scholarship at Georgia Tech."

"He told me just before we heard about Grandfather."

"Don't make any hasty decisions. You're part of our family now, so you don't need to think you need to move anytime soon. There's something else we need to discuss, and it's serious. There's been a huge shakeup in Cali. There was a woman who was financing a new organ recital hall at the university for your mother. As it turns out, she was Espinis's half-sister, Maria. She has discovered that all the money is gone. She has declared bankruptcy because, to save face, she depleted her own ill-gotten funds to complete the recital hall. She's mad as hell, and she's looking for you. Also, your school no longer exists. Between the information you deciphered and this latest news, the archbishop closed it. Father Xavier has disappeared, and Father Arturo has returned to France. Luis managed to convince the archbishop to use some of Espinis's money to remove all the ornaments from the chapel, and they will be used in a new Catholic Church near Charleston, South Carolina, which has been designed to replicate the old chapel."

"And the organ?"

"All of it—the windows, altar, painting, silver, vestments, organ, and bells—are going to Charleston. The organ will be restored, and once the new church is finished, it will be placed in the new rear gallery. The old school site is being redeveloped as low-income housing. Oh, and Luis found a music journal in the organ loft with your name on it. It's waiting for you at home."

Hew just sat there. He took a long sip, drained the glass, and poured himself another. "Dirty drug money laundering. She will never think to look in Atlanta, and she will never learn my new name, so I'm not going to let it bother me. She'll be looking in Catholic churches, and there are millions of those. I'm glad to have my journal back, though. I'll write Luis a note."

"Fine. I hesitated to tell you, but you need to know. Changing the subject back, have you thought about Potomac House?"

"I have decided I'll sell Potomac House. I've never liked the place. Would you consider finding someone to inventory the contents and appraise the place? I know there are a few items I want to keep, but anything else of value will be sold. I'll keep the paintings, the dining room breakfront, the sideboard, the silver, the library books, and the stuff in my pool house. I will give Douglas and Maybell, you and Tippy, Jeffrey and Mary, and Pink and Roller anything y'all want, but sell the rest."

"I know just the team. There are plenty of very valuable pieces in the house. We'll get an international auction house to run the sale. What about XI's New York office suite?"

"I've never been there, but from what he told me, I just assumed you would move in. If so, keep whatever you want, and I'll decide about the rest. I'll keep the apartment in the Carlyle Hotel, so whatever you don't use from the office will go there when I redecorate it."

"I want to keep XI's office exactly as it is, but I will move my personal things in there, if you don't mind."

"Done."

"I can tell that you've made up your mind about moving, so let me ask you if you have noticed the construction across Peachtree Road from the cathedral?"

"Yes, but I haven't paid much attention to it except for the noise."

"Before you moved here, the site was home to a very large active Baptist congregation. They voted to move and build a new church with a K-12 school. They took an option on a hundred-acre site inside the perimeter ring interstate beside the Chattahoochee River. The price they were asking for the existing property was enormous, but finally, a developer purchased it."

"Why would a church move? It looks like a big property to me."

"It is big, but they wanted large athletic fields and plenty of parking. The Baptists call it repitching the tent. If they decide that God has called on them to move, they move. It was a huge gamble for the developer's financial backers, but they thought anything in Buckhead would sell for big dollars. The national recession hit, and the banks stopped the financing.

"Everyone associated with the project lost enormous amounts of money. Some of them may never recover their businesses. One of my associates, Katherine, worked on all of the zoning, environmental permits, and land disturbance permits for the developers. When she found out the land could be purchased at much less than the appraised value, she convinced XI and me to invest. We used some of the Bishop family money in the Swiss account to finance it, just as we did to build our office tower. The bank just couldn't resist."

"So we are in the money laundering business now too?"

"No! Absolutely not. You have so much old family money in Switzerland you can never spend it, but you need to invest it. XI swore that some of Capt'n John's profits are still there. New American Swiss accounts need to be reported to our government, but this one was set up long before that law was passed. Nevertheless, it's all legal now."

"I've studied enough international policy in school to understand what you are doing, and I don't have a better idea. Tell me more."

"Our building is well under construction using a fast-track, just-in-time design and construction method even though we scrapped the old plans and brought in our German team, Eberhart Environmental Associates of Cologne. The skin is already being applied to the lower floors, but the columns and floor slabs haven't been started on the upper levels yet. They had the financial power to get good prices during the recession too. They were the site designers for the area where our office tower is located. Cleaning up an old steel mill site and getting permission to extend a city street over the interstate was a monumental project, but together, Katherine and Eberhart got it done in record time. That's why our office tower is there. XI loved working with them."

"Tell me more about this German company."

"Eberhart is an architectural, engineering, interior design, landscape architectural, property management, development, and construction company. They have offices and projects around the world. They have won major awards for their environmental work. You and I are part owners in their development company. We're ready to begin marketing the units to early buyers. It will be a net-zero building and is certain to win environmental awards here and in Europe. We think it will win a National American Institute of Architect's Honor Award too. It is the first net-zero building in Atlanta. Since you now own XI's shares, if you are interested, the only costs would be whatever changes you want to make to your unit."

"Sounds interesting. I want to look at the building plans tomorrow. What is net zero?"

"Net zero basically means the property creates all of the energy it needs onsite to operate. The next step is what the environmentalists call regeneration. That means the site produces excess energy and sells it to the utility company, offsetting some of the world's dependence on fossil fuels."

"Regeneration. That sounds impressive. I know that word. I heard the word *regenerate* from my grandfather. He said it referred to being reborn, as in Baptism, and as in my new identity, but I can see why environmentalists like it too."

"Katherine and I will show you the plans. She can answer more questions than I."

The next morning, they walked into a beautiful sales office complete with a large model, drawings of each unit, and full-size renderings of the views from each direction. As she pointed to the large model, Katherine told him, "One of the points of environmental design is to reduce the building's footprint on the earth. Like the Seventeenth Street project, this site is considered a brownfield site, meaning it had a previous use, so we aren't disturbing new land. The parking is therefore under the building. To avoid a massive excavation resulting in vast amounts of material being hauled away using more energy to move it, we've put the parking above grade but under the condo units. The amenities level is between the parking and the first level of units. This has the added advantage of raising all of the units above the tree line to give better views."

"I don't see the parking levels."

"Look closely at this rendering. The horizontal slats are hiding the cars. There's no glass behind those slats. The darker color of the glass slats helps too. The slats on the south facade are actually solar collectors. The angle of tilt is perfect for Atlanta's solar latitude. All of the slats all the way up the facade provide balcony rails and winter sun shades for each unit. Each unit has a deep terrace on the south facade that provides summer sun shade, but the sun in the winter is lower in the sky. These slats, along with the high-tech German glass help keep the cooling loads down. The new concept of in-slab radiant cooling uses the groundwater as a heat and cooling source. The combination reduced the construction cost and the operating costs. The lack of ductwork reduced the building height, and that saved on the construction cost too."

"But I thought the winter sun was a good thing."

"Not necessarily in the South. On cold winter nights, mornings, and cloudy winter days, we do need heat, but because the heat gain on a bright sunny day in the winter can be huge, by midday, we often need cooling."

"I love the sleek, modern design, but you could have just reduced the amount of glass."

"Sure, but there is still some radiant heat gain through a solid wall, and besides, when you get inside, you'll agree that the panoramic views add to the value of the units. There's really nothing else around with these stunning views. The building is forty stories tall and is set well back from Peachtree Road on the site of the church's parking lot. The other nearby condo towers are right up at the road and would have blocked the views of midtown and downtown if we had built the new tower up there as originally planned. The front area and the site of the old church will be landscaped with native plant material and developed as a bioswale to control site water. We will plant stands of XI's longleaf native pines, and there will be live grass tennis courts, a grass croquet pitch, a grass soccer field, and a grass putting green. All of these help control water runoff. In fact, we don't produce any stormwater runoff from our site. Each unit has grand south-facing and/or north-facing views. The upper-end units have views to either the Blue Ridge Mountains or Stone Mountain. The concept will be similar to a five-star hotel with a fine in-house restaurant and on-demand gourmet food. There will be a café beside the indoor pool and a first-class restaurant open to the public."

"That sounds great." He laughed. "The soccer field can also be used for parking when I host large parties. Maybe Douglas can manage the building, like a CEO, and Maybell can be the executive chef."

"Can they qualify?"

"He ran officer's clubs while he was in service, and she trained at the Cordon Bleu. Grandfather trusted them to manage his life."

"I think we can make that work."

"I want the top two levels. I'll be able to see the cathedral from the west side of the building."

"Two levels?"

"Yep. I'll move the Potomac House library here, and it will require two levels."

Shocked, Katherine replied, "That will require us to redesign some of the floor structure. Let me ask the design team if that's even possible at this late date. It might set back the sales."

Ignoring the caution, Hew continued, "I'll start working on a plan I can give to the architects."

The following week, Edward told him, "You and I have business to discuss. I need to make some decisions about Bishop Hardy since you aren't going to study law, and I'd like for you to be included in the decisions. You probably don't realize this, but you are the majority stockholder, which isn't allowed under the law. We need to fly back to Swan Bay and meet with Jeffrey."

On Friday morning, Edward and Hew flew up to the farm. During the trip, Edward told Hew he wanted to spin off, as he called it, the entire Ops Center to the DEA. They would lease the land and facilities. He didn't want to involve another attorney in the Center's secrets. He would still be available as a private consultant if they needed him, but he was going to increase his focus in environmental law. He also wanted to give the breeding program to Jeffrey and Mary.

"I doubt they can afford to buy it. May we say XI left it to them in his will? They can operate without paying rent. If you agree, only you and I will know."

"Great idea, Edward. What about our Ops Center staff?"

"I think the DEA will keep them on, but let's see if Jeffrey has a problem with it first."

"Edward, I went from being a miserable boy trapped in a Colombian prison school to this almost overnight. I have no idea how to manage any of it. I'm not even sure I know what 'IT' is. Now I'm hearing that I'm the major stockholder in an international law firm. Tell me what to do. I'm clueless."

"For now, just know that it's all under control and working well. Everything is in what we call a trust, and XI engineered an easy transition for you. You can learn as you go, if you are so inclined, or you can continue to let us manage it for you and we'll fully brief you as we move forward."

"I'm not going to rock the boat, so continue as is."

*****

Jeffrey and Mary were dumbstruck. "XI had never even hinted at that."

Jeffrey wasn't eager to turn the Ops Center over.

Edward had thought this might be the case, so he had prepared another document that transferred ownership of the center to Jeffrey and made Jeffrey the president and CEO of the Ops Center, and he left it to Jeffrey as to when and what to tell the other team members. The new documents created a new center and erased all evidence of its past. Hew was still the landlord, and the Center would pay rent. They would work out the terms as soon as possible. They all knew the terms would be favorable since Hew didn't need the money. Edward was relieved. The work of the Center was in good hands and would continue. He made an afternoon appointment with the director of the DEA and took Jeffrey to the meeting, while Hew drove around the farm in his Corvette. The director was pleased. Edward called his secretary with all the details. She transmitted the documents to all parties the next morning for signatures.

*****

Edward and Hew flew nonstop to Germany in Eberhart's new Boeing business jet to meet with Eberhart Associates regarding Hew's ideas for the top floors of his apartment. Edward breathed a sigh of relief.

"It wouldn't have been the same without XI, Hew. The whole ops idea was his brainchild, and now, the firm is in the clear."

The senior partner at Eberhart, Axel Hague, welcomed them and led them through a beautiful lobby down a corridor papered with awards and photographs of their work. They walked into a high-tech conference room. He offered coffee, which Edward gratefully took and Hew diplomatically declined. Hew hated coffee. Colombia was all about coffee, and he absolutely despised the taste and the smell. He was introduced to the heads of the design team.

Johan was a handsome young blond guy slightly shorter than Hew. He had a good command of English and spoke with a British accent. He explained, "My father is Danish, and my mother is German. They met after the war while living in England. I was a boarding student at Lansing College until I graduated and went up to Cambridge and took my undergraduate and graduate degrees in architecture."

He and Hew bonded immediately. The lead engineer, Hans, did not speak English. He was an athletic-looking guy, but from the looks of his expanding waist, he really enjoyed drinking German beer. The third person on the team was Heidi. She was a petite blond German with beautiful clear skin and blue eyes. Her English was passable, but with a German accent that Hew found charming. She was head of the interiors group. She and Johan were both thoroughly schooled in the language of International Style midcentury modern architecture and environmental design. Hew presented his concept.

He apologized for the crudeness of his drawing. The team sat there for a moment. Johan and Heidi had heard that the plan might utilize the entire top floor, but they both doubted this kid understood scale drawings.

Johan began. "Hew, this is very interesting. Let me see if I understand. I take it you want to redesign the top floor and make one unit."

"Actually, it's the entire top two floors, but I've got some wasted space on the top floor over the bedrooms, I'm afraid. Beginning from the west, there is a large terrace with a lap pool. I've placed the pool over the building columns to help transfer the weight. That's the hot afternoon sun side, but the sunsets over the mountains will be nice. Next, along the south side with the great views, is the great room."

Johan was translating. "Excuse me, Hew, Hans asked what a 'great room' is."

"That's the latest concept. I've seen them in magazines. The kitchen, dining, and living areas are in one open space. This space is two floors high."

Hans squirmed. Katherine had warned him in advance about a library, but this would require even more structural changes, and all those terraces will require major roof redesign as well.

Hew continued, "The space down the center is an art gallery. I have inherited thirty French Impressionist paintings. The library is on the east end. It's also two stories high with balconies with bookshelves on three sides. I am thinking about a piano-style curve on this east glass wall, but I can't quite decide. I really don't need that terrace. The bedrooms are straightforward."

"Hew, I see a fireplace in the library, but what are the two rectangles?"

"That will be my practice pipe organ."

Hans made a comment in German. Johan and Heidi giggled, but the senior partner, Axel, was aghast.

"What did Hans say?"

They realized that neither Hew or Edward had understood the complete German expression, but they didn't know that Hew understood the term *Gott verdammt*. He'd heard it enough from his old German art history priest!

Johan quickly replied, "He just commented that the volume—ah, sorry, translation issue..." Johan was struggling to get his wits together. "The, uh, 'vibrations' might disturb the unit below, but don't worry, we'll get the acoustical engineers on it."

What Hans had actually said was no one in the building would be able to stand the goddamned racket. Axel was relieved by Johan's tact. Hew suspected that it wasn't quite true, but he admired Johan's quick thinking and diplomacy.

Johan continued, "Hew, we are impressed. Give us some time to develop this by adding closets and other smaller areas, and I'm positive we'll have something you'll love."

Axel spoke up. "Edward, with your approval, and as a thank you to an outstanding client and now business partner, we want to send your family and Hew on a complimentary Rhine River cruise aboard one of Viking's newest ships, *Kara*. You will fly first-class round trip from Atlanta. You will land in Basel, Switzerland, where you'll meet the ship, and you'll fly home from Amsterdam eight days later. The ship departs in two weeks, and Katherine has already gotten Tippy to clear her schedule."

"Amsterdam. Amsterdam? Holland!" Hew was suddenly excited. Hans thought that he probably wanted to visit the brothels and drug dens.

"Yes, we would love to go. Thank you very much."

Hew asked, "If possible, could you set up a meeting for me at Flentrop Orgelbouw in Zaandam? Oh, and at Sint-Laurenskerk in Alkmaar and the Grote Kirk in Haarlem, please?"

"Certainly, Hew. It will be done as an add-on at the end of the cruise."

"Why those places?" questioned Heidi.

"I'm going to ask Flentrop to build my new practice organ, and the two churches have fine historic Germanic organs. I will need letters of introduction to play those instruments."

"Good," replied Axel. "The ship makes a call at Cologne on the sixth day, so we'll pick you up and bring you here for a briefing. We should have everything ready by then."

*****

"Paolo, I need a report. Where are you?"

"I haven't found him yet. I've been in New York and New Jersey. Nothing."

"Have you asked the bishops? Just ask about blond-headed, blue-eyed organists. There can't be that many."

"That's a joke, right? The bishops don't know anything about organists, and this place is huge. I need help. Send more guys."

"You don't get it. I can't afford to send anyone. I'm barely hanging on as it is. I've sold everything. The cash burned in the fire, the gold has been stolen, and the Cayman account has been wiped out. We tortured the bank president until he died, and all we know is the date that everything was transferred to another account. That's a dead end. I've changed my thinking. I want you to find the boy and kidnap him for ransom. We'll kill him once we get some money. Where are you going next?"

"I'm headed to Boston. I'm told there a lot of Catholic churches there."

*****

Two weeks later on Saturday afternoon, they took an Uber to the Buckhead station and rode MARTA, arriving two and a half hours early at Hartsfield-Jackson International Airport in Atlanta. Tippy didn't want to be late. Their new TSA and Global Entry passes allowed them to easily avoid the gestapo-style cattle lines and pass right through, but she hadn't ever used the new passes, so she didn't really trust them. Edward took them to the Crown Room to wait.

Hew had never flown on a commercial jet. He wasn't happy about it until he saw the first-class section on the KLM 777-200. They had individual pods with small TV monitors and noise-cancelling headphones. The seats fully reclined. Hew texted Jeffrey with a picture to suggest the rear seats in their corporate jet needed to be replaced. The superb flight attendants served a cocktail they called the Flying Dutchman. It was their signature drink made of Dutch gin by the legendary distiller Bols. It had Damrak gin, Bois blackberry liqueur, fresh lemon juice, and sugar syrup. Edward allowed the boys to have just one each. They ate their dinner as the plane flew above the coast of Canada. Hew selected the roasted cauliflower soup as his appetizer. He ate white lasagna with pesto cream and béchamel sauce, blistered tomatoes, and broccoli for his main course and warm apple pie strata for dessert. He washed it all down with a fine white wine. He pushed the button. It flattened his seat into a bed. He was reminded of the answer Peter Pan gave Wendy about the location of Neverland: "Second star to the right and straight on till morning." He noticed the plane made a slight right turn in front of a full moon as he fell asleep.

*****

The flight was fantastic, but the immigration process in Amsterdam was a lengthy nightmare! Edward didn't know it at the time, but someone in the airport stole the information from his American Express black card. XI had made Hew keep his AmEx card in an RFDI sleeve. Finally, they arrived in Basel, and the cruise line took over with the baggage.

The boat was superb. Eberhart had booked Edward and Tippy into an Explorer Suite. Hew and Charlie were in a room with a balcony and two single beds. The food was outstanding. The shore excursions were fascinating. Hew bought Tippy a German-made contemporary necklace with matching earrings in a small shop in the Black Forest. Charlie bought her a similar set. They surprised her with the gifts at dinner. The highlight of the trip, however, was unquestionably the cruise down the Rhine with castles rising up on the hills. The boat had a large sundeck with a large awning. They lounged under the awning, sipping Bloody Marys while the castles passed by. There wasn't a cloud in the sky, and a gentle breeze kept the air cool. It reminded Hew of a fine garden, but instead of specimen trees, there were castles and forts rising on the hills out of the landscape. He filled his iPhone with pictures. When they docked at Cologne, there was another car waiting. Tippy and Charlie went to the cathedral for a tour. Hew and Edward went to meet with Eberhart.

CHAPTER 11

Holland

More coffee. Hew thought, *Ugh.* He wanted to get on with it. He found a seat upwind from the fumes. There were highly detailed renderings and a beautiful set of plans for his condo. They projected the plans onto the large multipaneled video wall.

Johan began. "We have made a few changes, but your basic concept remains. Let's start with the great room and gallery. Your private elevator will open into the gallery. We suggest making the gallery wider. We will move the kitchen to the north exterior wall and make it a bit more narrow, but there's more than enough room for the kitchen, utility room, and a very large butler's pantry. Heidi learned from Mary and Maybell that you have an extensive collection of china, silver, and crystal, so the pantry will actually be two stories with a small spiral stair and a dumbwaiter. The stair will be against the window wall, giving the room a two-story with balcony effect. The dumbwaiter will also allow food delivery to the bedroom level. The second level of the pantry will contain a small undercounter refrigerator with an icemaker, and we'll include a microwave to heat soup or water for coffee or tea."

Hew studied the drawings and listened.

"We'll move the bedroom suites to the upper level. We want to locate your master suite on the south wall over the living/dining room with the other bedroom suites along the north wall over the kitchen and utility areas. Note the large contemporary spiral stair. Hans has outdone himself with the cantilevered frosted glass treads and clear glass railings. He projected a plan of the second level. "Each of the spacious guest bedrooms will have a large walk-in closet and a bathroom. Katherine told us that you'll need a unit for your help, so we propose putting them one floor down under the kitchen." They showed him a rendering.

"Yes. Okay. Douglas and Maybell can live there. I'll move two antique furniture pieces and three old paintings from Potomac House to go on the wall between the living/dining room and the gallery. They will be a great counterpoint to the midcentury pieces and the piano. And the art gallery idea is great."

Axel continued. "The acoustician will work with your organ builder and will design an absorptive mat to go under the organ, He is still a bit worried about the resonance of the pedal pipes, but perhaps you might like having a guest suite underneath the library as a compromise. This rendering of the organ is based on Flentrop's pictures of similar instruments, so I think you can see that the instrument will work nicely in the room."

"Yes, I agree. You're correct. The concept is fine."

"We also want to move the organ to the south side and the fireplace to the north as shown here. There will be a small study with a balcony behind the fireplace and a small workroom with a balcony behind the organ. We don't want the heat gain from the south windows to affect the tuning of the organ. The two-story concept will remain for this room."

"No, I would prefer the natural light coming through the east windows to come over my right shoulder if possible, but I do like the two small rooms. The one behind the fireplace needs to be outfitted as a bar with glass-faced cabinets for my collection of single-malt scotch. The one on the north side needs to become a study with spaces for my computer, printer, scanner, and paper storage."

"That's no problem. Heidi proposes a reclining lounge chair in the nook by the northeast window wall and a small desk in the other nook behind the small spiral stair. She has already designed the reclining chair for Edward and Tippy's mountain house. The light there will be perfect for reading. I couldn't get a piano curve into the east window wall as you suggested. It looked odd, so we've expanded the library to extend to the building's east edge. You'll need the volume to keep the organ from looking cramped, and it will increase the reverberation time. The north, west, and south terraces will be covered with newly marketed flat semitransparent solar collectors. They have been successfully used at the California Academy of Science in San Francisco."

Hans projected several pictures. "We'll reframe the roof over the terraces, and we'll actually be able to increase the number of solar collectors for the building."

"Regeneration," commented Hew.

Hans was surprised when he said that. He understood the English word, and he was impressed. Hans added that the structural and other engineering changes can be accomplished.

Johan continued. "We want to move the pool to the south side of the west terrace. We can locate it over the columns, and we will raise the pool up five feet and surround it with an ample terrace for lounge chairs and tables. New steel beams will span under it to spread the load. It will be four feet from the south rail with an infinity edge along the south side. There will be a large spa on the east end, and the main area will be fitted with a swim-in-place feature that provides a resistant current. You can swim for miles if you like. When you are in the pool or on the raised terrace, nothing will restrict your view. We will build a toilet, shower, sauna, and changing room against the stair wall. This will be balanced with a large fireplace and outdoor kitchen against the other stair wall."

Hew sat quietly for about fifteen minutes looking at the images.

Everyone on the design team held their breath. He stood and applauded.

"Absolutely incredible! I approve. How did you accomplish this so quickly?"

"We use a computer software modeling program. Everything down to the pipe sizes and electrical runs are modeled. The parts arrive on site ready to install with no cutting."

"I want to learn more about that, but we need to leave. I don't want to miss the ship. Holland awaits."

They gave him a flash drive with the entire presentation, and the design team left for the beer hall and their beds.

That evening, the dinner aboard the boat was a delicious German feast. Two musicians appeared and played, and everyone sang the old German drinking songs "Roll Out the Barrel" and "Ein Prosit." Hew had no idea what the lyrics to "Ein Prosit" were, but everyone was toasting, swaying, and having fun. He later Googled the lyrics. Basically, it translates as "A toast, a toast to cheer and good times." The repeated refrain was "I poured you one, drink it up." The man played an accordion, and the woman rolled the action wheel on a portable barrel organ. By the end of dinner, he was exhausted.

When the ship docked in Amsterdam, Edward and Tippy left for the airport. Hew and Charlie went to the train station for two days of freedom. At Flentrop, they were warmly welcomed. Hew started the conversation and immediately told them, "I want a copy of the 1958 Harvard instrument for my new condo."

He showed them the plans and the renderings. "I would like for you to begin immediately."

"We have a large backlog, but fortunately, we are about to begin production of a copy of the same instrument for another university, so we'll make two at the same time."

Hew toured the facilities and then went through the details of the contract. He only changed the species of the wood in the case to match the woodwork in the library, and per their suggestion, he increased the size slightly to match the post installation changes. "Please send the final contract to my attorney in Atlanta, and he will wire the deposit to your account immediately."

*****

They took the train to Alkmaar.

"I'm starving. Let's get lunch at that little sidewalk café over there."

"You're always starving, Charlie. This place is crowded. There's an empty table for four. Quick, grab it."

Just as they were about to sit, two college-aged girls walked over. Margot was a petite brunette, and Collette was a slightly taller brunette. "Are you two guys on holiday?" Their accent was French.

Charlie never met a stranger, so conversation just naturally flowed. "Yeah, sorta. We've been on a Rhine River cruise, and we're going to some big church here so Hew can play their organ. I'm just his page-turner."

"Oh! Another organist! We're both organ students at the Conservatoire de Paris. We are going to a place in the States called Oberlin for an exchange semester. Do you know it?"

"Yes, I've heard it has a fine program, but I've never been there."

"The cheapest tickets we could get are from Amsterdam in two days so we are just traveling around. Are you playing at Sint-Laurenskerk? We were hoping to be able to get inside to look at their famous instrument."

"I think I can do better than that. If y'all will be my console assistants, I can even let you play. I have reserved the entire afternoon, and we can swap around."

At the suggestion of playing and swapping around, Charlie's brain immediately turned to sex. "Yeah, if y'all do it, I won't need to turn pages, and he won't be yelling at me about messing with those little knobs at the wrong time."

"That's a deal," exclaimed Colette. "Charlie, you can use our iPhones and video our sessions. Maitre probably won't believe us when we get back to Paris without the proof. Are you staying overnight? We need to find a youth hostel first."

Hew was slow on the pickup line. "Not here. We're taking the train later this afternoon to Haarlem. I'm playing at the Grote Kirk tomorrow afternoon. We've booked a room there for the next two nights."

Collette pouted. "Only one room?"

Charlie seized the moment. "It has two large beds and a private bathroom."

Hew quickly caught on. "Come with us and you can play there too."

"Excuse us while we powder our noses, please."

"Charlie, do you have any protection? I've never done this before."

"Yeah, I've got you covered." They both laughed.

The girls returned smiling. "That works for us, guys."

Charlie was excited at the promise of two sex-filled days and nights. Suddenly, two boring days turning pages in moldy old churches might become the icing on the whole trip. "Okay, ladies, let's get it on! This will be fun!"

They climbed into the organ loft and spent the afternoon enjoying the instrument. Charlie was bored, but he took videos on each of their phones, hoping he was building points for being a good sport for later. Hew loved the clean sounds.

Once they were naked in bed, Collette, quickly judging the situation, climbed on top. He wasn't her first virgin. "Just lay still, Hew. Let me do this for you."

No one slept much that night, and Hew quickly learned the basics. The next morning, they had another round.

When they climbed into the Haarlem organ loft, Charlie started giggling.

"What's so funny?"

"Look at the butt print on the organ bench! That's just gross."

The girls started giggling too, but Hew snapped, "Just get over it. You don't have to sit there. This bench is as old as the organ, and many great men and women have sat on this bench. They weren't naked, you know."

As they neared the end of Hew's appointed time in the Grote Kirk, he decided to go for broke. He figured all the church could do was kick them out. He pulled his copy of "Dies Parentales" out of his backpack, penciled in the changes that the girls would need to make to compensate for the differences between this organ and the one he had composed his work on, and started playing. He wanted to hear it on this style of instrument. The church organist had been downstairs listening for the last half hour because he was ready to lock up and go for a drink, but he perked up when he heard this piece and walked up to the gallery.

"Let me see that music, please."

"I'm sorry, I'm just playing something new. We'll leave. Sorry if I offended you."

"No you didn't offend me at all, but this piece is difficult! It's almost impossible. I've been working on it for months, and I didn't think it should be played that way. No one that I've talked to does."

Hew was surprised that anyone knew about this piece until he remembered that Father A had sent it to a friend. "You just need to follow the composer's written notes. They're very complete."

"I would have said that you were wrong, but I just heard you do it! Some of us have assumed that some of his choices were wrong. We've been discussing ways to 'correct it,' but your way makes it all work. Why do you think the composer did that? Do you know who wrote it? It's not signed, and everyone wants to know who this genius is."

Hew deflected the question. "My copy doesn't have a signature either. I think it needs revisions for your instrument, though. I think this is registered for a French instrument."

"Yes, you're correct. That's what's throwing everybody."

"Maybe I can make some suggestions. Let's try it."

Charlie was bored and getting horny again. He started thinking about last night. The girls were standing on either side of the organ bench, and he was standing slightly behind Collette. He rubbed up against her. "I'm starved. Let's go, Collette. Karl can take your place if he wants to learn this." Her eyes widened as she realized what he was doing. She discreetly reached back and moved her hand down the inside of his thigh. He pressed into her hand. She smiled and announced, "You're right. We're leaving."

Standing off at a slight angle, Margot had seen the action happening. Hew and Karl were completely focused on the score. Remembering the fun last night, she started to get excited too. Hew, as usual, was oblivious to everything except his work.

"Would you play it again and let me observe, please? I'd like to set up my camera phone and video it."

When he finished, Karl asked more questions and then asked, "May I take you both for a coffee?"

Margot was ready to go to the hotel and repeat last night's action, so she spoke before Hew could answer. "Thanks, but we've got an early plane in the morning and need to get to bed."

Hew knew he didn't want coffee, but the girls drank it like water. Suddenly he understood.

"Yes, we need to go, and to thank you for your hospitality, let me give you this annotated copy with the stop changes." Using his pencil, he then scribbled, "To Karl. Thanks for letting me play this outstanding instrument." He signed it "JBXIII."

Hew left Holland with a better understanding of why he liked the Dutch organs. He also was fascinated by his introduction to sex.

*****

"I've finally found the little bastard!"

"Where are you, Paulo?"

"I met a woman in a bar in Boston and—"

"Spare me the details of your conquests."

"No. It wasn't that. She's your age. God. No. She was in Boston to sing for a family funeral. She's a choir member at the Catholic cathedral in Atlanta, Georgia. She told me they have a new young blond boy organist who sometimes subs for the regular organist for the Hispanic Mass because the regular organist doesn't speak Spanish and can't tell when the priest has finished a prayer or is just pausing. They all speak with a different cadence according to her. She said that the women in the choir can't keep their eyes off this guy."

"I'll fly up today. I'll use a private plane so I can bring my Glock and silencer. We'll go to Mass on Sunday and check this out. I'm ready to end this."

"Come on up. He's not there every Sunday, but there's a bishop from Argentina scheduled for Sunday's first communion for that Mass, so it's a good bet."

Maria's plane was late. Mass had ended by the time they parked and began walking down Peachtree Road.

"Look down there. There he is. He just came out of the door, and he's still wearing his robes. He's talking to the people standing behind the MARTA bus. They'll probably all get on. We'll follow him. Hurry up."

"Damn it, Paulo, I'm dressed for Mass. I can't run in these shoes."

"Move it. This is our best chance."

As they passed the open doors of the bus, Hew stepped off of the curb behind the bus and ran across the road to St. Philip's Cathedral. He was assisting at the next service there.

"He's crossing behind the bus. Turn around. We'll run in front of the bus and cut him off."

Paulo nearly collided with his mother, but they stepped off the curb just as the driver pulled away. He had closed the doors and was checking his rearview mirror for oncoming cars. The driver felt the crunch and then heard the screams of people waiting for the next bus. Hew heard screams but couldn't see anything because the bus was blocking his view. He was running late and went on into the choir. He was annoyed by all the sirens during the service.

*****

"Edward, would you top off my wine please?"

"Yep. I'm pouring myself another wee dram. Turn on the TV. I want to watch the Sunday evening news for a weather report. I'm flying to New York tomorrow."

The news reporter began a story about the deaths at the cathedral earlier in the day. She reported from the scene. "Two people were hit by a bus and killed following Mass at the Catholic cathedral on Peachtree Road this morning. They have been identified as Maria Rodrigues and her son, Paulo, from Cali, Colombia. Anyone who knows them is asked to contact the police."

"Oh my god, Tippy. Back that up."

She grabbed the remote. "Did you know them?"

"Not exactly. She was Espinis's half-sister. I've got to call Luis."

Hew and Charlie walked in from the pool ready for supper. "What's going on?"

"Hew, did you sub for Mass at Christ Our King this morning?"

"Yep. It was first communion for the Hispanic kids. Why?"

"You remember that I told you about Espinis's sister and you said that she would never find you in Atlanta? Well, she found you! She and her son were killed when they stepped in front of the MARTA bus after Mass this morning."

"That's why I heard screams. God, they were close. I crossed behind that bus."

"I'll make a discreet inquiry with a contact at the police department tomorrow, and Luis will try to find out more from Colombia, but your ordeal with the cartel has ended!"

"Tell Luis I'll pay to have them cremated and shipped back to Colombia. I don't want them left here."

CHAPTER 12

Temptation

Her long blond hair moved in waves as she walked. She was nearly naked! He saw a small bright-yellow string with two small triangles pretending to cover her ample breasts. A matching string around her tiny waist had one small yellow triangle. Her graceful body seemed to be completely devoid of hair except for her head. He forgot about his cramping injured knee.

"Hi. I'm Susie. I live next door. You can only be Hew. May I join you for your swim?"

"Sure. Charlie isn't—"

"Oh, I know. Charlie is at orchestra practice today, as usual, Tippy is in surgery, and Edward is God knows where." She jumped in.

"Charlie has never mentioned you. Why haven't I met you before now?"

"I'm two years older than Charlie. I'm in school at University of Virginia also called UVA. I'm in premed. I want to join my mother's gynecological practice when I graduate from med school. I had to run home for a dentist appointment tomorrow. I prefer my old dentist."

"How long have you lived next door?"

"I was born here. I was six when the Hardys moved in. Charlie was four, but he was tall and mature for his age. We were very much alike. Charlie and I are great friends. We've done everything imaginable together, if you catch my drift." She was grinning. "We started playing house in the trees behind the pool house. Then we played doctor and explored our little naked bodies. We lost our virginity to each other, and we've been at it ever since. I hope he gets home before Tippy does. I'm horny as hell. The guys at UVA just can't match Charlie. He's a real swordsman, if you know what I mean." She wasn't laughing.

Hew was almost speechless. He had never heard the word *horny* before, but he suddenly knew exactly what is meant. He didn't know what a swordsman was.

Without thinking, he blurted out, "Tippy will be late tonight. Charlie will cook salmon." He realized the moment after he said it under these circumstances it sounded stupid.

"Great. Let's make it a threeway then. Charlie will love it. We'll do it on the bearskin rug of the pool house in front of the fireplace. It's one of our favorite places."

Hew managed to say apologetically, "Susie, as fantastically wonderful as that sounds, and believe me, I'm ready, Charlie is my best friend in Atlanta. The Hardys have welcomed me as a son, and they are my only family in the entire world. I won't do anything to make him or them hate me. I'm afraid your offer might cause friction."

"Oh, there won't be any friction." She laughed.

"That's not what I meant."

"I know, I know. I was just making a little joke. Now I'm embarrassed. Well, actually, no, I'm not. The offer stands. You're a real gentleman, aren't you?" She floated over and gave him a long wet kiss with tongue.

Charlie walked through the shrubs as they were kissing.

"Susie! What a great surprise. You should have texted me!" He stripped off his T-shirt and boat shoes and jumped in. He gave her a long welcoming kiss.

"God, I've missed you. I'm horny as hell."

"Charlie, I've tried to get Hew to join us, but he's afraid it will mess up his relationship with you. Tell him I'm right."

"Hew, it won't bother me at all. We have threeways with Susie's cousin Katie every chance we get. We're not in love, we just love sex."

Hew wasn't sure. He declined. "No, thanks, but y'all go ahead. I'll just be in the way."

"I'll teach you. Threeways are very easy, but maybe next time. Hurry up, Charlie. Let's get it on."

They jumped out of the pool and ran into the pool house. Hew got out and moved to a lounge chair in the shade, but he could hear them. He was wet from the pool. He couldn't go in to change. He didn't have his shoes, so he couldn't go for a run. His only option was the piano. He dried himself off and took the towel with him. The groans and shrieks were getting louder. He walked into the living room and put the towel on the padded piano bench. Tippy had a Steinway grand. He started playing random dissonant ideas, but he was pounding the keys with all his strength. Maybe he had made a mistake. Charlie seemed okay with the idea. He stopped playing and stood up to go join them.

"What the hell?" He heard the garage door start to open. Someone was home early. Forgetting about the towel, he ran out the dining room French doors and down to the pool house to warn them. He burst into the pool house to see them lying naked on their backs laughing with each other.

"Someone's home early! I just heard the garage door start up."

Susie jumped up and struggled into her bikini bottom. She asked Hew to help her put her top on. Hew had no experience with this, but he managed to do it, while Charlie just lay there laughing. Susie ran out the back door.

"Relax, Hew. Mom never comes down here. She'll just—"

Charlie's phone chimed. Tippy sent him a text. "*I'm home. Where are you?*"

Charlie replied, "*We're in the pool house. Just got out of the pool. I'll start the grill. We're starved.*"

Tippy had been standing in the great room window when she started texting. *Ravished is a better word than starved, son,* she thought. *You are no longer starved.* She laughed out loud. She had seen a bright yellow flash moving quickly behind the trees and the large azaleas between the houses. Jane had told her Susie was coming home. That's why she canceled her late surgery. She thought Hew might need rescuing from the nympho neighbor. She chuckled. *Too late.* Tippy and Jane knew all about their kids. She wondered if Hew had joined them. As she walked through the foyer to get the mail, she spotted the wet towel on the piano bench. *Poor Hew,* she thought. *Not yet.* She wondered how long he could hold out. She and Jane would laugh about it during lunch tomorrow. They had never told their husbands. Katie's mother didn't know either. She tried to keep a tight rein on Katie.

The following Saturday morning, while they were eating breakfast, Edward turned to Charlie and reminded him about the coming weekend.

"I don't want to go to Asheville. There's nothing to do. We'll be stuck in the hotel while y'all party."

CHAPTER 13

Highlands, North Carolina

"The inn and the hotel are completely booked." Tippy sighed.

"Highlands is probably the best solution. They can't get into trouble there, they don't know anyone, and Uber won't pick them up." Edward laughed.

Hew overheard the comment. "What are y'all talking about?"

"We're going to Asheville to a wedding, and we can't leave you boys alone here, so y'all are coming along."

"I need to stay here and practice."

Charlie overheard the discussion as he walked in. He looked at Hew and winked. "It'll be fine. Trust me."

At noon on Friday, Edward and Tippy came home to pack. Edward was driving a new custom-built Desert Silver Metallic Mercedes G65 SUV.

It had just arrived at the dealership the day before. The rear seat entertainment system was similar to the units on the KLM jet. Charlie began loading bags into the hatchback.

Hew was astonished. "I've never seen so many bags for four people." He had a simple gym bag.

They piled in, and Edward headed for the perimeter interstate at the end of West Paces Ferry Road. They stopped for lunch at Tippy's favorite restaurant, Blue Ridge Grill. He took the ramp onto the interstate and headed north. After about thirty miles, traffic became lighter, so he set the radar-based cruise control and sat back. Charlie whispered, "This is the longer, easier route because he's not sure about this car yet."

Hew asked, "Where exactly is Highlands?"

Charlie explained, "Highlands is in the southwest corner of North Carolina, above Atlanta. It will take about three hours to get there, but the altitude is above four thousand feet, so it will not be as hot or humid as Atlanta."

Hew made a mistake and decided to have a little fun with Edward to pass the time. "Edward, why this huge car? I thought you of all people would drive the sweet Jag electric SUV on this trip."

"Ha!" he replied. "Did you notice the very large bag? That's full of Tippy's shoes and purses. The second large bag is her portable hair, makeup, and nail salon. There's a curling iron, a hair dryer, a nine-foot extension cord, a steam iron, and a bottle of distilled water in there too because she claims that hotel irons can be 'icky.' The third bag is her casual clothes, and the hangup bag is her formal wear."

Tippy snapped, "Yeah, and we know those damned titanium golf clubs in the alligator bag you just had to bring won't get used. At least my stuff will be used. Don't forget, I'm Mrs. Edward Hardy on this trip, NOT Dr. Hardy! They're YOUR client-friends, not mine. I can't stand them!"

Charlie broke the tension. "Don't worry, Hew. We go through this on every trip. It's a family tradition."

Tippy laughed.

Edward added, "Actually, now that we are a family of four, we need a larger vehicle. Has Charlie told you about our mountain house?"

"Let me tell him. Y'all go into too much detail. Dad used the same German firm to design the mountain house. It's only two years old, and it's very modern. Some people call it Mountain Contemporary, whatever that is. It's mostly stone and glass, and it has a dynamite view. There's even a solar heated pool."

"That sounds good to me. Contemporary is my favorite style."

"Then you'll love this place."

"Charlie, if y'all look in the seat pockets, there are two pairs of Bluetooth noise-cancellation headsets. I've already loaded a few action movies into the entertainment system so y'all can watch one while Tippy listens to her opera. She has her own pair up here."

They crossed into South Carolina on I-85 and took exit one onto Cherokee Foothills National Scenic Highway 11 and then drove up to Highway 28. Highway 28 was a winding, hilly mountain road. As they passed a roaring river, Charlie said, "On our next trip, we might go whitewater rafting on the river if the water level is right. The name of the river is the Chattooga. It's classified as a National Wild and Scenic River, and it's world-famous with whitewater rafters."

They drove into Highlands and turned onto Horse Cove Road. They arrived at a fir-tree-lined section of the road and turned between two long moss-covered stone walls. They stopped at a stainless-steel gate, and Hew noticed a small solar panel on top of one of the walls. Edward punched in a code, and the gate opened.

"Is everything here solar powered, Edward?"

"Yes. The whole property is net zero. We sell most of our power to the utility company. Charlie can show you how it all works."

"Regeneration," he remarked.

"Yes. We make much more than we use. There's a large solar array in the old pasture above the house. All the lighting is LED, and the heating and cooling is a groundwater in-floor radiant system, so we are only running pumps."

"Maybe I can write a small program to work with the GPS system in the SUV to open the gate as you approach."

"Hew, you're going to make a billion." He laughed. "Go for it. Let Charlie help. He needs the money."

The driveway turned and started down a steep slope. At the bottom, a small stream ran out of a rock outcropping and down alongside the drive until it turned under a contemporary bridge and fell down the mountain in a splashing waterfall. The stone wall picked up intermittently on the right side. The walls were low, and the stones appeared to have been stacked by a farmer at some point in history. The landscaping along the driveway appeared to be both manmade and natural. They started up a steep slope, and the running wall became taller. Hew saw a massive stone chimney rising up through the trees ahead of them. The stone wall became the front of the house. It was only broken by an opening which turned out to be a recess for the wooden front door. A sloped green standing seam metal roof hovered above the stone wall without any visible means of support. The roof was low over the entrance and high at the back. The 3,000-square-foot house was very linear and rode just below the top of the ridge above a dramatic 1,500-foot sheer drop. They got out and stretched their legs. Hew's knee was bothering him from the hours of sitting.

"Why not a green or solar roof?"

"We have a solar farm behind the hill above the house, and a green roof would be dangerous here. The danger of wildfire is great up here due to periodic times of drought. This house is designed without flammable materials. There are no gutters to trap leaves either. Notice the gravel around the perimeter? It matches the stone, and we have a maintenance guy who keeps it free from debris. Windblown embers will not have a place to start a fire near this house."

Charlie unlocked the door. "Notice the door opens out, and the doorknob is round. Bears don't have opposable thumbs, so they can't grab the knob. That keeps them from pushing the door in."

"Bears?"

He laughed. "Yep."

"This is a great room!" The view was only apparent after walking through the front door.

The house sat near the top of a ridge at the center of a three-sided bowl. Views of the surrounding mountains commanded the left and right sides. The south view went on forever. "That rock face is Whitesides Mountain," said Charlie. "You are looking south into Horse Cove. The headwaters of the Chattooga River start near here. The mountains beyond are part of what you will see from the north side of your terrace in Atlanta."

Tippy reminisced, "My brother still owns our family summer house up here. I remember going down into Horse Cove to visit my great uncle Sam Stoney. He was a Charleston architect and owned a small log cabin in Horse Cove. We played in the small creek. Uncle Sam told us the water in his creek flowed all the way to the Atlantic. The river forms the state line between South Carolina and Georgia. I love sitting up here, looking down at old Uncle Sam's Horse Cove."

The great room had a heart pine wooden floor. The quarter sawn flooring came from trees that had fallen at Swan Bay after an ice and wind storm several years ago. The ceiling consisted of large Swan Bay poplar beams with a wood deck above. The ceiling was about eight feet tall over the entry door and sloped up to sixteen feet at the window wall. The window wall formed a large bay about thirty-six feet long and eight feet deep. The roof was supported on four wood columns sitting just inside the glass. The glass ran from the baseboard up to the ceiling with very few mullions between. Charlie noticed Hew looking at the sizes of the glass.

"The glass is the largest size we could get up the mountain. Notice that it is slightly canted out at the top. That reduces the reflections at night, so we only see stars rather than our reflections."

A large stone fireplace commanded one side of the room, and an open kitchen was across from the fireplace. The seating group in front of the fireplace appeared to Hew to be the steel-and-black leather furniture designed by Le Corbusier, but something was different.

"Edward, do you know the work of Le Corbusier? He was an early twentieth-century Swiss-born architect who practiced mostly in France, but this furniture looks like his work."

"Not really, but I'm told that this design is based on his work. Johan redesigned it for, as he put it, modern lazy Americans." He laughed. "The sections of the sofa recline. The two side chairs recline too."

Charlie demonstrated.

"This is the design Heidi described for my library. I'm going to text her and tell her to use this group. I'll put two side chairs and the sofa in front of the fireplace. We can put one of my Eames chairs and ottomans in the reading niche, and we can move the other Eames chairs and ottomans to the bedrooms."

There was a large quilt hanging over the fireplace. "The quilt was handmade by my grandmother," said Edward. "It slides up to reveal a one-hundred-inch Sony flat-screen TV behind."

Charlie gave him a quick tour of the house. A glass door beside the fireplace led out to a large screened porch. There was another fireplace behind the main fireplace and a large gas grill. Charlie remarked, "We do have a few bugs here, and we like to eat out here in the summer. The food attracts the local stinging yellow jackets and horse flies. They're like bees but worse, so we added the screening. I love to build a fire out here on cool nights."

The kitchen had a large island with a wooden top. Tippy said, "The wood top has a natural edge and is made of three wide pieces of Swan Bay poplar."

There were six Bertoia wire bar stools with dark green leather cushions.

"Tippy, I feel right at home here."

The large subzero refrigerator was hidden behind wood doors, which matched the cabinets. All the woodwork was finished in a waxed, limed oak. It was stained pale white in color, which was a very subtle form of whitewash, but it took away the harsh orange of the natural wood. Behind the kitchen and down a short hall, a large pantry, two guest bedrooms, the master suite, and three and one-half baths completed the floor plan. The master suite was large. The other two suites were smaller but more than adequate. One bedroom had two queen-size beds, and the other was designed with three sets of bunk beds. Fortunately, Johan and Heidi sized the bunks for Charlie. All the bedrooms had full window walls looking toward the view.

When they had returned to the great room, Edward and Tippy were preparing to leave but gave them stern warnings about not burning the place down. They would pick them up on Sunday afternoon.

"I'm ready for a swim and a martini," quipped Charlie.

"I'm ready for the pool too. My knee needs a workout." A broad stone terrace outside the great room window had five wide steps leading down to the pool. The pool was low enough that when sitting on the terrace, the railing didn't block the endless valley view. The pool had a large jacuzzi built into one end.

They quickly changed into soccer shorts. Charlie took two martini glasses out of the glass cabinet over the bar beside the fireplace. He took crushed ice out of the small undercounter refrigerator and put the ice and some water into the glasses while he prepared the martinis.

"Won't your parents notice the missing liquor?"

"Nope. I brought it."

"How?"

"Fake ID, my friend."

While the glasses chilled, he pulled a bottle of the Botanist Gin Islay Dry out of a small bag hidden in his gym bag. "This gin was distilled in Scotland and has twenty-two locally foraged botanicals, so you should love it."

He picked up a lemon. Hew had never seen anyone make a martini, much less taste one.

Charlie cut slivers of lemon peel using a small peeler. "We only use the peel, the zest, they call it. The white stuff underneath is bitter."

He put the gin into a silver cocktail shaker with a few cubes of ice, a 7:1 amount of Dolin French Vermouth, and started shaking the container. Once it was too cold to hold, he stopped. The glasses were frosty with condensation, so he dumped the icy water out and poured the strained cold gin into the glasses and added a sliver of lemon peel.

"Now that's good, Charlie. It really doesn't taste like alcohol. How did you learn to make martinis?"

He laughed. "Yeah, it'll sneak up on you though. I worked as a tennis coach at the club last summer. The bartender taught me to mix drinks. But he wouldn't let me taste them. I had to do that at home. Cheers, Hew. Welcome to Highlands with no parents."

They jumped into the pool, but the first sips were starting to relax them.

Charlie heard the gate alarm. "Oh great! Our guests have arrived."

"What guests?"

"Just wait. You're going to have the time of your life!"

A small Mercedes convertible drove up. Susie got out from the driver's side, and she had another girl with her. "Is THAT Katie?"

"Yep. Let's get the bags."

Katie was as beautiful as Susie. She had short brown hair, but otherwise they could pass for twins.

"Y'all are dripping wet. You started without us."

"I've just made martinis. Jump in with Hew while I make y'all one." The girls stripped naked and jumped into the pool. The unusual weekend had begun!

Katie, an architecture major at UVA, looked around and exclaimed, "Charlie, I *love* this place! It's so…unexpected…so fresh and modern, but warm and mountainy at the same time." She swam over to Hew. "Now, Hew," she purred, "I'm here to help you with your 'batting' practice this weekend. Susie says she doesn't think you have much experience, so let's not waste any more time." She sipped her martini. He quickly downed the rest of his.

Charlie came out with another round. "Oh, he's already got a very good grasp on the mechanics. He's no virgin."

Hew quickly reached for one, but Katie said, "We'll see about that. No more for you just now. I want you to remember this. Come on."

She pulled him out of the pool and led him into the bedroom. She turned and kissed him as she pulled his wet soccer shorts down. He stepped out of them, and they tumbled onto the bed. She jumped on top of him. "Let's get this first one over quickly. Lay on your back and let me lead. I know what I'm doing." She didn't realize that he also knew what he was doing.

An hour and a half later, they walked out to the pool and rejoined Charlie and Katie, who were lounging naked in the pool.

"Susie, we have a new swordsman in our stable. I had to make him speed it up on the third one. These two guys could be twins. You're right, Charlie. He wasn't a virgin."

"Third? I'll test your theory after supper. Charlie, we're starving."

"Fine. Let's grill steaks and bake a few potatoes."

Hew chimed in, "Great. I could eat a horse. I'll start the potatoes. They'll take a little longer, and then I'll grill the steaks. Y'all make a salad."

"Men. Pierce the potatoes with a fork and put 'em in the microwave. We don't have all night. We've got better things to do."

Hew covered himself with a towel, which Katie immediately ripped off. He started the grill, and Charlie brought another round of martinis out to the screened porch. It was only Friday night. Hew didn't know if he would live through Saturday, but he knew he would die a happy fellow! They sat around the glass-topped table on the screened porch. After supper, Susie said, "My turn, Hew. You ready?"

"Actually, I'm going to beg off. I don't think I have another one in me right now." He moved off to begin work on the gate opening app. Susie pouted. Hew had already determined that he liked Katie better than Susie. Katie was quiet and thoughtful, but Susie was loud and bossy.

Susie grabbed Charlie, and they ran toward the bedroom. At nine thirty, Susie wandered into the great room and said, "We're going to the jacuzzi to relax. Let's have another round of martinis, Charlie."

Katie yawned. "No, it's time for sleep. I'm exhausted."

Katie and Hew slept in one of the queen-size beds, and Charlie and Susie slept in the other. Saturday was a blur. Hew lost count, but he artfully avoided Susie's advances.

On Sunday morning, Charlie and Hew were hungover, but the girls jumped on them anyway and then afterward got up, and Susie started giving orders. "Roll out, guys, and hit the showers while we strip the beds and start washing the sheets. Party's over," barked Susie. "When you've showered, Hew, cook breakfast while Katie vacuums. Charlie, you round up all the liquor bottles and put the trash and our bags in my car. Katie will put the sheets in the dryer, and we'll shower. Charlie, when the sheets are dry, you and Hew make the beds."

Susie made one last trip to the powder room, and with one last kiss and a promise to do it again soon, they left. Susie wanted to get away in case the Hardys decided to arrive early. The place was spotless. Charlie and Hew folded the towels and then began finalizing their app.

*****

While Edward and Tippy were finishing brunch, she quietly remarked, "I think I'll just text Charlie now so Susie and Katie can have time to get away."

"What the hell are you talking about, Tippy?"

"Oh, Edward, when have you ever seen Charlie so excited to be going anywhere to do nothing?"

"But why Susie, and who's Katie?"

"Katie is Susie's cousin. Susie and Katie have been screwing Charlie for years. I think this was Hew's initiation weekend."

"You're just joking with me."

"Nope. Jane got home early one afternoon and found Susie on top of Charlie. They were so involved they didn't notice her. They were on the floor of the playroom. Susie had her back to the door, and Charlie's eyes were closed. Jane quietly left and went shopping for two hours, trying to decide what to do. She made a lot of noise when she returned, but by then, the kids were in our pool. Later the same day, Katie came by, and Jane overheard Susie giving Katie a detailed description of Charlie's ample anatomy. She then heard Katie ask if Charlie would show her. Susie readily agreed. Jane pulled out her cell phone and immediately got two prescriptions for birth control pills. Jane invited me to lunch in the hospital cafeteria the next day. She hesitated to start, but I told her to just spit it out. She told me the kids had started having sex. I nearly fell over laughing because she was awkwardly trying to discreetly describe the scene. Tears came streaming down my face. Jane was relieved by my reaction. People were watching us howl with laughter. Of course, Katie was fifteen, so it wasn't a total surprise."

"But then he was only thirteen!" Edward was practically shouting.

"Control your voice, you old codger. We started early too, if you remember."

"Yeah, but we weren't thirteen, for God's sake. I can't believe Charlie has been at it for this long. How many other girls has he been with?"

"You were supposed to have the talk with him as I remember, and you said you would. Obviously you didn't."

"The time never seemed right."

"Chicken! Too late now. He probably knows more than you do now."

"Well, I've certainly never had a threeway!"

"Sounds like you're jealous. You know I would never have agreed to THAT! I don't know about other girls except Katie. Jane swears they are a threesome and have been for a while. Jane and I agreed we couldn't unscrew them, and once they had started, it would be nearly impossible to stop them. We agreed neither you or Joe could handle it, so we didn't tell you."

"Thanks for that! You're right. I can't handle it very well now. Why Hew, and how do you know about, what's her name, Katie was it?"

"Katie's mother is Jane's sister. She tries to keep a tight rein on Katie, but Jane says it has just made her wild. Jane actually overheard Katie and Susie discussing a recent threeway with Charlie. Apparently our Charlie is quite a swordsman, as the girls call it."

Edward smirked.

"We think Hew is still a virgin, or at least he was until this weekend. We've done about all we can do to protect them."

"Good god!" But Edward laughed. "Yes. Text him. I sure as hell don't want to walk in on any of that!"

*****

"I just got a text from Mom. They'll be here in about two hours."

"Should we do anything else to make sure the house is clean?"

"No. I think we're okay. Susie is always very thorough."

"I don't want to even think about sex for a month at least."

"Ha! You'll be ready to go again tomorrow. The girls are driving back to UVA today, so we'll probably be horny until Christmas! Katie's designing a big project that'll take all semester, and Susie has more work than I even want to think about. Both the schools pile on the work in the first years to see who they can weed out. I don't know any more willing girls at the moment. My last girlfriend was a prude."

"Okay. We'll find another way."

Once Edward and Tippy arrived, she did a discreet survey of the house, looking for evidence. At first, she didn't find anything, but just as they were leaving, she went to the powder room and spotted a single long blond hair on the floor beside the toilet. Tippy simply smiled. She was correct. She hummed most of the way home. She couldn't wait to tell Edward and Jane. On the drive back to Atlanta, they took the back roads and avoided the interstates entirely. Exhausted, Charlie and Hew slept the whole way.

Work was well underway on Hew's unit. Hew was fascinated by the modeling program. On one of Johan's observation trips, Hew started questioning the process. John described how the design team, the fabricators, the subcontractors, and their in-house construction team all worked with the same integrated model. Even the billings and pay applications were integrated.

"Johan, How do you keep track of the workers' productivity?"

"That's the various supervisors' job."

"Yes, but how do you know that? The supervisors can't be on every floor of a large building."

"That's a good question, and I don't have an answer."

"Okay. Let's work on it."

Johan agreed just to placate a good client, but he wondered exactly what this kid could possibly know about computer programming. Hew launched into a full-scale search for managing worker productivity. He learned that the large parcel services used GPS to locate their trucks and manage the routes. He decided to write a program to utilize a similar concept. He and Johan wrote endless emails back and forth testing his ideas. Many were impracticable for construction sites, but after two busy months, they had something both thought might work. Hew explained the idea to Edward and Katherine. She was impressed but not really sure. Edward had no idea, but he sensed that if it worked, Hew would make another fortune from his computer skills. The three of them flew to Cologne on the company jet and presented the ideas.

CHAPTER 14

Construction

Hew explained. This time, he was the one with the high-tech presentation. "The process utilizes existing GPS technology. We'll probably need to pay to use their process, but it will be worth it. The construction workers will get a new entrance badges with a small unobtrusive GPS transmitter. They will be required to wear it at all times while on the job. For this test project, the subcontractors and workers will not be warned in advance. There is a scanner installed into the workers' entrance to the site, and scanners will be installed in construction trailers and throughout the penthouse. Every movement will be tracked and recorded into the monthly pay applications. There will be cameras and scanners hidden in the smoke and air monitoring devices. Those are Johan's custom unit designs with my custom circuit board architecture inside."

Eberhart loved it. They agreed to use his penthouse as their test run. Hew agreed to fund the setup. Eberhart also agreed to have the German fabricators try it on their factory workers. Edward quickly filed patents on the software and the custom equipment.

*****

At the end of the month, the subcontractors were asked to attend a meeting and brief Hew on the past month's pay request. They all arrived with pay applications to proudly show how much they had accomplished. When the last one had finished, the accountants for Eberhart walked in. They projected two sheets of numbers on the screen. One was the workers' time sheets, as had been presented for payment. The comparison spreadsheet was of the actual productivity. Every time a worker had been idle for more than fifteen minutes or left the room to go elsewhere, the computer showed it in red. The subcontractors protested. The accountants took a worker as an example and, using the GPS tracker and hidden cameras, showed them exactly where the worker had been. Hew even had installed a discreet video surveillance system along the site security fence that worked with his software. It caught one guy selling tools over the fence, and another guy was buying quantities of small bags, which turned out to be cocaine. Edward was particularly glad when that guy was sent to jail. The Ops Center team busted a major drug and prostitution ring in Atlanta thanks to Hew and Johan's program.

The accountant continued, "Now let's take two other examples. This first guy is listed as a drywall installer. He reported 160 hours this past month. Here we see him in the first two weeks helping to install sheets of drywall. Notice, however, he plugged his phone into our power. Also notice that he spent a total of an hour and five minutes in the toilet every day, and he took his phone with him. During the next two weeks, he sat on the floor for fifty hours plugged in playing with his phone. At this point, he jumped up waving his arms. We checked the internet." The accountant showed a video of a soccer match. "See, his team obviously scored at this same exact moment. We noticed no drywall was hung during that period. For the sake of time, we aren't showing your other crew members, but it is all here.

"Now here is an electrician. He is running conduit and installing rough-in boxes. He takes three toilet breaks on this day for a total of fifteen minutes. He stops for lunch, but otherwise, he worked his required hours. That is true for the entire time he is on the job. Ladies and gentlemen, most of these other actions are legally known as fraud. Using our electricity to play on the internet is theft. Note that all of your time will be reduced, and we will provide proof. You will be given a flash drive if you want to show your workers. Several badges, as of this morning, no longer work. Those people will not be allowed back on site."

"Now wait just one damned minute," cried the drywall sub. "I'm not going to pay for all of this hardware or the time it took to prepare this charade."

The accountant parried, "This is a cost-plus contract, and some of you guys are hiring useless workers, paying the minimum, but charging us for all of the time just to pad your profits. The hardware will be reused in the common parts of the building, so nothing is wasted. The computer will serve as part of the final building security system. It's not manned because the program reports all anomalies, so your argument won't pass muster."

Several subcontractors were fired for filing false reports. Thirty workers were fired immediately. Eberhart was very pleased. The pay application for the month was reduced 25 percent. Hew and Johan were pleased and were heartedly congratulated.

After the third successful month, the numbers rapidly improved. Everyone had gotten the message, and the production had markedly picked up. Edward got a call from the software company. They wanted to meet Hew. Edward set it up.

"Mr. Ramsay, I'm Matthew Davis, and I'm head of development for Vitruvian Solutions Inc. I'll get right to it. We are prepared to offer you one billion five hundred million dollars for the full patents and design of your productivity software. We think this will revolutionize the construction industry around the globe. We want to get in early and add this feature to our product. You are going to introduce a major missing piece and help bring construction into the twenty-first century."

Edward and Katherine excused themselves and asked Hew to follow them into another conference room. Katherine placed a call to Germany. Fifteen minutes later, they had an answer. "Take it. Take it immediately."

They walked back in, and Edward, using his best poker face, said, "Two billion, five hundred million dollars. That's our best and final offer."

Eberhart had told him that if he negotiated, he might even get a better offer because this program was revolutionary. It has applications far beyond construction. Without batting an eye, the deal was struck. Katherine excused herself and drafted a memorandum of agreement. They all signed it right then. A final contract followed. The money was split fifty-fifty with Hew and Eberhart. Eberhart gave Johan a $500,000 bonus and welcomed Hew and Edward as their newest partners. Hans and Heidi were rewarded with $100,000 each for their work on the penthouse design.

There were huge celebrations in Germany that night. There was a quiet dinner at their club in Atlanta. Katherine had been invited, and she showed up with a date whom none of them had ever heard about, much less met. Edward raised his glass and toasted Katherine on having just been made a named partner that day. She was totally surprised. Hew had also sold his stock in the law firm to Edward that afternoon.

*****

The building was finished. Sixty units were already occupied, and several more potential owners were going through Katherine's extensive background checks. There had been other issues. The interior painting contractor had been fired for thinning the paint with unapproved solvents. He had caused the general contractor to rip out much of the drywall in Hew's unit. Heidi helped solve the problem by covering most of the walls with a pale gray Scottish wool fabric similar to that in XI's New York office suite. Edward called Hew to congratulate on the final completion of the penthouse.

"No rest for me, Edward. I'm flying back to Swan Bay tonight. I'm going to drive the Corvette to Philadelphia to see the Barnes Foundation exhibits of French Impressionism. If I like it, I will ask the curator to assist me with my paintings and then drive back to Atlanta."

"Hew, no. You don't want to drive to Philadelphia. The traffic between DC and Philly is a nightmare. I'm flying up tonight. I need to have a quick meeting with Jeffrey. Let's stay at Swan Bay overnight, and tomorrow, I'll drop you off on my way to Manhattan. You can take Acela to Grand Central Station and then take Uber up Park Avenue to our offices in the Seagram's Building. There's something there I want to show you. We'll fly back together, and we can stop at Swan Bay if you want to get the car."

"Good idea."

Hew loved the Barnes Foundation and contracted with the curator to hang the paintings while he was in England. The cathedral choir was going on tour. At Dr. Withersby's suggestion, Hew had decided to stay in England for the summer and study English cathedral music.

Edward ushered Hew through the main doors of the Four Seasons restaurant in the base of the Seagram Building. Hew couldn't believe it. The first thing he saw was a 361-square-foot tapestry by Picasso. It stopped him in his tracks. He had never heard of it. They turned left and were shown to their table in the Pool Room. Their table was across from the pool and had a commanding view of the space. Everything was midcentury modern right down to the tableware. The chairs were Miesian. The stainless-steel window drapes were shimmering. Edward suggested the Dover sole. "It is a white fish fresh from Dover, England, prepared with lemon-caper butter."

It melted in Hew's mouth. They finished with the restaurant's signature fancy cake. It was a layer of orange chiffon cake topped with a dome of Bavarian cream, and the whole affair was covered in chocolate.

"Edward, this is fantastic, but as much as I love being back in New York City, after Evensong at St. T's tomorrow, I really need to fly back to Atlanta and practice for the choir concert."

CHAPTER 15

Bloody Altar

"Stop that damned infernal racket!"

Hew thought for a moment that he had heard something, but he knew he was alone. He was concentrating. He had been at this for days, and it still wasn't right. His scar tissue was a nuisance. He really needed to stop and stretch it. Sitting on the hard bench of the cathedral organ practicing Bach's Toccata and Fugue in D minor, the Dorian BWV 538, the pedal work was causing him real pain. During this piece, his left foot must move across the entire left side of the pedalboard, but he was having trouble when he stretched and turned his left foot to hold the low D for five and a half measures at the end of the Toccata. The knife wound behind his left knee made pedal work difficult, especially after extended practice sessions. He knew better, and he knew he would never be a professional concert organist, but he really wanted to get this pedal line worked out. He was going to be allowed to play it as a postlude on the upcoming choir trip to England. Even though it had been two years since the attack, the weather sometimes caused odd pains in his knee.

11:00 p.m.

The cathedral organists practiced late into the night and early morning because the cathedral was very busy during the day. It reminded him of his practice time in Bogota. He only turned on a few lights immediately over the console, so the nave was very dark. He did that in Bogota to reduce the light showing through the windows and thereby reduced his exposure from passersby. He only had a few more measures to go, but it was time to stop for the night. The cathedral was built in the early 1960s, and even though it is Gothic in form and detail, the sanctuary was fitted according to modern liturgical practice rather than Gothic. Instead of having a high altar and reredos at the end of the apse, the planners located the organ pipework there. The choir sat in a concert rather than a divided monastic choir position in front of the pipework, and the console sat in front of the choir. Suddenly, he heard it again! A man yelled, "I said stop that damned infernal racket!"

Startled, he violently jerked his head up. He was surprised to see United States Senator Thomas Kalhan Sr. staring at him through the openings in the hand-carved oak Gothic parclose/reredos screen between the altar and the console. The senator had a gun.

"Senator, how did you get in here?"

"Shut up you little pissant and listen to me! Did you really think you could hide from a powerful senator like me? What about your high and mighty grandfather's secret ops organization deep inside the DEA? Contractor my ass. He thought he could hide it from Congress too, but when I get back to DC, I'll destroy the program, grab all the hidden loot, and ruin his memory. I'm sure there must be a massive amount of money somewhere. All that money will fund some very nice projects in my state and absolutely assure my seat in the Senate. It will make me famous for sure.

"I want you to know I'm the one who killed him. Yeah. Me. Dead. Now, thanks to your smart little coverup and my brilliant plan, no one can ever put this little charade together. I hold you both responsible for my only child's murder. You didn't do anything to help him during the trial. All you had to do was simply change your story and say he didn't do it, but no. You and all your friends just had to tell the truth. Idiots. Now, you're going to die too. I killed your grandfather, and now I'm going to kill you right here, but I wanted you to know. I didn't give your grandfather the courtesy. He didn't deserve to know. Killing him was easy, but it took a little planning. It was a beautiful thing. Knowing he would be driving back to DC after a long meeting at his Swan Bay farm, I took him out. That's a long, deserted, hilly, curving backcountry road, so I put a preserved full body deer in the road. I bought it from a local taxidermist who told me it was a Swan Bay deer. How poetic. He didn't see it until the last minute because I had carefully placed it standing in the road down a hill and at the end of a sharp curve. He was going too fast, and he swerved. His precious MG ran off the road with such force that when he hit the tree, he was knocked into the tree headfirst.

"The deer had been spun around, but I don't think he actually hit it. I made sure he was dead, then I put my deer into the back of my SUV and simply drove home. It was a perfect crime, if you can call it a crime. I don't. I call it justice. So here I am now. Your turn. Your death will be perfect too because my father's old World War II pistol can't be traced."

"But, Senato—"

The explosion was earsplitting! The noise bounced around off the walls, the floor, and the stone vaulting for several seconds. Suddenly, the senator had disappeared. Hew couldn't hear anything except the ringing in his ears. Bending over and looking through the opening, Hew saw a body with a bloody pulp where his face and neck had been! Blood was beginning to run all over the marble floor. The fair linen on the altar was covered with spray and pulp! Hew started screaming. He jumped up from the console and limped toward the narthex. Halfway down the aisle, he remembered that his cellphone was laying on the organ bench. He limped back to get it and limped up the stairs to the chancel, trying not to look at the bloody mess. He shouted at the phone, "Call Edward!" The damned phone was locked. He entered his security code and tried Edward again.

"Slow down, Hew. Oh my god! Don't touch anything. I'll call 911. Meet them at the parking lot door under the porte cochere. I don't want sirens and flashing lights causing a scene on Peachtree Road or Andrews Drive. We need to keep a lid on this if possible."

Edward arrived right after the first responders. After that, everything happened very slowly. The EMS team went inside. The police arrived next. He was told to wait outside, and a policewoman would wait with him. He didn't know what to say, so he said nothing. He was shaking. She got a blanket and wrapped it around him. A little while later, a black van arrived with the word Coroner written on it. The coroner went inside, and an unmarked police car arrived at the scene. The new policeman asked him if he were a key holder, and he said, yes. He asked if Hew could turn on more lights. Hew usually only turned the choir lights on when he practiced, so he went in and turned everything on. He asked Hew to take a seat in the atrium. Edward sat with him. Hew turned his back to the action. The cop introduced himself as the chief of detectives.

"Son, this is a very serious crime in one of the most prominent locations in Atlanta."

Hew thought, *No kidding!*

The detective asked if he could ask Hew a few questions. Edward said, "Yes, but I may tell him not to answer."

He asked his name and home address. Hew gave his full name and said, "I live just across Peachtree Road, in the new high-rise condominium.

He asked his age.

Hew answered, "Seventeen."

He asked if he were in school. "No, sir, I've just graduated from school."

"Why are you here alone at 11:00 p.m. on a Thursday night"—he checked his 911 notes—"um, Mr. Ramsay?"

"Call me Hew. Sure. I'm the assistant to the sub-organist here, and this is my assigned weekly practice time."

"I suppose someone will confirm this?"

"Yes, sir. The canon for music will. His name is Dr. Samuel Marshall Withersby. Do you want to call him right now?"

"No, no. I can get it later. Did you know the victim?"

"Yes, sir. He is—was US Senator Thomas Kalhan Sr."

"HMMM. This just keeps getting worse. How did you know a US senator?"

"I used to live in Arlington, Virginia. The senator's son, Thomas Jr., and I went to the same school and played soccer on the school team."

"So why was the senator in here with a gun?"

"Thomas Jr. attacked me with a knife one afternoon in the locker room. There was a huge trial. All the media covered it. After the trial, the court changed my name, and I moved to Atlanta. Thomas Jr. was found guilty and sentenced to prison for premeditated aggravated assault with a deadly weapon. The senator also confessed just before he pulled the trigger on me to killing my grandfather."

"What was your grandfather's name?"

"John Bishop XI."

"XI?"

"Yes, sir. He was the eleventh John Bishop. He was named in succession from his ancestral grandfather, Captain John Bishop. Capt'n John Immigrated from Scotland to Virginia. Grandfather has been called XI since his boarding school days at Exeter. That was his nickname, and it stuck."

The detective coughed to cover his stifled laugh.

The coroner came through and told the chief she had cleared the scene. Under the circumstances, she believed the death had been self-inflicted, but she asked to swab Hew's hands for gunshot residue. The detective wanted to call Hew's parents, but he told him he could walk home. Hew didn't want to tell them that when he moved into his new condo, Edward had allowed him to legally become an emancipated minor so he no longer had a guardian. The detective agreed not to call since it was 2:00 a.m. but told him to stay in Atlanta in case they had more questions after they had contacted the DC police. Hew gave him his key to the cathedral and left.

*****

At 11:00 a.m. the following morning, Hew's phone woke him with its annoying buzzing. The condo concierge said there was a police detective and an FBI agent in the lobby wanting to see him. He really didn't want them to come into his penthouse, so he asked if he would offer them coffee and show them into the club room. Hew had to shower and dress. The chief of detectives from the night before introduced him to the Atlanta FBI field office director.

"Mr. Ramsay, ah, Hew, we have some news. Actually, everything you told us about the senator, the son, and the trial checked out surprisingly quickly. My counterpart with the DC police was unusually helpful. The FBI lab here in Atlanta put a rush on the weapon. The weapon had not been fired or properly cleaned in years. In fact, the barrel was full of wadding from whenever it was last cleaned. Apparently someone left it there to absorb moisture or something. The senator also used the wrong ammunition. The combination was deadly, as you saw.

"We found his Mercedes on Andrews Drive. He had driven from DC, apparently because he couldn't get the gun on a plane or didn't want to leave much of a trail. He probably paid cash for the gas, food, and a hotel room somewhere. There were fresh pick marks on the lock of the side door of what I think y'all call the sacristy, and the case of pick tools was in his pocket. The door was still unlocked, so we know he gained entry there. He has no living relatives, so the FBI contacted his chief of staff. His body will be cremated here and transported to DC. The official cause of death will be from a sudden aneurysm, which isn't far from the truth. The explosion ripped into his throat.

"As far as your grandfather's death is concerned, I'm sorry to have to tell you, but with a great deal of overnight investigation by the FBI, this story checks out too. Agents found a fully preserved ten-point buck standing in the storage area of the senator's DC garage while going through his house. At the time of the accident, the forensics experts had found traces of old deer fur in the road, and they had found traces of fur on the right front bumper, but because it was a country road, and people hit deer on that road all the time, they didn't process it. Fortunately, it was kept in an evidence bag. On our way over here, they called with the results. Small areas of paint matching your grandfather's car were found on the deer's left front leg. The processing chemicals on the fur matched too. Your grandfather caught just enough of the deer to leave a sample. This case has officially been ruled a murder."

Hew was stunned. After a few moments, he asked, "Can y'all keep it out of the media?"

"Yes, we think so. His death will need to be reported in DC and his home state, but his office will release all of that and just say he was here visiting a close friend.

"It'll die a quick news death. He was powerful, but I was reliably informed that no one really liked him, so with your permission, we'll close both of these cases. I must say you are the luckiest young man I have ever met. You should not expect to hear from us again. Please sign this document showing I am returning your church key. Here are complete copies of the incident reports for your files."

They left. Hew was exhausted. He took the elevator up to his penthouse and collapsed onto the bed. In a few minutes, he had lapsed into a deep sleep.

*****

At one thirty, his phone woke him up again. The concierge said, "Hew, there are two priests and Mr. Hardy here to see you. The one in the purple shirt is actually demanding to see you right now."

"Oh hell! I forgot about them! Send them right up."

The bishop of the diocese, the Rt. Rev. Richard Kirkland; the dean of the cathedral, the very Rev. Dr. James Stewart; and Edward were in the lobby. Edward was also the chancellor of the diocese. Hew was glad Edward was with them. He quickly ran into the bathroom for a quick cleanup.

"Charter Hew Ramsay? Did I hear you correctly, Edward?" asked the dean.

He responded, "Yes, sir."

"Hew, are we related?"

The bishop broke in, "Let's get into that later!"

"Bishop Kirkland, Dean Stewart, Edward, please come in. I'm sorry. I should have called this morning, but I have been with the police most of the day. May I get you a glass of water or iced tea? I never drink sweet tea, but I do have sugar and lemon. Because of my age, I'm afraid I don't have anything stronger to offer."

"Forget the pleasantries," demanded the bishop. "I want to know exactly what went on in my cathedral last night."

Hew had actually never talked to either the bishop or the dean. He had seen them many times, but they had never been properly introduced.

The dean usually had his back to the choir and organ console, while Hew was busy assisting the sub-organist. Hew helped with the stop changes for each piece of music, and he turned pages. The canon for music directed the choir, and the sub-organist played. Obviously, Edward had filled them in on his position with some heavily edited information about his background.

"Certainly, sir, certainly, and again I apologize for my tardiness. Have you seen the official police reports?"

"Not yet. The police have arranged a meeting at four this afternoon. We immediately called Edward, and he has led us to you."

"Gentlemen, please come with me out to my terrace. I'm sorry, but my condo isn't quite finished yet. The interior designers are still here. I have a complete copy of everything. Perhaps you could read this while I get us a drink. My throat is very dry. Each part is separate and in order, so perhaps one of you would begin with the 911 call then pass the parts on. Bishop, would you like to start, please?"

Hew led them onto the terrace and left them at the table reading while he headed for the kitchen. He had only been in the building for one day, and very little of it was furnished. Maybell had shipped most of the pantry and kitchen items early. She and Mary had convinced him to keep all the family silver, crystal, and china. The architects had quadrupled the size of the butler's pantry, and the added second level was fully utilized. The warm hues of the quarter-sawn oak cabinetry gave the room a very updated English Edwardian look. Maybell had come down from DC and set everything up. He was grateful it would take him a little time to find everything he needed to put the tea together. He had to search for the sugar. Fortunately, Maybell walked in just as he was pouring the tea into the glasses.

"Land's sake, Hew! What are you doing? The hell's that mess?"

"The bishop, dean, and Edward are here visiting. I've made tea?"

She cackled. "Tea? That ain't even fit for dog water. Get back out there with your guests and let me do this. Tea!"

She used his late grandmother Bishop's best small silver tray. She put the tea into his Waterford cut-leaded crystal iced tea glasses. She also used the silver iced tea spoons and four linen cocktail napkins from the butler's pantry. She retrieved a lemon in the refrigerator and arranged several slices on a small plate. Hew always added a slice to his unsweet tea. The acid in the lemon cut the alkaline bitterness.

When Hew walked back onto the terrace, they were standing by the rail, talking, looking down, admiring the view of the cathedral.

Hew tried to lighten the mood with the comment, "Angels we have heard on high."

The bishop turned and quipped, "We're not angels yet." That got a laugh.

Maybell walked out onto the terrace, and Hew made the introductions.

Once she had left, Edward began. "As the attorney, I believe this is very complete and most extraordinary. I'm not sure what to say, but it seems everything was reported correctly."

The bishop spoke next. "Yes, Edward, I'm satisfied pending the meeting with the police this afternoon, of course, but what an ordeal. Hew, may I just say how profoundly sorry I am, we all are, this has happened to you. God was surely with you last night. I must ask, however, for you tell us more of this story."

Edward quickly came to his rescue. "Gentlemen, as far as the events of last night are concerned, I'm completely satisfied the documents before you contain the full and sordid facts of the case. Frankly, I'm still trying to process it all myself. I'm especially shocked and deeply saddened at this new revelation of the murder of my best friend and partner. I would ask you to leave it where it stands."

The dean saw his opening. "That's fine with me for now, but, Hew, I want to ask you a question of a more personal nature, if you don't mind."

"Sure. Fire away, but Edward may step in if he doesn't want me to answer."

"Hew, you are named, well, somewhat named, for one of my ancestral grandmothers. Is that a coincidence?"

He hadn't expected that! Fortunately, XI had told him the whole story in great detail.

"No, sir. It isn't a coincidence at all. You must be an ancestor of James Bishop. James and my ancestor, Capt'n John, were brothers. James had a daughter who married Lord Stewart. John and James' father was Sir William Bishop, and their mother was Charteris Hew, Lady Elizabeth Ramsay of Clatto, Midlothan, Scotland. She seemed to be my most interesting Bishop ancestor, so when I had to leave DC, I adopted her name. My grandfather was John Bishop XI, and my father was John Bishop XII. I was baptized John Bishop XIII. We changed my name hoping to avoid the incident that just happened. It almost worked. You and I are cousins, several times removed." He laughed.

"What a small world," remarked the bishop. "There are entirely too many Bishops for me to remember, but I'm the only official one here. Y'all seem to have your own House of Bishops, Hew. If we were Roman Catholic, y'all could be a conclave of cardinals."

"Or a house of English kings," added Edward.

"No, no. You would all need to be dead for any of that," quipped the dean.

"I damned nearly was." Hew put his hand over his mouth. "Oops, sorry." Everyone laughed, and it broke the seriousness of the meeting.

"Oh it gets better, sir. Dean, your name Stewart should tell you something. There are probably thousands of y'all in America at this moment. There are probably several in St. Philip's."

Edward was interested in the story. "Hew, why the spelling, Stewart rather than Stuart?"

"Grandfather said both are used interchangeably, but Stewart is usually associated with the Scottish side, while Stuart is used by the French side. Mary Queen of Scots changed the spelling while she was living in France to preserve the Scot's pronunciation."

Edward continued, "So you two are descended from British royalty?"

"I doubt it, but if it's true, then probably French too. Edward, I don't really know, and Grandfather never said much about it. The Ramsays were Norman descendants of Vikings and fought at the Battle of Hastings with William the Conqueror. It was so long ago it hardly seems to matter now, but, Dean, your connection to the royal Stewarts is probably stronger than mine."

"Oh no, you don't," exclaimed the bishop. "I'm the only bishop in this diocese, and I will absolutely not bow to any Scottish/English/French royal Bishops or royal Stewart/Stuarts in my cathedral."

More laughter. The man actually had a sense of humor after all. Edward quipped, "It sounds like you may not have a choice, Richard."

"So is your birth name John Bishop—I've lost track of the numbers, thirteen?"

"Yes, sir. At school in DC, before my name change, I was simply called John."

"Tell me more about your need to change your name."

Edward quickly responded, "I'll tell y'all later. That's highly confidential, and it'll take too long to go into now."

"One more question. I know a little of my ancestral history, but do you know anything about the title Charteris Hew?"

"Charteris is the name of the clan that came from Chartres, France, with William the Conqueror in 1066. They settled in the Scottish lowlands near Edinburgh. *Hew* literally means to hew wood, or maybe, anyone with the title Hew was a guard who chopped off the heads of the enemies." He laughed.

"More than I wanted to know with the last bit, Hew, but thank you. I too am sorry about your ordeal. Very sorry."

The bishop stepped in to bring them back to the matter at hand. "I want you to set up an appointment to meet with my archdeacon.

Her title is the venerable archdeacon Mrs. Carrington, but you may hear folks here simply call her Cindy. She and her four assistants manage all of the property in the diocese, and she manages all the welfare needs of our clergy, staff, and their families. She is a very fine musician, so y'all will bond easily, and I think you should talk about last night and anything else that may be troubling you. I would also like to meet with your parents as soon as possible, please."

Edward jumped to his rescue. Edward knew Hew could never open up to anyone, including the archdeacon.

He stopped the conversation short.

"One other item, Hew." Edward opened his briefcase. "Sign this will right now! Thank God you made it through the ordeal last night. I would have had a legal nightmare to deal with. Perhaps Richard and James will be good enough to witness this for you."

Hew half-laughed. "Thanks a lot for thinking about your problems first, Edward."

"We'll both be happy to witness this, Edward."

*****

Hew started to relax a little. He changed into his soccer shorts. He decided to go for a soak in his pool on the terrace. To help ease the stress of the past few hours, he went into what, in a few weeks, would be a copy of his grandfather's wine cellar. He had brought a few cases with him. He brought two cases of Franciscan Magnificat from DC. He liked the name because it reminded him of the song he sang as a small child with the choir before they stuck him in the hellhole school. The wine was a blend of cabernet sauvignon, merlot, and petit verdot. XI loved it, and Hew was looking forward to his first glass in his new home. He opened it and decanted it as he had watched Douglas do. He wanted to allow it to breathe. He planned to drink it later with dinner. He had found an unopened box in XI's wine cellar that contained a large crystal Riedel Amadeo Double Magnum decanter. Apparently it had been a gift and was very contemporary. The name Amadeo reminded Hew of Mozart, and he loved the clean contemporary lines. He also brought a case of Cade white and a case of Dominus. XI loved those wines, and the cellar had many cases of them. Hew opened XI's old humidor and took out one of his Cuban Cohiba Esplendido cigars. XI had let him smoke a few of those while they talked in his library in the evenings. Hew trimmed the tip with XI's cutter and struck a wooden match to the tip. XI said a fine cigar should never be lit with a nasty butane lighter. The smell ruined the taste. XI preferred to use the flame from a fine beeswax candle, but Hew hadn't remembered to pack one. He then opened a bottle of XI's rare Macallan 1926 single-malt scotch. This was a special occasion, after all. He poured himself a wee dram into one of his nosing glasses. XI had also told him that fine scotch should never be chilled with ice or diluted with water. Hew was not sure he would be able to follow that rule given the heat and humidity of Atlanta. He walked out onto his terrace, grabbed a float, and climbed into the pool.

Fifteen minutes later, his phone rang. "Hi, Edward. Tell me I didn't screw up."

"No, but you should have been a fly on the wall during the elevator ride down."

"I don't understand. Why would I want to be a fly on a wall?"

"Oh, sorry. I forget you've only been back in this country a few years. It is an American expression for eavesdropping. If a fly could talk, it could tell everything it had heard because no one ever notices a fly on the wall."

"Okay, you be the fly and start talking."

"Simply put, the bishop and the dean are convinced there is more to your life story than you told them. The bishop will instruct the archdeacon to get it out of you. I was, of course, in a very awkward position, so I simply stayed silent. You must be careful if you talk with her. The bishop asked if you always referred to your ancestors by number. I laughed and told him the family always did because it was the only way to keep them straight. Those old Scots weren't very creative when it came to naming their sons. I told him the boys at Exeter had simply called your grandfather XI. We're going to the club for dinner, so let me pick you up."

"Thanks, but I'm very tired. I already have dinner ready. I was just getting out of the pool when you called. I've made a salad." It was a small lie, but he intended to make a salad, so no problem.

"Okay. We're going to Canoe tomorrow night. It's my favorite restaurant. It's down on the bank of the Chattahoochee River. How about seven?"

"Sounds good. I'll be in the lobby."

CHAPTER 16

England

"Hew, you've got to go back into the cathedral. The choir's counting on you for the trip."

"I know, Tippy. Maybe I won't go back after dark for a while."

"Charlie will go with you when you practice if that's the problem."

"Ha. He would drive me crazy! No, I've got to face it sooner rather than later. I have been practicing for the trip, though. I stumbled onto a fantastic website while looking for new music. It's called Hauptwerk, and it's a group of virtual organs that are unbelievable. I ordered a four-manual console and purchased the Hereford Cathedral sample set. It runs on a large Mac Pro 5.1 with dual 3.33Hz 6-core and 128 GB of RAM. Once it arrives, I'll be able to practice at home."

Edward asked, "That's Greek to me. How does it work? You're going to have two organs in your library?"

Charlie chimed in. "I know what that is, Dad. It's a pretty sweet setup."

"Yes, Edward. The two organs will allow me to have maximum flexibility. To answer your first question, basically, a group of sound engineers got permission to set up microphones in the Hereford Cathedral and sample each individual pipe in its natural acoustical environment. They wrote code that lets anyone with the program play the sounds from their own consoles. The sound plays through my stereo speakers, and it's better than a CD, in my opinion. The full reverberation of the cathedral can be reproduced in my library. It's not quite the same as the instrument in Lincoln Cathedral, but it will allow Rob and me to practice using unique English sounds without working around other events in St. Philips. While my real organ is perfect for Baroque and early organ music, this one is a great substitute for practicing English cathedral music of the nineteenth- and early-twentieth-century works."

Hew showed up for the weekly choir practice, and life got back to normal. The venerable archdeacon, Mrs. Carrington—the bishop had been right, everyone just called her Cindy—was a guest soloist for the final fund-raising concert for the cathedral choir's trip to England. She had a fine, classically trained voice. Her priestly duties were demanding and didn't allow her to sing the services with the choir, but she had been asked to sing the alto part for Purcell's 1649 Canticles, Jubilate, and Te Deum in D major, Z 232, parts one and two. The music was written for a choir and orchestra and was considered too expansive for a normal modern Sunday service. Together they run about fifteen minutes. The orchestral brass opened with a beautiful but rather theatrical flourish. She could sing the difficult passages with ease.

The audience loved the concert, and they finally raised enough money to allow everyone in the choir to have a full scholarship for the trip. The tumultuous standing ovation ran so long that Dr. Withersby raised his arms for quiet and then turned to Hew and asked him to pick a hymn and accompany the congregation.

"We'll now have a treat. You'll hear from our new assistant sub-organist, Hew Ramsay. He's never played for you before, so this is his premier."

It took him by surprise. Was this a new position? He hadn't practiced anything, so he would just have to wing it. Without thinking, he picked one of his favorites from the hymnal.

Hew took the microphone and announced, "Number 665."

"Number 665 is Herbert Howells's great hymn, Michael. The verse begins, 'All my hope on God is founded.' Howells wrote the hymn about 1936 to the words of Robert Bridges's 1899 translation of Joachim Neander's 1680 German text. This hymn resonates with me, perhaps because Howells wrote it after his young son, Michael, died. He named the hymn Michael, and it is about hope." Hope was something Hew had never had, but Atlanta was beginning to teach him.

The sub-organist moved away, and Hew sat down on the bench and selected his stops. He whispered to Cindy loudly enough that the choir and orchestra could hear and asked her to take the fourth verse, "Daily doth the Almighty Giver bounteous gifts on us bestow," as an unaccompanied solo. She smiled and nodded. He began the introduction on the organ's trumpets using just the last few measures of the tune. He moved his hands to the great manual, and the choir and congregation came in spot on with the aid of Dr. Withersby and raised the roof with their voices. After her fine solo, Hew began an improvisation as an interlude working through a few minor chords to give it a more modern sound. He was just getting cranked up when he spotted Dr. Withersby urgently pointing at his watch, so he quickly started back to the home key. The brass suddenly joined in. It gave him goose bumps. The congregation, choir, and orchestra finished the last verse with gusto. He had just finished his first solo performance in the cathedral.

After the concert, there was a champagne reception in the Great Hall. Cindy came up to Hew to congratulate him and thank him for giving her the solo. She was very easy to talk with. Too easy, but Edward had warned him.

*****

They left Atlanta the following Sunday evening. The choir flew to Manchester and took the train to Lincoln. It was a little less expensive than going through Heathrow and then up to Lincoln. They would be one of the summer choirs in residence for a week at Lincoln Cathedral while Lincoln's choir was on holiday. Hew took the Stewarts, Cindy, Dr. Withersby—they all called him Dr. W—and the sub-organist, Rob, with him on the new Swan Bay long-range jet. He gave the Stewarts the aft bedroom. Everyone except Hew had cocktails. They ate dinner over New York. Hew had a small keyboard setup on board. Dr. W spied it.

"That's an interesting setup you've got there."

"It's a Casio single keyboard portable Hauptwerk digital system using my MacBook Pro. It's not as powerful as the one in my library, and the keys aren't the right touch for the organ, but I use this one to compose while I'm traveling. I can even edit a few notes at a time on my iPad. My preferred method, though, is still pen and paper."

"Ah, the wonders of the young computer age, but a pen? A pencil will allow you to make changes easier."

"But a good solid swipe through the wrong notes with a bold felt-tipped pen is more satisfying and reduces second guessing."

"Whatever. Here's the list of hymns I selected for the Evensongs. You've got a few hours. Why don't you compose a few interludes between some of the verses to add a little more festive sound to them. I'll select those I like."

"Dr. W." He laughed. "I provided the ride, the cocktails, the wine, and your supper. Now you want me to sing for it too? Besides, I don't want to intrude on Rob."

"Hew," Rob chimed in, "after that improvised work of art you just whipped up for the Howells, I can't wait to hear your next one. Go for it. Did you miss the announcement? You've been promoted to assistant sub-organist. I'm now called the canon organist."

"Did I get a raise? I can use the money you know." Everyone laughed.

"Sure," added the dean. "You were paid nothing, and we doubled that."

More laughter. "I know you will rise to the occasion. We've already seen you in action."

The weather was clear for the entire trip. They landed at Lincoln after having showers, a change of clothes, and breakfast over Iceland and Ireland. The choir was still on the train but would go directly to the hotel. The dean met with the dean of Lincoln. The organists went to find the Cathedral Choir School. They spent the remainder of the morning getting to know the cathedral organ. The choir sang their first Evensong that afternoon.

On Tuesday, Hew felt bad. It was jet lag. He had spent the entire night on the plane composing. Whenever the music began in his brain, he had to let it play out. He begged off his duties as Rob's assistant, and one of the choir members stepped in to cover for him. He stayed in his room for most of the day, but by Evensong, he was feeling much better and wandered into the nave to listen. In the long English afternoon light of that beautiful summer day, as he wandered around the empty nave listening to the music and looking at the windows, the choir began singing Stanford's Magnificat in C. He stopped. They had risen to the occasion. Dr. W, himself a Brit, had drilled the correct English pronunciation into them. He heard the piece as he had never heard it before. He thought it was grand when he had sung it as a small boy. He had practiced it many times when the choir sang it in Atlanta, but here, somehow, this was something special. After the second lesson, they started singing the Gloria Patri following Stanford's Nunc Dimitis. Hew was standing alone beside the South nave wall, far from the eyes of the choir, and he just sank to his knees on the floor and started sobbing! All his problems had suddenly burst forth, and he was glad for the solitude of that space.

Hew returned to the choir school after the service to congratulate them. As he was leaving with them to go to the pub, he heard bells. They sounded different. The ringing was ordered, but they weren't ringing a melody. He wanted to know more. Hew asked the Lincoln dean, "How do the bells make that unusual sound?"

The dean laughed. "That's called English Changing Ringing. It's done by a band of ringers pulling on the ropes. This is their practice night. I'll show you the stairs, but you're on your own after that. When you get to the top, wait outside until they stop and then walk in and introduce yourself. They are a very friendly group."

They walked back to the west front and into a small room on the south side known as the Ringers' Chapel. The medieval room was decorated with paintings and plaques commemorating several hundred years of ringing achievements and monuments to ringers who had died in the wars.

The dean pointed to a small door and said, "Good luck."

He hadn't told Hew there were 365 winding stone steps up to the ringing room. Hew was out of breath and doubled over gasping for air by the time he reached the door. When the ringing stopped, he walked in and introduced himself to a very friendly group. They asked him if he rang, and he said no, but he wanted to learn.

"Anyone who makes that trip and lives deserves to have a lesson. Would you like a quick pull on a rope?"

"Sure."

He was an old guy, but he was Hew's height. He handed him the tail of a rope. "Place your feet comfortably apart. Good. Relax. We're not going to get you hanged tonight. Put your right hand here, and tuck your left hand here with your left thumb resting in the palm of your right hand."

Hew did as he was told.

"Yes. Good. Now, don't pull until I tell you. Don't jerk or pull hard. The bell will do the hard work. You just guide the rope. Don't look up! There're hundreds of years of dirt up there. We don't want any of it in your eyes. Keep your eyes on me handsome face." That got a laugh from the band.

The teacher pulled the bright wooly part, and the rope went up quickly. Hew felt the rope pulling his hands up, and he looked up. "Don't look up, boy. Keep them eyes on me!"

On the next cycle, Hew did much better. After ten tries, he thought he was doing fine. The band agreed, and they all applauded. "You're a natural, boy. If you stayed in town a few weeks longer, I could make a first-rate ringer out of you. You're a real natural. Practice is finished. Come with us to the pub."

Hew thought their English beer was better than the stuff the guys drank in the Ops Center, but it was still beer. He managed to get his pint down, though. The ringing lesson was fun, and he sensed that the bells were larger and had a better tone than the chapel bells in Bogota. After the Eucharist on Sunday, the choir said goodbye to the good folks at Lincoln and took the train down to Peterborough for a week at another famous cathedral.

*****

The organists practiced for hours learning the cathedral instrument. It wasn't pitched at A440, so they had to work with it. The cathedral was huge! For Sunday Matins, the choir sang the Purcell again with Cindy as the soloist. After the Eucharist, they moved by train for their final week at Dr. W's alma mater, New College, Oxford. Dr. W had proudly told them that New College, Oxford, was old when King's College, Cambridge, was founded. They all visited the Bate Collection of musical instruments in Oxford. There were over two thousand instruments of almost every description on display. They also toured many of the colleges. It was another memorable week.

On Sunday, everyone departed for home, but by prior arrangement, Hew stayed. The organist at New College was off on his holiday, but Dr. W and Dean Stewart had sent letters of introduction to the dean at the Cathedral Church of Christ, Oxford. Hew had an appointment with the sub-organist for two months of lessons. The sub-organist was considered a master. Dr. W wanted him to experience English cathedral music in situ, as he called it. Hew arrived in the gallery early.

*****

"You can only be Charteris Hew Ramsay. I'm Colin Singen-Smith. Here's my card. You may reach me at any time you are practicing and I'm not here." Hew noticed that Singen was spelled St. John-Smith. He was going to need to learn a new language too, he thought. Colin had a dry, sarcastic "let it all hang out" wit, and Hew liked him immediately. "So what's in a name, Charteris Hew Ramsay? You do see that I know how to pronounce Charteris correctly, but I'll bet Singen took you by surprise."

Hew told him about his ancestor. "Oh god. I hope you didn't inherit her stubborn Scot's attitude. Englishmen can't teach anything to a Scot! They refuse to listen! Okay, I understand you want to be immersed in English cathedral music. We'll start with an Anglican chant. Show me what you know. I'll sing, and you play." He put a score of Psalm 23 on the music rack. "I shouldn't need to explain the meaning of this one to you."

The Oxford Cathedral organ was a modern instrument. Hew noticed that the keyboards seemed to overhang the ones below slightly more than the console in Atlanta.

"Oh, you'll get used to it. I'll be your assistant to help you get started, but you'll be on your own during most of your practice sessions. Let's get started. It's getting on tea time."

*****

"Well, you certainly accompanied it like a Scot. It sounded like the drone of a damned bagpipe."

"But, sir, that's the way it's written."

"Right. Call me Colin. I'm not knighted—yet. Well, I wrote it especially for today's lesson, and that score is intentionally vanilla, just to see if you would slavishly follow it." He laughed. "You did, but at least you didn't drown out the words, and the words are paramount. Here, let me play it using the final score, and you sing."

*****

"Damn! You've a fine voice. Do you see the difference? I played the notes as written, but I also varied the accompaniment to do just a little word-painting using various stops to add to the meaning. An English organ builder named Robert Hope-Jones is considered the father of the theater organ. He began experimenting when movies first became popular. He used an organ to add sound effects to the silent films. Very gradually, we church organists began adding certain 'effects' to color our psalms. I played the line 'Yea tho I walk' on the pedals only to add a slight emphasis to the idea of darkness, and I played the line 'and I will dwell' on a light flute to add a little descant of an angelic emphasis.

"It's subtle, but it helped to emphasize the words. That's the art, and that's what I'll be teaching you. Do you know the work of Sir John Stainer? He wrote a fine treatise on playing Anglican chant. You need to go to the library and find it. Essentially he said—and mind you, this was written over a hundred years ago—'The Anglican chant is simple as a musical form, but to play an accompaniment to suit the varying sentiment of the words materially increases the difficulties. In order to obtain perfect freedom in the accompanying of the Psalms, it is necessary that the player should have a thorough knowledge of the words.' You must absolutely memorize that! Above all, you must avoid exaggerations of your word-painting. A little goes a long way. No staccato 'drops of rain,' and that sort of theatrical claptrap. We're British, you know. In our tradition, organ music has tended to be a backdrop to the choir. I think you Yanks tend to let it all hang out. But we do have our preludes and postludes. Have you studied plainsong?"

"Yes, sir—er, Colin. I was a student at St. Thomas Fifth Avenue in New York and then a student in a Catholic Franciscan school in Colombia when my parents moved to Cali. In Colombia, that's about all we sang."

"Ah. So you played Catholic Masses as well. Show me how you accompany Gregorian chant."

Hew played the same psalm.

"That's actually very nice. Very ancient. You must teach me a thing or two for some of this. Improvise for me."

Hew played as Father had taught him.

"Very nice. French. Plainsong-based improvisation. I'll teach you the English method if you'll help me brush up on my French method.

"I'm going to introduce you to one of our choral scholars who is a master of the psalms. I know you've studied and sung them individually, but you need to fully understand the meaning of each one in context with the lessons and gospels to be able to properly accompany them. He's also a fine baritone. Now, I'm thirsty. Let's go over to the Buttery for a pint and get to know each other."

Hew took tea, while Colin drank a pint. Dean Stewart had also arranged for him to have temporary rooms in the college, and he arranged for him to take his meals in the Hall. Hew realized that the hall was outstanding. He recognized the stairwell leading to the hall from the Harry Potter movies. The dining hall was a sixteenth-century hall with hammer beam trusses, old wood paneling, and old paintings. Hew was a modernist, but even he could appreciate why people called this room one of the seven architectural wonders of the world. There was even an *Alice in Wonderland* window because Lewis Carroll had taught here. Hew started trying to devise a software program to allow a computer to reproduce and cut the timbers in the roof, but he decided no one would ever be able to afford another roof such as this. Still, there might just be a historic preservation use for such a program. He thought that perhaps this one could be scanned. He finally quit his daydreaming. He had other work to do.

*****

She saw him limp through the west door of the cathedral as she walked along the south terrace of Tom Quad. The sun produced striking shadows in his unruly, curly mop of blond hair. She thought he needed a haircut. He seemed to be stretching his leg, but when he started walking, he was very tall and trim. He turned left and walked toward the hall. His leg seemed fine to her. She dropped back and followed him up the grand stair of Bodley Tower. She was getting excited just watching him walk up the stairs! She was in line just behind him. She was a modern languages major from York, but she couldn't place his accent when he spoke to the cashier. Certainly not British. American, but with a very slight, almost imperceptible Spanish inflection. Miami? Southern California?

Perhaps a Spanish parent? She wanted to know more. She approached his table and asked if she could join him. They ate and played the "who are you" game. He dodged some of her questions.

"You have a slight Spanish inflection in some of your words and phrases."

He had no idea he still had a Spanish inflection. He had worked hard to eliminate Spanish from his life. No one else had ever mentioned it. She persisted about the Spanish inflections.

He simply commented, "I had a Hispanic nanny. Until I was six, I was with her every day until my parents came home from work."

It worked, and it really wasn't a lie. He felt her foot moving up the inside of his leg. "Let's skip dessert, Rose."

"We call it pudding, but yes, let's nip on."

A few minutes later, they were in his room ripping each other's clothes off. This time, he led. He only had an hour before his next lesson in the cathedral, but they made the most of it. They spent almost every night and weekend in bed. By the time he left Oxford, she had helped him obliterate his Spanish inflection. It was replaced with an Oxonian inflection, but he could live with that! He was going to miss Oxford.

Hew spent long hours in the cathedral. Even though it was summer, it was still a busy place, and his practice time had to work around the services and events. The evenings were quiet, though. On the first Tuesday evening, his knee was bothering him, so he left early. As he walked out of the cathedral, he heard bells. The sound was not coming from Bodley Tower, though. The sound seemed to be coming from across Aldate Street in front of Tom Tower. He started to follow the sound. The ringing stopped while he was crossing the street, and a small group came out of the church. Hew assumed they were ringers going to the pub, so he followed. He had been told that going to the pub after ringing was a required part of every practice.

"Excuse me, but are y'all the ringers I heard a few minutes ago?"

One of the women said, "'Y'all'?"

"Oh, excuse me, that's a Southern expression for *you all*."

"Yes, we know. And we learned another expression: *uh-huh*." They all laughed.

"Take a pew and join us, mate. Most of us have been to the States and your South many times. Our first trip was back in, oh, I think it was 1990, to Charleston, South Carolina. We've rung at all of the towers in North America. Are you a ringer at one of the Atlanta towers?"

Jokingly Hew answered, "Uh-uh." *No.* They doubled over laughing.

Hew had no idea there were two towers in the Atlanta area.

Hew introduced himself. The Brits had an odd way of never really telling a stranger their surnames. He had gotten used to it. One of the guys, Clive, bought him a pint. More beer. Oh well, when in Rome.

Again, someone asked, "Do you ring?" It was always the first question.

"I had my first lesson at Lincoln Cathedral two weeks ago. I had no idea there were bells in Atlanta. I'm the assistant sub-organist at the Cathedral of St. Philip in Atlanta."

"Lincoln? Well, you are special. After the trip up to the ringing room, most nonringers don't survive to tell about it!"

Everyone, including Hew, laughed. "I'm here until the end of August learning to play Anglican service music at Christ Church, and I have rooms there. Is there somewhere here I can take ringing lessons?"

"I thought you looked familiar. I'm the cashier in the hall. I've seen you several times. You're the polite one. From Atlanta. No wonder. Now I know why you aren't like all of the other snotty-nosed undergrads." That got a knowing laugh.

Hew bought the next round and now had new friends. "Yes, Hew. We are members of the Oxford Society of Change Ringers. The society was founded in 1734, and several of us will be happy to give you lessons."

The wife of one of the ringer quipped, "They won't tell you, but you've just stumbled into one of the premier ringing societies in the world."

"Now, now, enough of that, Shirley. You're giving him the wrong impression." More laughter as the beer started to do its work.

Hew asked, "I do have a question, well, many questions, but I didn't recognize the tune y'all were playing. Tell me about it."

"Oh, well, we don't play tunes. We have eight diatonically tuned bells, so there are only a few tunes that could even be chimed on these bells. The revolution of the bells takes about 1.5 seconds between sounds, so we couldn't manage repeating notes. We memorize methods, and each ringer plays the same method but at a different time. It's like the little song 'Are You Sleeping, Brother John.' As a musician, you'll understand canon theory."

"Sure. I get it. In a way, it's like a fugue."

"Oh, yes. We're all masters of the fugue!"

One of the guys quipped, "Sounds a bit bawdy if you ask me."

Everyone had a good laugh since most of them had very little knowledge of the meaning of the word *fugue*.

"We have several towers at our disposal around town, and many of us can work to your daily schedule. We are normally restricted from ringing at Carfax except on special occasions, and we only ring at Lincoln College when invited because the tower is part of the old Christopher Wren-designed chapel, and it's now used as the college library, but you're in luck. Friday of next week is the Queen's actual birthday, and we'll ring all of the bells in all of the towers for that. Come with us and we'll give you a pull so you can say you've rung in all of the towers. We'll have you in a quarter peal before you leave Oxford."

"There's a service in the cathedral tomorrow morning, so I have some time."

"Meet me at nine at St. Aldate. That's across from Tom Tower. You saw us there tonight. I have time between breakfast and lunch, so I'll give you your first lesson before we start the day's ringing."

Hew started again with the tail of the rope. He spent every available hour for the next two weeks with various members of the society, but finally, he was able to control the bell. He heard the phrase "You are a natural" several more times. Hew went to every practice night. They had a minder standing behind him, telling him when to pull and how to make small adjustments in his rope work.

"Ring the bell. Just relax and do it."

That was easier said than done. After a practice in July, he was told, "Hew, we've scheduled you to ring the tenor for a quarter peal of Grandsire Caters on the ten bells at St. Thomas tomorrow at two. It lasts about forty-five minutes. You'll be a pro when you finish."

"But I don't—"

"It's about learning the rhythm. Don't worry, we'll all help."

Standing in a circle facing each other with a rope in their hands, the opening words were always the same. The treble ringer shouted, "Catch hold. Look too, treble's going. Treble's gone."

In order, from smallest bell, called the treble, to the largest bell, the tenor, they pulled their ropes in turn. They rang down the musical scale, and they called this ringing rounds.

More English oddities, he thought.

He was feeling positive about his ringing, but about ten minutes into the ringing, the old guy on the treble yelled, "Get that bell up, boy. You ain't been in the right place yet!"

Oh hell. He wondered, *How?* The other ringers began to nod to get his attention, and suddenly he realized it was a sign for him to just ring after each of them. It didn't take long to actually see a pattern, and his ringing improved.

Afterward in the pub, they bought him a pint and congratulated him. The treble ringer apologized for yelling. "I wern't criticizing, boy. I needed to git yer attention, that's all."

"No need to apologize, sir. It worked. Thanks."

By the time Hew had to say goodbye to his new friends in Oxford, he had rung the tenor to a respectable three-hour peal of Grandsire on the bells at St. Thomas Church. The treble ringer didn't need to yell at him either. Afterward, they threw a party for him. There was a bell-shaped chocolate cake, and they all drank from their large porcelain bowl. It reminded Hew of the chamber pots in the sideboards at home, except this one was brown! He invited them all to Atlanta on their next trip.

*****

Hew and Colin were sitting in the Buttery. "Look at this score for the Magnificat and Nunc Dimittis. I think you'll like this since you've also become an English change ringer. It was written by the twentieth-century composer Kenneth Leighton, and it includes a small passage imitating bells. We'll sing it at your final Evensong with us. You'll play it. Do you know Louis Vierne's 'Carillon de Westminster'? With your abilities with French works, you must learn it. You can play it for your final postlude. Oh, and I must introduce you to Sir John Stainer's 'For God So Loved the World.' You can wow everyone in Atlanta with it during Holy Week. God, I've really got to teach you to drink beer."

"I've never heard the Leighton pieces or the Vierne. I know the Stainer. I think I'll start composing organ pieces to include bells when I get home."

"Bells! No doubt they'll work their way over here. Send me your compositions. Oh, do you know the work of the contemporary Estonian composer Arvo Part? He has created a new style he calls tintinnibuli, from the Latin word for *bell.* You'll love it. It's modern, minimalist, classical music based in part—no pun intended, well, yes, it was—on Gregorian chant. His religious music must become part of your development." Colin laughed at his own cleverness. "How about the 'Ringer's Hymn'? Do you know it? It's based on the eight bell changes, and my friend John Rutter has written a new Christmas piece called 'All Bells in Paradise,' and an organ score named 'Festive Bells.' Oh, oh, I heard your Bach yesterday as I passed by. Do you know his Prelude and Fugue in C Major? It's BWV 547, if I remember. The pedal part in the prelude repeats what some say is a bourdon bell like ding-dong theme. I like to play it using a sixteen-foot reed for extra punch. Lots to learn, hmmm? But back to basics. Come on, we need to get to work. I want you to be able to compose your own Anglican chants before you go back to the colonies. I want you to apply to be our organ scholar next year. You'll learn to play proper English services better than anyone you know!"

"I wish I could, but I'm starting med school in the fall, so there just won't be time, unfortunately."

"Medicine? Ah yes, well, at least you won't be another starving musician. I have a radical idea. You block out next summer and come back here. I'll give you a crash course, put you through the ringer, so to speak." Colin was on a roll now as the pints began to kick in.

"That I can do!"

"Okay, now here's another idea. Since you'll be studying all the time and can't always go to your cathedral to practice, look at www.Hauptwerk.com and buy yourself a virtual pipe organ digital practice organ for those late nights in your flat when you can't sleep. They have virtual instruments you can download, and the sound is amazing. It'll work on a digital keyboard, but if you can spare the dollars, buy yourself a three- or four-manual console. Just use headphones to keep the neighbors from complaining. You can get several very nice English cathedral instruments to play that way. It's amazingly convincing, even for a purist like me. I've just ordered a four-manual setup for my flat. Of course, I've got to sell my dining room furniture to have a place to put it but, hey, can't have my tea and biscuits or a martini in the cathedral when I practice, so there's the bright side."

Hew didn't tell him about the setup he already had or about the Flentrop that was waiting on him.

"You must come to Atlanta and stay with me. Atlanta is different from most of the rest of the US."

CHAPTER 17

Scotland

"Sir, if I'm reading this correctly, I want to leave Oxford at 9:39 a.m. tomorrow from platform 4. One first-class ticket, please."

The train traveled up the coast, and at certain points, the tracks were only a few feet from the North Sea. Hew ate breakfast in the dining car and watched as Peterborough and Durham Cathedrals came into view. He also saw an amazing twisted spire on a church tower in the distance. He took a cab from the station to Dalhousie Castle. It had been built in the thirteenth century as one of the Ramsay castles, but now it was a twenty-nine-room inn, and he would spend his first night there. He had changed into his Ramsay kilt on the train.

"Welcome tae Dalhousie Castle, Mr. Ramsay."

The young man standing behind the desk seemed surprised at both Hew's age and Ramsay kilt. Hew noticed the guy was wearing a kilt. Hew handed him the black AmEx card.

"Would you wait a moment, please? There's someone here awaitin' yer arrival, sir."

Hew had a difficult time understanding the brogue. He wondered whom it could be.

"Hello, laddie. Ah was expectin' someone older. Please excuse me. You're wearing the Ramsay tartan?"

"I'm a direct descendant of Charteris Hew, Lady Elizabeth Ramsey."

"American's have it wrong, laddie. Bishops are th' direct descendants."

"Yes, I know, and for reasons I can't discuss, I'm the thirteenth generation. I still own the original tobacco farm in Virginia."

"Swan Bay? It still exists?"

"Yes, it does. May I ask your name, sir?"

"Forgive me for my surprise. I'm Sir John Cochrane. Somehow, we're cousins."

"My mother was a Cochrane."

"En we're dooble cousins an' ye may call me John. Dine wi' me tonight in th' dinin' room here. Ah want tae hear aw about yer lineage.

"James, show our cousin to th' Simundus De Ramseia Suite, please, and, Hew, put yer card awa'. You'll be our guest tonight. You'll like this suite, I think. 'Tis th' area which still has th' charm of th' auld castle before everythin' was Americanized."

He was right. The ceiling was of vaulted stone, the walls were original stone, and there was a well in the sitting room. It was once the guard room for the old well. Hew loved it. On his way to meet his cousin in the library turned bar, Hew noticed a huge ancestral chart on the corridor wall, and he saw the names of Lady Elizabeth's relatives. There was a description of the various kilt patterns as well. He was clearly in the right place. At dinner, they drank a wee dram. Hew had changed into his blue-and-black Ramsay kilt, which seemed to surprise and please his cousin. Sir John was wearing a kilt also, but his kilt was the Cochrane tartan. It was predominately green with blue-and-red grids.

"Get yourself one of ours too."

Hew said, "Do I need three kilts? Between my kilts and my choir vestments, I might never need to wear pants again—or underwear!"

Sir John just laughed. Hew told him about his name change and the Bishop ancestors, and Sir John told Hew things about his mother's ancestry that XI had never told him. At the end of the meal, he asked Hew about his plans for the remainder of his stay.

"I plan to go back to Edinburgh and take the train to Glasgow. I want to see the Bishop dock area, and then I want to try to visit the Macallan Distillery."

"Not Ochiltree Castle too?"

"I understand it's in private ownership and not open to the public."

"But ye arenae 'public,' are ye, laddie?"

That hadn't occurred to Hew. "I have two portraits hanging in my new condo my grandfather told me were my ancestors who were married in St. Gile's, and the entire family stayed at Ochiltree."

"An' those portraits would be by John Singer Sargent?"

"Yes."

"En forget th' train. I'll pick you up and' take you to Glasgee and to Bishopsgate. I'll show you the Coltrane and Bishop houses on the Tobacco Lord's row of houses, and you'll bide th' night in my castle. It's only about three miles from here. 'En we'll set out for th' Macallan Distillery. We'll have a great time, laddie."

Hew had a fantastic time. Sir John drove his restored British racing green MG convertible. It was a five-hour trip through Scotland. The distillery tour took about two hours, and Sir John purchased three more cases of XI's favorite for Hew since he was underage. They managed to get them into the boot and started back. Hew had noticed at dinner cousin John liked a cigar, so he texted Jeffrey and asked him to put one of XI's boxes of Cuban Cohiba Esplendidos on the plane. The next afternoon, Sir John took him to the local airfield where the Swan Bay jet was waiting. James, the concierge, was standing by the jet wearing his Coltrane kilt with his bagpipes ready to send Hew off with a tune. They were very impressed by the Bishop coat of arms on the tail of the jet. James helped the pilot load the scotch, and Hew invited him aboard. He presented Sir John with the cigars.

"Ah, laddie. Thank ye. We Scots dorn't usually spend this amount on our pleasures, so ah'll enjoy them durin' may lang winter nights by the fire while ah sip my wee dram an' remember th' grand time we had together."

"Perhaps you will visit Swan Bay next winter. I'll send this jet."

After his flight attendant had served him lunch with two glasses of Franciscan Magnificat wine, He began to think about his new condo. Except for the installation of the Flentrop organ and a few other touches, it should be finished by the time he arrived. Going home. He relaxed and let out an audible sign and then remembered Sir Henry Bishop's melody, "Home Sweet Home." He googled it. The lyrics were by an American, J. H. Payne. He started reading, "Mid pleasures and palaces although we may roam, be it ever so humble, there's no place like home!"

He laughed out loud. Nothing humble about his penthouse. Then he remembered that Tippy had a piece of artwork—hand embroidered on a worn, stained cloth—framed over her desk with those lyrics. She had said that her great-grandmother had made it one summer in Highlands. He began to remember the words Ms. Mamie used—*sugar*, *honey*—all old Southern words of endearment. He began to remember his class on the history of Georgia, and he opened his composition book and started scribbling down notes. He lost track of time, but by the time he landed in Atlanta, he had composed a rough draft of his first symphony. This was for organ and orchestra. He called it "Home Sweet Home." It needed refining, but he was satisfied.

CHAPTER 18

Symphony

On Saturday evening, the Atlanta Symphony Youth Orchestra held a concert in the symphony hall. Hew, Edward, and Tippy had choice season ticket seats together in the center of the orchestra. The hall was full. At precisely 8:00 p.m., the conductor took the podium, acknowledged the applause, and raised his baton and launched into Beethoven's Fifth Symphony. Hew was not familiar with the work, but he loved it from the four-note opening through the tragedy to the triumph. He sensed a parallel to his own life.

During the intermission, Hew wandered through the lobby, observing the audience. Edward and Tippy were drinking wine while making the social rounds. The lights had flashed once, and he was about to return to his seat when the girls approached him from the side.

"Are you Hew Ramsay?"

She was a blond knockout. He smiled. "Yes, and you are?"

"I'm Amanda. This is my friend Lois."

Lois was a knockout brunette.

"I'm very glad to meet y'all."

"Is Charlie the one on the drums?"

"Yes, he's the principal percussionist. How did you know our names?"

"A friend at UVA told us to look for you at the youth concert. We missed it last time. She described you perfectly. My brother's in the orchestra too, so here we are. If you guys are free after this, we would love to meet you at a party."

"Sure. We can meet you there. Charlie has to mingle for a few minutes before we can leave." The lights flashed for the second time. "Text me the address. Here's my number. I've got to run."

The second half was Dvorak Symphony No. 9 in E minor, "From the New World." Charlie and the orchestra were nearly flawless and got a standing ovation with shouts of bravo resounding through the hall.

"Come on, Hew, I'm starving. Let's go eat."

"You're always either starving or horny. We're invited to a party by two knockout girls. You can get something to eat there."

Charlie started to put the address into his GPS but then decided he knew about where it was. They drove west on Tenth Street, through some streets west of GA Tech and onto West Marietta Street. They passed a railroad yard and started seeing old warehouses.

"Charlie, this area is dark and very run-down. I don't like the looks of it."

"Oh, don't worry. It's becoming very trendy now."

They saw cars and parked. They heard the thump of music and went inside. The old warehouse was packed. Charlie immediately went to the bar, where they were selling beer. Charlie bought three even though he knew Hew didn't like beer. He simply didn't want to fight his way back for another one. Hew was looking for the girls. It took him about ten minutes, but he found them. She and Lois had their backs to him, and they were talking to two other guys. The light was dim, but Hew saw the flash of white as the two guys raised their thumbs to the girls' noses. The girls snorted! Hew quickly turned to find Charlie. Charlie had just stepped up beside him and was already drinking his third beer. Hew grabbed his arm.

"Let's get the hell out of here. Now!"

"We just got here. I like this place."

"Now, Charlie. RIGHT NOW!" Hew was yelling and pulling on Charlie's arm as forcefully as he could. He was dragging Charlie toward the entrance.

"What the hell has gotten into you?"

"Drugs, Charlie. Drugs. Everywhere. Everywhere. Look." Suddenly Charlie saw a deal going down. "Oh shit! Come on, but you gotta drive. I'm a little tipsy. The beer hit my empty stomach very quickly."

As they were fighting their way through the throngs of people, Hew became very frightened. He hadn't felt that way since Jorge died. He was repeatedly muttering under his breath in Spanish, "Never put yourself in the way of sin. Never put yourself in the way of sin. Never…" It had been drilled into the boys by the priests, and he hadn't thought about it since his rescue, but it seemed appropriate now.

"What? I can't understand you. Speak louder!"

"Forget it, just move."

They drove back toward downtown. He was trying not to speed. They were less than three blocks away from the warehouse when they saw a caravan of flashing blue lights coming toward them at high speeds. It looked like a military invasion. Charlie turned to look back. "They're raiding the party. God! We just made it."

"We need an alibi right now, Charlie. Think."

"I don't really know…"

"Get in the game, Charlie. Think."

"I'm too hungry to think, and I'm a little drunk, but…"

"Okay. Food. That'll work. Tell me how to get to that Varsity drive-in restaurant you've been talking about. Is it near here? Get us there as fast as possible."

"Dammit!" Charlie muttered as they drove back toward town.

"What?"

"I said damnit. I was all set for a little sex. Now I'm just horny."

"You're always either thinking about sex or food."

"Yeah, and you're always thinking like an old man, Hew. Lighten up. Live a little. We're teenagers. It's okay to live, man."

"You're probably right." He sighed. "But at least I didn't get us arrested. Your parents would never let us forget that."

"Turn left here onto North Avenue."

The Varsity was a ninety-plus-year-old drive-in restaurant near the campus of Georgia Institute of Technology, known as GA Tech.

The Varsity was a Southern institution and had doggedly refused to change.

"What'll ya have? What'll ya have?"

"Two glorified burgers with strings, one large unsweet tea with lemon, and one large Coke, please."

Hew quickly paid with his AmEx card.

"Why the rush? We escaped. Let's enjoy the food. Settle down."

"I'm making this up as I go, but I want a time stamp on this receipt to show we were miles away when the raid started. Eat up. We need to get home as quickly as possible. Wolf it down or leave it, but we need to go."

"Slow down. I'm hungry."

"No, dammit. Take it with you then. If anyone you know saw you, they might squeal to save their own hide."

"Oh. Okay. I've never done this before. I didn't recognize anyone, though."

"But they might have recognized you, or me for that matter. We do stand out in a crowd. Let's get home before Edward and Tippy see it on the 11:00 p.m. news. Get up, dammit."

Charlie took one more large bite and left everything. He knew his mother didn't like the smell of food in her car. Hew was right about the news. It was the third story following a murder and a bank robbery. The cameras were live at the scene. Police and TV helicopters were buzzing overhead with bright searchlights, looking for escapees. They made it to the pool house without incident. Edward and Tippy were fast asleep anyway.

At 6:45 a.m., Hew's phone rang. "Um, good morning, Roller. What time is it?"

"Get up and turn on the local news. Get Charlie up too. Y'all need to see your work in action."

He walked to the sofa and turned on the TV. Charlie was still in his bed. "Okay, Roller, what will I be looking at?"

"Big raid in Atlanta last night. One of our DEA kids scored a big haul at a party in an old warehouse out in a seedy area."

The pictures were coming in. The announcer said nearly five hundred kids and scores of adults were still being arrested and loaded into vans. The arrests had been going on all night. Several cocaine dealers had been busted with bags of the stuff. There was a vast quantity of weed too.

"You and Charlie should be proud. That's our program."

"Wow! Just wow. Thanks for telling us, Roller. Talk again soon." Hew hung up just before he got sick. Charlie was just rolling out of bed when Hew came out of the bathroom. He backed up the show for Charlie and broke the news to him. Charlie started laughing uncontrollably.

"You think this is funny? You think this is a damned joke?"

"Damn right, Hew. We nearly got stung by our own sting!"

Hew thought a minute, and they both started laughing and rolling on the floor.

They were enjoying their early morning coffee while sitting at the table on the terrace. Edward was examining the commercial real estate section. Tippy had the social scene. The boys walked up from the pool house. Charlie poured himself a cup of coffee, but Hew declined, as usual.

Edward had been ignoring their discussion as he grabbed the front page and immediately saw the article above the fold on the front page. "Oh my god. This could kill us! That's our project."

"What's happened, Edward?"

"There was a big drug bust in a warehouse on Alabama Street last night. We own the property. Someone's going to catch hell for this. Guys, did y'all hear anything about this last night?"

Charlie rather sheepishly commented, "Yeah. It was on the eleven o'clock news last night. Roller called Hew about it this morning."

"Roller? Why did she call?"

"Apparently it was a DEA sting using our program."

"What?"

Not fully understanding the magnitude of the discussion, Tippy checked her watch and told them they needed to get dressed or they'd be late for church.

Edward looked over the top of his new reading glasses. "Guys, after church, we need to talk."

When the adults left to dress for church, while eating toast and scrambled eggs Hew had made, Charlie asked, "Tell me again. You said the girls were friends of Susie and Katie?"

"Yeah. Let's go back to the pool house. We need to call 'em."

"Put her on speaker."

At first, Susie and Katie didn't recognize the two girls. Then Susie remembered meeting them at a tea last semester.

"Y'all went to a tea?"

"Yes, but we just went for laughs. The hostesses were a bunch of uppity know-it-all Virginia girls who think they rule the campus. Their parents are all members of some hunt club on the James River, so they're supposed to be special."

"The Princess Anne Hunt Club?"

"No. That wasn't it. I don't remember anything except James River, but they didn't mention a princess. I'm sure of that. I really wasn't terribly interested, you know? How do you know about them, Hew?"

"Never mind. Not important. Continue your story."

"These two girls were there too. Turns out, all four of us were from Atlanta. I was seated at a little card table with the blond and two of the hostesses. Apparently we were going to be taught how to drink tea—like girls in Atlanta don't have tea parties. Katie and I had on our most conservative outfits and our pearls, but the other two girls were not quite as conservatively dressed. I was asked to be 'mother.' Me! I clasped my hand to my breasts and said in my best old Atlanta voice, 'Why, I've never poured tea in my life. We have servants for that. I might spill it onto your pretty little yellow dress.' I then turned to the blond and talked with her for the remainder of the little charade."

"Surely y'all didn't mention our 'exercises.'"

"Oh no. But we did tell them how drop-dead handsome y'all were. I thought y'all might want someone to fill in while we're up here."

Charlie said, "Well, it won't be with those two. Let me tell you what happened last night. Y'all won't believe it."

Hew quickly made a cut-it sign with his hand across his throat and grabbed the phone. "Amanda came up to me during intermission at our concert and invited us to a party after the concert. She texted me the address, but Charlie was hungry as usual so we went to the Varsity. By the time we were a few blocks from the address, there were cops and flashing blue lights everywhere, so we turned around and came home. This morning it was all over the local news. It was a big drug bust."

"Oh, it was on the morning news up here too. It's going national. The director of the DEA just held a live TV news conference. He's headed to Atlanta to personally lead the investigation. Much ado about nothing, if you ask me. Who cares about drugs anymore? We don't touch 'em. I'd get booted out of med school, and besides, I always need to be in control of myself, don't I? Gotta run. See y'all in a few weeks. Bye."

"Sorry, Hew. I don't know what I was thinking."

"Don't ever tell anyone about last night, Charlie. Ever!"

The lunch crowd had nearly all departed by the time they all got to the club. During lunch, Edward casually but probingly asked them what they did after the concert. Charlie quickly said, "I was starving. Y'all know how nervous I get before a concert. I showed Hew the glories of the Varsity."

"What time did you arrive?"

Hew read the situation and jumped in. "I don't remember exactly, but we left at, um, let me check…" He pulled out his wallet and looked at the receipt. "Ten fifteen."

That seemed to stall Edward, but he continued, "But you heard about the big drug raid last night on the late news?"

"Yeah. And as I said, Roller called and woke us at six forty-five this morning. We watched it on the news."

"Roller thinks it was one of our college stings?"

"Yep. She said it was one of our stings. She wanted us to watch." That stopped Edward cold for a moment, but he added, "Oh my god. Y'all need to fine-tune that program, then. If the local DEA agents rented the warehouse, and I'm sure they did, they need to remember to find a place that's at least legal. That old warehouse belongs to us!

We also own most of the others around it, and everything is scheduled for demolition. We've already got permits. Demolition permits are ridiculously easy in the City of Atlanta. We walked in with drawings and walked out with a permit. Eberhart has been quietly working on a masterplan to match Atlantic Station on Seventeenth Street for nearly a year. We're scheduled to begin demolition next week.

"Hew, I bought some of the property in your name, and, Charlie, you also own some of the adjacent properties. Johan is one of our partners too. We did it that way to keep the owners in the dark. If they had known it was for a single large development, the prices would have skyrocketed. It's a standard developer's ploy. The remainder was bought by a corporation I set up. We're all partners in it as well. Katherine called a few minutes ago, and she was livid until I reminded her that the demolition contractor actually owns the building at the moment. We own the land. He has the salvage and recyclable rights, so he's the one who would have rented the space, and it would be his insurance that would have taken the hit, but I'm not exactly sure how to get out of this mess. The doors were chained, there are no exit lights, emergency lights, sprinklers, or other fire safety devices. If there had been a fire or a shooting, OH MY GOD! I don't even want to think about it. Five hundred kids!"

Hew commented, "Edward, you're right. We never considered this sort of thing. Neither we nor the DEA know anything about building safety regulations. How should we correct this?"

"Hew, you and I can't be involved in any discussions with the DEA at all. Leave out the details of our ownership. I'll get Jeffrey to call the DEA director and get this program error changed. This might get real messy very quickly. The DEA can sort out the property issues, but the civil trials might drag on for years. What a mess, and, guys, I wasn't born yesterday. I've been to the Varsity, and I know that time stamp was when you paid for the food, not when you left. Charlie, you implicated yourself when you insinuated that you saw it on the late news. You've never watched a news show in your life. There's more to your story. Now, tell me again about last night, and start from the exact time you left the concert. Where were y'all between the time the concert ended and ten fifteen? That's roughly two hours. I need to know everything if I'm going to keep us out of this mess."

Hew came clean but then added, "That's the whole truth, Edward, but this works both ways. We had no idea there would be drugs there, and if I had known I was the owner of that warehouse, I never would have gone in."

On Wednesday, Edward told Hew that the demolition contractor was at fault, and the DEA had quickly discovered that the guy was, as they had suspected, a major drug dealer in the Southeast.

"It turns out, this was an orchestrated local sting. Washington knew all about it except no one had bothered to check the building for life safety issues, and the crowd got very large very quickly. Between this raid and his other dealings, the DEA netted over a ton of cocaine and weed.

"Someone was even setting up a small meth lab in the lobby of the warehouse for God's sake. They confiscated fifty million in cash and hard assets, and since this was a sting set up by y'all's program, our Ops Center will split the money with the government. Fortunately, the criminal trials won't involve us, and we suspect the parents will want to keep this as quiet as possible. We expect it to die quickly unless the press fires it up again. We've postponed the demolition for at least six months while we find another subcontractor. By then, the public won't remember it."

CHAPTER 19

Celebrations

Before he left for England, Hew had planned a formal celebratory dinner for the choir when he returned. The music staff agreed to send out the invitations. With the bishop, dean, and their wives, other clergy and partners, music department staff, the Hardys, four from Eberhart, Mary and Jeffrey, Pink, Roller, and the choir and their partners, one hundred people were invited. The dinner party was a grand affair. Ms. Mamie had flown down to help Maybell and Douglas. One hundred five people attended and were decked out in their finest evening attire. Hew wore his Ramsay kilt. He had quietly put out the word that kilts would be welcome. Six other men came in their kilts. The dean wore his and discovered one of the women was a descendant of his Stewart clan! The bar had been set up on the terrace. Along with beer, wine, and assorted spirits for cocktails, Douglas made very liberal mint juleps. Between Swan Bay, Potomac House, and Hew's mother's parents, he had a hundred sterling silver julep cups and linen cocktail napkins.

Mary had told him that his grandmother Cochrane had learned a little trick early in his grandfather's Naval career. "Each time they changed commands, the base officers gave them a piece of presentation silver. It's a Navy tradition. At the first change, they received a large, heavily engraved hand chased sterling silver tray, so she started dropping hints saying they never seemed to have enough silver julep cups for a decent cocktail party, and voilà, sets of sterling silver cups began to appear."

His guests thought his master bathroom was scandalous. It was entered through the dressing room. The floor and three walls were of polished gray granite. The fourth wall, on the north side of the building, had floor-to-ceiling clear glass. The water closet was in a small room on the left side, and the large two-person walk-in shower was on the right side. There were two clear, crackled glass vessel sinks sitting on granite counters. The views from the toilet and shower were terrific! Hew purposely hadn't told his guests that Hans had installed a wall switch which electronically turned the glass from clear to frosted when he needed to use the room at night. After the guests toured both floors of the condo, they would return to the punch bowl for a refill.

"Douglas, I want you to teach me to make mint juleps. Everyone loves these, just as Grandfather said."

"Boy, you aren't old enough to drink yet. I don't know 'bout teaching you. You're just like XI. He drank his scotch straight because he never could get the amount of water right."

"That's not what he told me."

"Hot as this town is, your throat's gonna be on fire if you drink that scotch neat here, so okay, I'll write it down for you. This is Hunt Club Punch, though. It's similar, but I make it in big batches so's they don't have to wait. XI insisted that I make it with Macallan single malt and simple syrup. These bourbon drinkers don't know what's about to hit 'em. You best go tell Maybell to start the buffet. XI never let the Hunt Club folks have more than two of these, and some of these people are about to start number four. These Atlanta folks sure do love their cocktails."

While Hew was talking to Johan, as if on cue, Mary walked up to him and said, "You need to get them started with a blessing."

"Who? Me?"

"You're the host. It's your job."

Trying to weasel his way out, he protested, "But they are so spread out, no one will hear me."

Johan said, "Open your iPhone and let me show you something." He touched a few apps and said, "There are speakers for your sound system behind all of the wall coverings. Just use the phone like a microphone."

That had given Hew a few seconds, and a thought popped into his head. He walked toward the grand piano, spoke into the phone, and said, "The Lord be with you." This was the standard Episcopal prelude to prayer.

Naturally everyone responded, "And also with you."

"Let us pray." He then sat down and began to play an introduction to the hymn. "When in our music God is Glorified…" and everyone joined in.

Dr. W was astounded. He didn't know that Hew had a fine baritone voice. The bishop, dean, and archdeacon were astounded too because normally, people just deflected the prayer to the nearest priest.

Dinner included Swan Bay's own Virginia ham, fried chicken (Hew's favorite), huge bowls of rice and boats of gravy, and a sideboard full of vegetables. Ms. Mamie and Tippy concocted a mixture of shrimp and grits. Tippy boiled the shrimp using an old Charleston family receipt—as they called the word *recipe*—in a mixture of spices, and Ms. Mamie had cooked the grits all night long. His guests loved it, but grits? No! Not Hew. Ms. Mamie also made her famous farm biscuits. He could eat his weight in those. Ms. Mamie and Maybell helped Tippy make small Huguenot tortes using Swan Bay Pecans.

The cathedral flower guild had graciously provided table arrangements for all the tables. After they visited the penthouse to plan their arrangements, they took one look around and decided to go minimalist. These tours de force floral arrangements were spectacular and would probably never be seen at the altar, but they might reappear in the cathedral's great hall.

Maybell had wrapped the old sideboard chamber pot so well that the movers didn't find it when they came for the furniture. Mary drove to Potomac House and took it back to Swan Bay. Ms. Mamie hand carried the old porcelain chamber pot with her on the trip from Swan Bay.

"Ms. Mamie had rewrapped it in fine linen napkins," joked Douglas, "but, Hew, when they unwrapped it yesterday, they joked about the old lazy men until I thought they might double over laughing and drop it."

The flower guild saw the old bowl sitting in the butler's pantry and, without asking, used the old pot for a spectacular arrangement on the large round Platner glass table sitting in the curve of the spiral stairs in the gallery. It was overflowing like a fountain with yellow calla lilies and yellow tulips. They allowed some of the blooms to droop over the edge of the bowl. The whole arrangement looked like a fountain. When Ms. Mamie and Maybell saw what the ladies were doing, they started laughing and continued to giggle every time they passed it while they arranged and set the tables.

Mary had spent the morning in the kitchen, so they finally said, giggling uncontrollably, "Mary, you best come look at this!"

Mary tried as politely as she could to tell the flower guild ladies the chamber pot story. The proper Atlanta ladies were aghast, but Mary assured them, "Oh no, it's fine. Hew's going to love it, and so will everyone else. It may even be the hit of the evening! It'll certainly make the rounds at the Hunt Club Ball for years to come too. They had already heard the story of the Westover punch bowl from Tippy, so they felt relieved.

As the mint juleps flowed during cocktails, the chamber pot story ran through the guests. Now everyone had to get another look. Some tried to be discreet, but the bishop simply guffawed when he saw it. "Good old Anglo-Saxon humor, I'd say," he remarked between fits of laughter.

Heidi's interior designer team had arranged the old George III Chippendale breakfront and sideboard from Potomac House at Hew's suggestion. The breakfront was now centered on the wall behind the glass-topped dining room table, and the sideboard was placed off center of the wall between the dining room portion of the room and the gallery. The family silver was back in the breakfront. Those two pieces made quite a contrast to the Miesian chairs and tables. His mother's ebony Bosendorfer concert grand piano graced the corner of the formal sitting area in front of the wall of glass. Sheer pale gray drapes were carefully arranged against the glass to further reduce the heat gain on the piano. The two portraits by John Singer Sargent were hanging beside the sideboard, and the Canaletto painting of the River Thames was hanging over the sideboard. Heidi's selection of fine pale gray Scottish wool fabric for the walls in the condo was splendid. She thought it would be better than flat white paint and less obtrusive than wallpaper, very minimalist, yet elegant. She and the painting's conservator had convinced Hew that the wool was a perfect backdrop for the paintings and a modern equivalent to the classical French silk wall coverings at Swan Bay. The curator had done a fine job with arranging the paintings in the gallery, and just as Johan had predicted, the north light was perfect. None of the paintings were crowded on the walls. Each could be viewed for its own statement. All the other movable furniture had been moved to an empty condo downstairs, and thirteen tables of eight had been spread out throughout the main level just in case a few others showed up, but there was still ample room for people to mingle. The tables were laid with all of Hew's inherited linen table cloths, napkins, china, crystal goblets, and sterling flatware. The ladies had arranged the various patterns nicely.

The library was the most impressive room in the penthouse. The library was on the east end and had a full two-story-high wall of windows that looked out toward Stone Mountain. The other three walls held XI's ten thousand books.

As the host, Hew was the last to serve himself. Charlie had saved him a seat at the Hardys' table, but Hew decided to sit at the mostly empty table in the library with a few people he didn't know. They were elderly members of the choir, and some of them obviously didn't have spouses. Until he sat down, they weren't saying much.

One of the men said, "Thanks for hosting this elegant affair, Hew. We've been members of the choir for many years, too many for some of us." That got a chuckle and started the conversation. "We usually leave immediately after practice before it gets too dark, and we leave early on Sundays to get to lunch at the club before the food runs out, so we've never had a chance to talk with you."

One of the ladies added, "Tell us about yourself, Hew."

He gave them the highly edited story and quickly said, "But enough about me. Tell me your stories. You've watched Atlanta change quite a bit." Their stories were fascinating. Several of their parents had been parishioners when the cathedral was built.

"This is a very unusual room, Hew. I'm a retired librarian. Are any of these books rare?"

"Yes, ma'am. Some of the books are considered rare, and some are the family collection dating back to 1638 and my ancestor, Capt'n John Bishop, including his 1559 *Book of Common Prayer*." He got up and walked over to the shelf and brought the prayer book back and let them look at it.

"Well, it's certainly been well used! Every page is lovingly worn. I love to see a prayer book that has been prayed through."

"Do you plan on reading all these books?"

"Oh, no, sir. They're really just here to help the acoustics." They all laughed.

Hew continued, "The second level is a three-sided balcony reached by either the small oak spiral stair in the corner by the fireplace"—he pointed—"or from the great room gallery. The balcony railing is made of wood paneling to reduce the visual scale of the room. The paneling is contemporary. The stiles, rails, and panels are in the same plane rather than raised as in traditional paneling. Only a small black reveal gives the panels' definition. Johan, my architect, told me this detail was quoted from the woodwork on the study carrels and balcony rails in Louis Kahn's famous library at Philips Exeter Academy. It's a small reminder to me of all my family who had been students there."

"That's where I've seen this detail! I was a student there when the library was built. I can tell you, the modern design without a proper front door caused quite a stir. It looked like an old New England textile mill. I was in there just last week. My son also graduated from there, and my granddaughter is a new student."

"In this room, the German acousticians set the panels so they were slightly angled and canted to reduce sound reflections and aid sound disbursement. I used limed and waxed quarter-sawn English oak. I prefer the lighter color. The walls of the room are not completely parallel. The two long walls are two degrees out of parallel to reduce echoes.

One of the ladies remarked, "The color of the wood is exquisite, Hew. I'm going to redo the paneling in our den in this technique. It's just what I've been looking for."

"My new three-manual, twenty-seven-stop mechanical action practice organ was built by Flentrop in Holland. The architect located it in front of the books on the south side to balance the fireplace on the north side. The ceiling rises twenty-four feet. The ceiling is made of white slatted aluminum. There are hidden baffles above the ceiling that are hung at multiple angles to help disburse the sound. They work like the groin stone vaults of a Gothic church, except they're hidden.

"The builders will be back next week. Maybe y'all can make another visit in the near future. I will be able to walk behind the organ and the fireplace to reach the books on the main level and the balconies. The large painting over the fireplace is me! I hadn't recognized 'me' at first. It's one hundred inches by eighty inches and it's a digitized, highly pixelated photograph. Heidi, my interior designer, found the original on my late grandfather's chest of drawers in his bedroom. Someone had taken the photo when I scored the winning goal in Arlington. It is a high-resolution picture, so she had it made as a surprise."

He hadn't had the heart to tell Heidi it represented both his best and worst days in DC. "The painting rises up to reveal a Sony flat screen A1E Bravia OLED TV."

One of the women laughed. "Of course it does. Boys and their big TVs! My guys would kill you to get this."

"The TV sound and the sound from the state-of-the-art sound system comes through the TV screen and the speakers behind the wall fabric and ceiling. I can operate the TV and sound system, and almost everything electronic in the entire condo from my iPad or iPhone, as you heard during the prayer."

"Do us a favor and don't discuss that during the party. We can't be rewiring our whole houses."

"Johan and Hans designed the large rectangular polished stainless-steel and glass library table we're sitting around. Johan said the size is proportionally based on the classical golden section. They built three identical units. Two are in the dining area. Johan wants me to put them together in the gallery for large dinner parties. They are so beautifully engineered they can be easily rolled from one place to the next. The legs sit on hidden Swiss stainless-steel ball bearings and will roll right over the area rugs with ease. I think they will all fit in here nicely. I can have a dinner party with a concert afterward."

"Please do consider inviting us to that dinner. We'll provide the wine if you'll have Douglas make those marvelous mint juleps!"

"Okay. It's a date."

The moment Hew had been dreading had come. The bishop, the dean, the archdeacon, and Edward had had a long talk with Hew the day before. Reluctantly Hew had agreed. The dean rose and asked Hew for the microphone.

"Friends, I want to thank our host for one of the finest parties I've ever had the pleasure of attending." Everyone applauded. "There are rumors that have been spreading, though, so the bishop, Edward, and I agree we need to explain. We were able to keep the death out of the media at the time, but some of the story got out anyway, as we all know. Without going into all the sordid details, I must tell you that it was not a suicide, as has been spreading, but the attempted murder of our young host, Hew. We were trying to protect him because of his age and circumstances, but we really need to clear this up because it's spiraling out of control. Certainly you will understand why it was kept quiet." He did a fine job of telling some of the background and circumstances without mentioning the victim by name.

Afterward, most of the choir members came up to him wanting to hug him and offer their condolences. Hew wasn't much of a hugger, and even less of a kisser, but he tolerated it. He was glad it was finally over. The evening ended with everyone standing on the west terrace drinking coffee and eating the Huguenot tortes while taking in the late-night August breeze. There were brilliant flashes of lightning over the mountains, and the rain-cooled breezes from the approaching storms were refreshing. Several of the men had taken up his offer for a wee dram. In a moment of weakness during the evening, Hew agreed to host a dinner for the bishop and dean when the Consortium of Endowed Episcopal Parishes gathered at the cathedral later in the fall. The bishop also rather matter-of-factly told him that there would be an organ concert following the dinner. After everyone except the Hardys left, Hew chatted with Edward, while Tippy and Charlie helped Douglas, Maybell, and Mis. Mamie. Charlie wanted the leftover biscuits, and Tippy wanted the shrimp and grits. Hew hadn't been drinking at all during the evening, so he and Edward were having a ritual Macallan.

"Edward, I want to give St. Philip's some money as an act of atonement for my part in causing blood to be spilled on the altar. The money is part of my share of the sale of the software. The government will get a huge chunk, so rather than pay taxes on it all, I'm giving some of it to the cathedral."

"Hew, I know better than to argue with you, and I have already seen the contracts from the Whitechapel Bell Foundry. I knew something was going on in your mind."

"On behalf of the dean and chapter and the entire cathedral, I thank you. May I ask if you have other specific projects in mind?"

"Yes, two. First will be a new bell tower. The cathedral's central tower simply isn't accessible for ringers. I have tentatively arranged to have ringing instructors from Oxford rotate through Atlanta teaching people to ring. Second, I want to replace the cathedral's surface parking lot with a large six or seven hundred car garage with the same horizontal solar panels covering the garage roof as on our condo building. Johan wants to build green walls around the garage to keep it from looking like a standard parking garage. I also want to build a cloistered walk from the garage to the north lobby. I sent Johan a little sketch for a tower, and he has turned it into a spectacular piercing needle. By the way, since Johan has been named a partner and is moving to Atlanta, I've offered to give him a condo here."

Edward chuckled. "Great idea, Hew. He'll appreciate the condo. I'll start transferring the funds to my escrow account tomorrow."

*****

After everyone else had gone to bed, Hew and Charlie were relaxing in Hew's pool with martinis. Charlie got a text. "Surprise! Susie and Katie will arrive in town about two tomorrow and can't wait to see your new condo. She's pissed they weren't invited to the party, though. You'll need to make it up to her, she says."

"Damn, Charlie. Why wasn't I asked first? That's going to be tight. I have to drop the Swan Bay folks off at the airport. We're having brunch with your folks at the club. And I will not be making it up to her either."

"We can make it work. I'll pick up the girls. They're arriving at the airport on someone's jet."

"Why do I know something will go wrong?"

Brunch ran long, and the girls were early. They almost met at the curb at Peachtree-Dekalb Airport. Jeffrey whispered to Mary as they walked toward their jet, "Wasn't that Charlie with those two bombshells?"

Mary whispered, "Yes. Tippy told me all about them. Our boy Hew has become a man. This isn't his first time either. The next party is about to begin."

Jeffrey chuckled to himself.

*****

As they walked in, Katie just stopped in her tracks and looked around.

"Oh, Hew! This is fantastic! I want the whole tour immediately. I need to see it all!"

"Not me! I didn't fly all this way for a tour. Let's go find a bed, Charlie." When they were out of earshot, Susie commented, "Jesus, Charlie, I know your folks are loaded, but Hew must have inherited a fortune!"

"I don't know. He owns a huge farm in Virginia and a house in DC, and he made a bundle on a couple of apps he wrote, but that's all I know."

Katie's tour naturally ended in Hew's bedroom. Afterward, while they were all sipping martinis by the pool, Katie asked, "Did you really design this yourself?"

"It was my idea, but Johan, Hans, and Heidi took my sketch and turned it into this."

"Well, it's absolutely perfect."

"Not to me," snapped Susie. "I want to be surrounded with Louis XIV. You've been brainwashed by those old architecture professors, Katie. This isn't what Atlanta girls do."

"Less is more," retorted Hew.

"What's the other saying, less is a bore? It is if you ask me."

Needing to change the conversation, Charlie said, "Let's get in the pool."

"I need another martini," ordered Susie.

Later that night, as the two were lying in Hew's bed, he and Katie talked long into the night. They woke about eight and took full advantage of his two-person shower. Luckily, Dr. W had given Hew Sunday off, because the next morning he was exhausted from Saturday's horn buster, as Charlie called it.

During breakfast on the terrace on Sunday morning, Susie casually commented, "Charlie, why don't you move in here rather than the dorm? You're too sophisticated to live in a dorm. And, Hew, get rid of that staff. They'll only get in our way when we visit."

The girls had to leave early to get back to UVA. Charlie drove them to the airport.

Hew was already lounging in the pool. Charlie brought a pitcher of martinis out to the pool.

"Charlie, I think Susie's idea about having you move here is great. I'm sorry I didn't think of it. Would you like to live here rather than a dorm?"

"Thanks, but no! Not that this isn't the greatest place in town, but your practicing would drive me nuts, and there's no place for my drums. Susie is right about the dorm, though. I'm going to continue to live in my pool house and commute. Our arrangement worked because I practiced when you went to the cathedral to practice, but now that you have that monster in the library, I don't think this is for me."

"Okay, that makes sense. You need to know that Katie won't be coming back. We talked late into the night. She only wants a career, and I want a wife and kids. It won't work. We parted as friends, but Susie won't be welcome here from now on. She presumes too much. I will not dismiss Douglas and Maybell either."

*****

Johan brought a preliminary concept for the new bell tower to the cathedral property committee meeting. During his presentation, he explained, "The glassed-in ringing room is at ground level. This has an added advantage of avoiding fire, safety, and access regulations. Otherwise, the city would require a fire stair and an accessible elevator even though the room only holds twelve able-bodied ringers. The bells are just above and behind glass too. People can see the ringers and watch the bells swinging. The sound comes out through an operable set of louvers in the metalwork above. This will allow practices and peals to go on for hours without disturbing your neighbors."

The dean and chapter loved it. They suggested locating it beside the Peachtree Road driveway to the new parking garage so everyone could see the ringers as they entered, exited, or drove by.

Edward asked, "Johan, we're a little concerned about the parking garage. We need to be able to park somewhere while the garage is under construction."

"The garage is easy. We plan to phase it. All of the parts will be prefabricated off site and delivered as they are needed. That will reduce construction time. We'll build the first half without disturbing the remainder of the lot, and then we'll build the second half. The south facade will be covered in solar panels, as will be the cover over the top level. We will drill deep wells for heat exchangers to use the ground temperature for new heat pumps in most of the existing buildings. We plan to get you to net zero and then finally to regeneration."

One of the committee members asked, "What is regeneration?"

"Oh, I can answer that," boasted Edward. "It comes from Archbishop Cranmer's first Baptismal service. 'You must be regenerate'—born again. The environmentalists have adopted it to mean make more energy on site than you need and return it to society."

"Wow," exclaimed the archdeacon. "That'll preach."

"Great idea, Cindy. I'll schedule you to preach at the next Baptism."

The committee members left more excited than when they entered. Edward called Hew on Tuesday night. "There's a documentary on ETV tomorrow night I want you to watch. Call me after you've seen it, and we'll discuss it."

*****

"Tell me, Bubba," whined Erik to his cellmate, "how can one kid just disappear? I've looked on the computer everywhere. My parole has been granted, and I'll be out of here within the week."

"I'm telling you for the last time. Get on with your life and forget him. He's not worth getting caught again, dude. You admitted that it was your knife. Don't wind up like the senator and his son."

CHAPTER 20

Regenerate

Hew was tired, so he recorded the show just in case he fell asleep, but he had actually managed to watch it. It was a program from Berlin announcing the return of paintings, gold, jewelry, and a very large rug that had been stolen by the Nazis. The rug had been on the floor of the Bema of the great 1887 Synagogue in Gdansk, Poland, before the war. Everyone thought the rug, along with the Torah scrolls and the fine chandelier, had been destroyed. These items had just appeared at the museum door on a recent morning. They thanked whomever had returned them. A number of heirs had already been reunited with their family property. Those people were interviewed.

The moderator also made a passionate plea to the Swiss government to release the loot stored in their bank vaults. After the war, whenever a Jewish heir approached one of the banks to claim their inheritance, the Swiss simply asked for a death certificate. The Nazis, of course, hadn't kept concentration camp death records. The moderator finished with a similar story about some old church silver in Charleston which had been secretly returned and would be reconsecrated during the coming Sunday Eucharist.

Hew called Edward. Edward explained the connections.

"Let's go to Charleston, Edward."

Tippy called her brother, DeVeaux, in Charleston. He and his family lived in the large old family house on the East end of Tradd

Street. It had been in the Mazyck family since old Isaac Mazyck fled France and moved his family to Charleston following the Revocation of the Edict of Nantes. She grew up there. They now use the carriage house and other outbuildings as a bed-and-breakfast. She was looking for accommodations, but the B and B was already booked. He asked about the sudden visit, and she told him Hew wanted to hear the bells at Grace Church Cathedral. DeVeaux, his wife, Missy, and twin teenaged boys, Daniel and Issac, were members. They had recently joined Grace following a secession from the Episcopal Church by their family parish.

"Be early. The place will be packed. Our old silver has been mysteriously returned. Let's all have lunch at the club afterward."

Edward, Tippy, Charlie, Hew, Jeffrey, Mary, Roller, and Pink stayed in a large old mansion turned hotel and walked to the church. As they approached, Hew was surprised to hear the sounds of ten well-struck change ringing bells. They were early, but the congregation was already arriving. He ran ahead, hoping to get a chance to ring with the band. He was warmly welcomed in the air-conditioned ringing room. In addition to the parish band, a visiting band from England known as the Society of Royal Cumberland Youths were in town. They and several local members of the Cumberlands were going to celebrate the occasion by ringing an original composition after the service, named "Bellum Civile Argentum Caters" (Civil War Silver on Ten Bells). During a break in the ringing, the standard question was posed to Hew by the tower captain, "Do you ring?"

"Yes. I learned at Lincoln Cathedral and with the Oxford Society. I rang my first peal at St. Thomas, Oxford, in August."

The Cumberlands began asking Hew if he knew certain of their friends in those groups. He knew them all and started to relate stories, but the tower captain quickly stopped the chit-chat by calling, "Catch hold."

"You too, Hew, grab a rope."

Hew took the rope of the 1,800-pound tenor. They wisely called a method which only required Hew to keep his bell in tenth's place! Ringing with an all-Cumberland band was a rare treat for him. Afterward, Hew announced the new tower and invited them all to visit. They exchanged email addresses. Hew also made an appointment for Charlie and his cousins Daniel and Isaac to have a quick lesson after the service. By the time the service started, the church was packed, and people were standing. The service was livestreamed to the parish hall for the overflow crowd. The program notes described the silver. It had been made in 1848 in Charleston by Hayden and Gregg, silversmiths. It was the gift of an unknown benefactor. The silver was coin silver. Coin silver was graded .900, whereas sterling was graded at .925. Made from old coins, the silver was rather soft, so this silver would only be used on certain occasions.

After the Peace, the organist played an extempore fanfare using the trumpets en chamade located high over the entrance doors. The horizontal polished brass trumpets sounded splendid. Following the verger, crucifer, the chancellor of the diocese, and the two wardens, members of the altar guild processed down the aisle as a part of the offertory and presented the old silver at the altar. The bishop reconsecrated the silver, and the choir sang Sir Hubert Parry's great anthem for Psalm 122, "I Was Glad," as the offertory anthem.

When the bishop elevated the old chalice, Jeffrey was struck by a sobering thought. He had an epiphany. He began shaking while trying to control his emotions, so he started shifting around on the little needlepoint-covered kneeler. Mary noticed but thought his knees were bothering him.

He had realized that this was the first time this chalice had held consecrated wine in nearly 153 years! He realized he had not been to church since he had planned an assassination. Mary had noticed, but she knew he had to work out whatever was bothering him on his own. Her best help would be to stand by and be ready whenever he needed her. He suddenly felt the weight of all the lives lost during the war when the silver was stolen. He thought about the lives lost to drugs. He thought about the Colombian assassination. He decided he was ready to give up the drug-busting business and return to breeding horses.

Pink looked up and suddenly recognized a face in the stained-glass window over the altar. His ancestor, Dr. Charles Cotesworth Pinckney, was standing on the right hand of Jesus in the window. He laughed at the sight, but he was in awe as he started thinking about the hardships this man endured. His family had a similar portrait hanging in their living room. Now, he thought, it would take on a new meaning.

After the service, while the adults went to the parish hall for their much-needed coffee fix, Hew sent the guys for their rope lessons, and he went to the console to speak with the organists.

DeVeaux had reserved the small map room at the club for lunch. After the usual family updates, the discussion turned to the service. Hew, Mary, Missy, and Tippy were seated next to each other. They began to dissect the service and discuss the events of the day. They agreed the liturgy, bells, and music were very well done. They particularly praised the fine choir and organists.

"Two organists. What a fine treat," remarked Mary. "I was lucky to have found one who would drive to Westover for me today."

Hew started to comment on the sermon when Missy stopped him. "Hew, whenever our favorite former now late bishop sensed we might be heading in the wrong direction with our comments, he would preface his wise advice with the gentle phrase, 'May I suggest.' May I suggest to you that we never serve roasted sermon at Sunday lunch in our house, so may I suggest you not start here?"

Tippy, now well into her third pinot grigio, chimed in, "We don't either, Hew, but we do love having the dean for cocktails."

Everyone at the table howled with laughter at yet another one of Tippy's one-liners.

They flew back in the afternoon. Hew was able to hear a few minutes of the bell peal before they left for the airport. He decided after having rung those bells before the service, and after listening to the well-struck Cumberland's peal, the managing director at Whitechapel was correct. He would ask Edward to call in the morning and amend the cathedral contract to twelve bells plus semitones in a size of the director's choice. Hopefully, the tenor could weigh at least one ton.

Fifteen minutes out of Atlanta, Jeffrey's phone rang. "Oh my god! When? Who is it? Hold on while I find a pen and some paper." He walked back to the table where Hew and Edward were sitting.

"I think y'all might need to hear this too." He put the phone on speaker. "Go ahead, Mac. Hew and Edward are listening too."

In his usual military style, Mac simply said, "We found a body near the perimeter fence early this morning. It's too much info to go into now, and the Surry county sheriff has just called in his counterpart from DC. He's coming in on one of our helicopters as we speak. Edward, you and Hew need to come on to Swan Bay. We think this involves Hew."

"Me? I've been in Charleston. I haven't killed anybody!"

"The guy's name, according to his driver's license, is Erik Wilson. Isn't he the other guy that went to prison?"

"Yeah, but he should still be in prison."

"That's why we need you here."

When they landed in Atlanta, Tippy and Charlie got off, and the plane immediately left for Swan Bay.

Mac met the plane at the airstrip. "Before I forget, Ms. Mamie is serving supper for everyone in the dining room. This place is crawling with cops, so we've invited them all, and they will brief you."

Edward pulled Hew aside and said, "Don't say a word unless I say you can. Just be quiet and listen."

Ms. Mamie had been there all day and had a full plantation spread on the antique sideboards. When everyone was seated, the sheriff started with a question for Hew. "We need to establish one fact first to clear up some confusion."

Edward asked to hear the question but advised that his client might not answer.

"Hew, is your birth name John Bishop XIII, and were you commonly called John?

Edward nodded at Hew who answered, "Yes."

"Okay. That's all I needed to know from you. Thank you."

"You could have asked me that over the phone!"

"We needed to see your reaction. Now, here's what we know. Our victim got early release last week. Detective Jones here, from DC, has spoken with the victim's cellmate, and it seems that Erik was obsessed with finding you, John—I mean, Hew. He spent every available minute searching the internet for you. He even used your grandfather's news articles to establish an ancestry tree of your family all the way back to the 1638 arrival of John Bishop. He always claimed that he didn't know that you were going to be stabbed and that he was unfairly locked up. He blamed you and the black kid who testified. He was planning to go after him next. We found his rental car on Cabin Point Road right beside the fence, and we found rubber gloves and a bolt cutter where he came through the electric fence, right under a No Trespassing sign, I might add. Apparently he entered sometime last night. He made his way in the dark until he was bitten by a snake, probably a very large copperhead, judging from the fang marks. We found the puncture wounds on his leg. He was allergic to bee and wasp stings, and we think the bite probably triggered anaphylactic shock. We found his EpiPen in the car. It either fell out of his pocket, or he mistakenly left it. The autopsy will tell us, but either way, he died trying to get back to his car."

Hew just sat there. Several others asked questions, but Hew appeared to be stoic. Finally, he excused himself and left the room. He went into his cabin and just lost it! After all these years of holding everything in, he couldn't stand it any longer. Sensing Hew's need to be alone, the group finished supper, and after thanking the cops for quickly solving the situation, the Swan Bay folks all went to bed.

The next morning after breakfast, they held a briefing in the Ops Center on an entirely different matter. They were very uncomfortable with the topic of the grisly body and the events of the day before, so they didn't bring it up. Pink began, "Hew, we need to brief you and bring you up-to-date on some upcoming changes now that Jeffrey has retired. I didn't want to discuss this on our trip to Charleston, as I'm sure you and Edward will understand. We're closing the DEA center and our Ops Center here. Roller and I will join the DEA, but we'll be based in DC. Our operations have yielded great results, but without XI, Edward, and now Jeffrey, we think our mission has ended."

"What about our employees?

Jeffrey took over. "Some of them want to stay on here and work for the breeding center and the farm. We'll keep them at their same salaries. The others know guys in the DEA and will join their task forces. If their pay isn't up to ours, we'll quietly supplement them. Every one of our team members is happy, as best as we can tell, and Swan Bay will no longer be in the drug enforcement business.

*****

While he was sitting on the front porch of his cabin later in the evening, Jeffrey walked up and asked what he was studying so intently. Hew had his iPad out.

"Several things. I have been trying to find my Colombian roommate, Tomas. I want him to know I'm okay, but he's not on any social media site and doesn't seem to have an email address either. I'm also trying to decide on my route back to Atlanta. I'm going to take the Corvette, and I don't want to spend all of my time on the Interstates. I can get more than enough of them around Atlanta."

"Then why not try the Blue Ridge Parkway. Look it up. It's about 469 miles long, but you won't need to take the whole route if you don't want to. The curves will show you something about your car. The low posted speed limit won't get you killed. You'll love it. The leaves haven't started changing yet, so the traffic won't be as bad as in the fall."

"That's a great idea. I can see those mountains from my west terrace. I'd love to compare them to the Andes. I used to be able to see the Andes from my perch in the chapel bell tower."

They discussed the route. "Oh, I can go all the way and go down through Highlands!"

"I hope you know the Corvette isn't practical for everyday driving."

"I know. For one thing, it's not air-conditioned! I ordered a new Jag SUV while I was in England. It was shipped last week. It will be my everyday car. Edward wanted me to buy something electric or hybrid, but I'm not convinced they are quite ready for the open road yet. I'm familiar with the route from Highlands. Edward uses it. I'll call Edward. Maybe I can stay in their Highlands house one night."

"Sounds fantastic. See if you can wrangle an invitation for Mary and me sometime this fall," he said as he laughed. "By the way, the monuments guys finished setting the new headstones late today."

"Great. I'll go up to the cemetery tomorrow before I leave and check them out. You should also know that I have changed my major from premed to business. Emory has an outstanding business school, and I will concentrate on international finance. Tippy convinced me that I'm really not interested in science. Edward thinks that with my position with Eberhart and my money, I should learn to manage it and make it grow."

"I agree. I know some folks at Clemson University who might interest you too. They have a program called MRED. That stands for Masters in Real Estate Development. You might qualify for distance learning."

Mary walked over and joined them. She had a large covered basket. Hew thought it might be some of Ms. Mamie's biscuits for the road. His mouth began to water. Instead, it was a chocolate Lab puppy. Hew was delighted. He reached in and picked the little sleeping fellow up and got a face licking. It was love at first sight for them both. Mary told Hew the puppy was Buster's son. Pink's chocolate Lab was the mother. The vets had bred them.

"He's the runt of the litter, and he isn't rambunctious. Jeffrey will puppy proof the Corvette for the trip with a plastic floor mat, and we have a traveling container for him."

"I'm going to name him Sebastian."

"Of course." Mary laughed. "How appropriate for an organist."

Early the next morning, Hew walked up the hill to the old graveyard. The air had turned a little crisp overnight. Fall was not far off for Tidewater, Virginia, and a light fog floated over the James River and Upper Chippokes Creek. He had asked Johan to work on a new headstone for his parents' graves.

Johan had designed a rough-hewn granite stone, and a firm of artists in Cambridge, England, had carved the word Bishop in freehand script on the reverse side and added the family crest with the words *Pro Deo et Ecclesia* above a shield using precious stones and Granites. Hew had spotted the firm's work on many inscriptions in

Oxford. His parents' Christian names and dates were inscribed on the front sides. Hew thought the work was stunning, but he thought it ironic that the Bishop family motto—Pro Deo et Ecclesia (For God and the Church)—had unwittingly played such an important part of his life. He stood for a moment reflecting on the past and what might have been, but he finally had realized that the time had come to leave it all in this place and move on. He would never forget the past, and he was sure that it would surface from time to time, but his new family and his new life in Atlanta was beginning to show him a way forward. He suddenly began to remember part of a poem he had studied in his English lit class in Atlanta.

The Rubaiyat of Omar Khayyam

> ***The moving finger writes, and having writ moves on, nor all your piety or wit shall lure it back to cancel half a line, nor all your tears wash out a word of it.***

Sebastian was sniffing around the oak trees. Hew picked him up and started the trip home. It was time to regenerate.

*****

"My god, it's turned cold. I'm freezing, and it's only four o'clock. How did you know to wear a jacket?"

Hew was standing in line in the university café when the guy behind him spoke to him. "I saw it on the weather report this morning. They predicted a sudden change by afternoon with snow and ice tonight. It is February after all."

"Guess I need to start watching the news. Weren't you just in that lecture about drone delivery systems? That's fascinating."

"Yep. I agree." Hew picked up a cup, a tea bag, and a wedge of lemon. He paid, and as he turned, he spotted an empty table for two just in front of the cashier's station. "Want to join me?"

"Thanks, but I've got to run."

Hew took the table, put his laptop bag in one chair, walked around, set his cup down, dropped the tea bag in the nearly boiling water, and squeezed the lemon into the mix. While he waited for the brew to reach a civilized temperature, he reached over and took out his laptop. He looked up and spotted her as she turned away from the cashier. She had short sporty blond hair, and she was dressed in black with tall black boots. He immediately decided that she was the most beautiful woman he had ever seen. Her hands were full with a teacup and a croissant. He raised his hand and waved her toward the empty seat. She smiled and walked toward the waiting chair. He stood and walked around the table, dropping his bag on the floor while holding the chair for her. She had him with her smile. He had her with his gentlemanly gesture with the chair.

"I'm Hew Ramsay."

"It's nice to meet you, Hew. Thanks for letting me sit with you. I'm Alexis Williams."

"What's your major? I'm in the business school."

"I'm an art history major."

"Interesting. I own a few old paintings myself. How do you intend to use your degree?"

She sipped her tea. "Actually, I have a scholarship to Oxford for the summer as an intern in their painting restoration program, but I still haven't earned enough money to pay for the flights."

"Hmmm. I'm going to study at Oxford this summer too, and I have access to a private jet with a seat for you too if you want to hitch a ride."

*****

Ten Years Later

The Thanksgiving lunch was a traditional Tidewater, Virginia, banquet. Hew had invited the entire Swan Bay staff and their families. They had arranged two long parallel tables down the center of the ballroom with family silver, china, and crystal for every person. The old silver punchbowl filled with the traditional "julip" punch graced the sideboard. When the meal was over and people began the ritual of the long Southern goodbyes, Hew turned to young John.

"When we go downstairs, stay by me at the door. Once everyone has gone, you and I are going for a walk."

"Can Eddie go with us?"

"Not this time."

They walked up to the old family cemetery. The afternoon shadows had not yet begun to stretch out along the river. The sky was a brilliant blue, and the temperature was unseasonably warm. They sat down on an old tombstone, and Hew began the story. They sat for two hours, while Hew recounted most of the family history, only omitting the details of most of the murders and attempted murders.

"Our known family roots go back to 1470 in Scotland with a man named James Bishop. His great-grandson, Sir Knight William Bishop the Elder, married Charteris Hew, Lady Elizabeth Ramsay, and one of their younger sons, John, sailed to Virginia. That's his tombstone in front of you."

SEPARATING FACT FROM FICTION

This is a work of historical fiction. The main story is one of generations of a family. The base story is the family. I chose an organist as my main character because, to my knowledge, no one writes fiction about organists.

In my thirty-seven years as an architect, I worked with many organ builders while I designed or restored churches.

I am a direct descendant of Charteris Hew, Lady Elizabeth Ramsay of Dalhousie Linlithgow, West Lothian, Scotland, and Sir Knight William Bishop the Elder through my maternal grandmother, Hattie Viola Bishop Summey. The family history has been thoroughly researched. The Ramsays of Dalhousie are recorded in the Scottish Peerage. I am a part of the tenth generation of Sir Knight William Bishop and Lady Elizabeth's line, through John Bishop of Jamestown, Virginia, but the preceding generations were not all named John, and all my direct ancestors were not male. Only Capt'n John, his son, and his grandson were named John. James Bishop was one of Capt'n John's older brothers, but James was not the firstborn son. James did own a tobacco dock in Glasgow. Capt'n John's tobacco farm was on the south bank of the James River near Charles City, Virginia, and it was called Swan Bay. He made numerous trips back to Scotland and England. The land patents quoted in the chapter "Spring 1638" are quoted from the actual land patents in the Virginia records. The names listed are in the patents. Swan Bay, however, no longer exists and must not be confused with the nearby historic site, Swann's Bay. There was no manor house or Potomac House. My maternal grandmother, Hattie Viola Bishop Summey, was orphaned as a child. Her parents died in the influenza epidemic, and Granny never knew of her Scottish ancestors. She would have been proud to have known that she had a connection to people who knew King James because even though she was illiterate, she loved to carry around his version of the Bible.

The Cathedral of St. Philip, Atlanta, Georgia, exists. I am a parishioner of Grace Church Cathedral in Charleston, South Carolina. The Grace Church silver was stolen during the Civil War and has never been recovered. Hayden and Gregg Co. was a fine Charleston silversmith company.

Until just recently, the Whitechapel Bell Foundry, London, existed. I am a bell ringer in the English change ringing tradition. As a member of the Society of Royal Cumberland Youths, one of the premier English ringing societies, I am often invited to places that I otherwise would not be invited on my trips to England. On one such visit, the elderly lady of a manor we were visiting invited us to tour her manor house. She told us the story of the Chippendale dining chairs.

The story about the WWII pilot instructor is true. My late father was the instructor.

The story about the lady of the plantation keeping the Yankees from burning the plantation by lying about diseased soldiers is often told at one of the Charleston plantations, but without the fake burials.

I do not know, nor have I ever used cocaine or manufactured cocaine. It just made a good story. The village in the Andes does not exist. The tunnel lab does not exist, the drug lord Espinis does not exist, and the Jesuit school does not exist.

The other schools do exist, and all are very fine schools.

Sadly, the stories about stolen gold and works of art by the Nazis are true.

The Flentrop Organ Company exists. The historic French and Dutch organs exist, and there are many working French instruments in South America, but not in Colombia.

The Viking Cruise Ship *Kara* exists. My wife and I enjoyed a cruise aboard sailing down the Rhine.

The German Architectural, Engineering, and Construction Company does not exist.

With the exception of Hue's program to track construction worker's productivity, the software design program exists and is widely used all around the globe. If anyone reads this and decides to write such a worker management program, I want the creative royalties!

The fox head sporran event happened to a friend of mine while we were at a formal bell ringing party in Charleston.

While visiting Fairfax House museum in York, England, on one of my ringing trips, the docent showed us the chamber pot in the side of the sideboard. That story is true! The use as a flowerpot is not.

Members of my Grace Church tower bell ringers did climb all the stairs to the ringing room at Lincoln Cathedral on June 17, 2001, and we rang with their fine band before a Sunday Evensong. I rang my very first quarter peal with the Oxford Society at St. Thomas Church, Oxford. They ring all of the bells in Oxford on the Queen's birthday. I was invited to join them. The Christ Church dining hall is as described but is much finer than my description.

I hope you have enjoyed reading about the despair, hope, and regeneration of one young boy.

I am indebted to my late great uncle, Carl H. (Bishop) Trammell and his son, Larken whose pre internet research started my interest. Great-uncle Carl was adopted after his Bishop parents' death. This extensive research led me to Jeff Bishop's paper, "From Scotland to Spartanburg, SC" which fills in details of the Scottish research.

ABOUT THE AUTHOR

W. D. Beaman is an architect living in Charleston, South Carolina, USA, with his wife of forty-four years.

Lightning Source UK Ltd.
Milton Keynes UK
UKHW010632100821
388622UK00001B/63